WITHDRAWAL

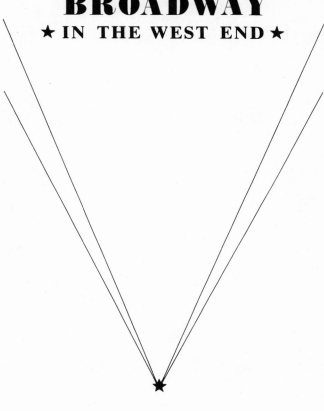

BROADWAY
★ IN THE WEST END ★

WILLIAM T. STANLEY

BROADWAY
★ IN THE WEST END ★

AN INDEX OF REVIEWS OF AMERICAN THEATRE IN LONDON, 1950-1975

GREENWOOD PRESS
WESTPORT, CONNECTICUT • LONDON, ENGLAND

Library of Congress Cataloging in Publication Data

Stanley, William T.
  Broadway in the West End.

  Includes bibliographical references and index.
  1. Theater--England--London--Reviews--Bibliography.
  2. American drama--20th century--History and criticism--
Bibliography. I. Title.
Z2014.D7S77 [PN2596.L6] 792.9'09421 77-89108
ISBN 0-8371-9852-6

Library of Congress Catalog Card Number: 77-89108
ISBN: 0-8371-9852-6

First published in 1978

Greenwood Press, Inc.
51 Riverside Avenue, Westport, Connecticut 06880

Printed in the United States of America

10 9 8 7 6 5 4 3 2 1

*For
Mary*

Contents

Preface

Critical and scholarly interest concerning American theatrical influence in Great Britain is well established. A number of works representing a variety of approaches to the study of American theatre in Britain have been produced on both sides of the Atlantic. Yet no substantial survey of the postwar American theatre in Britain, listing the works and the basic facts of each production with citations to critical reviews, exists. In this bibliography I have made the essential facts of American theatrical works produced in London from 1950 through 1975 more accessible.

My research was supported by two grants: a three-year fellowship, provided by the U.S. Office of Education under Title II of the U.S. Higher Education Act of 1965, and a Winston Churchill Fellowship, awarded by the English-Speaking Union, Los Angeles Branch. I spent four months in Great Britain and read nearly half of the reviews listed in the bibliography at the British Museum Newspaper Library in Colindale.

During my stay in Great Britain, I read reviews for the works produced from 1950 through 1961. I read reviews for works in the period from 1962 through 1975 at Doheny Memorial Library, University of Southern California; University Research Library, UCLA; Robert A. Millikan Memorial Library, Caltech, Pasadena; and the Library of Congress. In addition, the University of Southern California Library borrowed many items on microfilm from the Center for Research Libraries in Chicago. I also used collections at the Los Angeles Public Library, Central Branch, extensively.

Theatre reviews generally appear in the late morning or final editions of daily newspapers on the day after the official opening of the production. This pattern can be observed by the reader for those works produced in the period from 1950 to 1961, the reviews of which I read at the British Museum. For reviews in daily newspapers for the years from 1962 to 1975, I had to rely heavily on microfilms in the collections of the Library of Congress. As a result, reviews cited in all the morning papers except *The Times* will show variation from the usual practice

and will be dated as much as two days after the opening. This is because the Library of Congress films the edition it receives, which in
many instances is the first or city edition of the papers listed here.
These editions appear too early to have the theatre reviews. In theory,
the papers will carry over all items in the final edition that were missing in the city editions. With this peculiarity in mind as far as the
daily morning papers are concerned, those wishing to find the reviews
should be able to find them as listed. Unfortunately, errors will undoubtedly be discovered, and I ask the reader to accept my apology
in advance.

Scope: The bibliography covers commercial productions of American plays, musical shows, and revues in the West End from January 1,
1950, to December 31, 1975, comprising roughly 3,000 reviews for
339 productions. Of these productions 203 are plays, 82 are musicals,
and 8 are revues. The productions also include 45 revivals. The writers
included are natives of the United States or individuals whose writings
for the theatre were written in the United States and through associa-
tion are generally considered American. Anglo-American writers, including T. S. Eliot, W. H. Auden, Christopher Isherwood, and others
whose work for the theatre is primarily associated with the British
theatre, are not included in the bibliography.

In addition to the commercial productions, the bibliography lists
works that were produced by the major subsidized companies in
London, important club theatres, and three suburban theatres. Productions by the National Theatre Company, the Royal Court Theatre,
the Arts Theatre Club, the Hampstead Theatre Club, the Lyric Theatre
in Hammersmith, the Pembroke Theatre, and the Ashcroft Theatre in
Croydon were included because they generally received wide coverage
in the London press and in any view must be considered a part of the
essential theatre activity in London. Often the works from the club
theatres and the suburban theatres were restaged in commercial
houses in the West End. Reviews for such productions are listed in
their proper sequence in the bibliography. This extended life of productions is also true of several works that opened at the Royal Court. Experimental theatres such as the Open-Space Theatre, amateur houses
such as the Questors, and theatres in educational institutions such as
those that produce shows for the Royal Academy of Dramatic Art and
the London Academy of Music and Dramatic Art did not, on the whole,
receive wide enough coverage to meet the needs of my study. Their
omission is in no way intended to suggest that they do not provide a
vital and interesting theatrical experience but simply that for purposes
of this study they did not receive enough critical coverage to warrant

inclusion. Opera, ballet, one-man shows, cabaret, and other forms of live theatre are also beyond the scope of the bibliography.

Three standard yearbooks proved immensely helpful in the compilation of the theatrical works that compose the bibliography. *Stage Yearbook* and *Theatre World Annual* provided the most complete record of the yearly theatrical activity, but valuable summaries of each London season also appeared in *Best Plays* up to 1975. The various editions of *Who's Who in the Theatre* contained a treasury of production information in an accurate and concise way. Another consistently useful source was the *Index to the Times.*

Slight disagreements in dates and number of performances are common in the published record. Dates have been verified by checking programs and the record in the press. In a few cases I have estimated performances by using the standard professional theatre measure of eight per week. These are marked with an asterisk.

Reviews selected from sixteen sources represent a cross section of the daily and weekly London press. The sources were selected on the basis of their being in existence during the entire period of the study, of having a review staff, and on being known to devote space to the live theatre. Only one source ceased publication, and one became a monthly. A list of these sources with their reviewers follows the preface.

Arrangement: The bibliography is composed of three parts. Section One is the bibliography of the reviews; Section Two is a chronological listing of the shows produced each year; and Section Three is a title list that identifies the author. Section One is the fullest of the three.

In Section One works are listed alphabetically by author and then by title. After the title the following information is given for each work in this order: 1) the name of the theatre, 2) opening and closing dates, and 3) number of performances in parentheses. For a number of works produced at the Arts Theatre closing dates and the number of performances had to be estimated. These items are indicated by an asterisk. Closing dates were estimated on the basis of the date the next work opened. By looking at calendars I simply chose the most obvious date for closing. For example, I surmised the closing date for *The Immoralist* to be Saturday, December 4, 1954, since the next production opened on Tuesday, December 7, 1954. Sunday and Monday were days the theatre was closed. This closing date seemed to me to be the most logical and would allow the work to have run the typical length of Arts Theatre productions. Only a dozen or so productions had to be estimated in this way. Since I wanted to give some idea of the run and the closing date for each work, and since for these works the informa-

tion did not exist in any published source and the Arts Theatre did
not answer a personal inquiry, it was necessary to try, in the way described, to estimate the dates and runs.

Authors are listed by the form of their name that is commonly
used with their works. This follows the basic rule of the *Anglo-American Cataloging Rules.* Works by joint authors are listed under the
author whose name is generally cited first in reviews and on programs,
and in the case of published works, on title pages. However, cross
references from the other writer direct the user to the correct entry
in the bibliography. For example, Jerome Lawrence and Robert E.
Lee, a writing team whose works appear in the bibliography, are listed
under Lawrence. If one looks under Lee, cross references to the titles
he wrote with Lawrence direct the reader to the proper entry. Musical
shows are listed under the composer, with cross references under writers
who contributed lyrics and librettos. Cross references are also supplied
for writers whose works are represented by adaptations.

The reviews for each work are arranged alphabetically by the name
of the reviewer. The form of the name is that used by the reviewer to
sign his reviews. Unsigned reviews (*The Times* had unsigned reviews
until 1965) are alphabetized by the title of the reviewing source. Citations from newspapers and magazines are given in alphabetical sequence.
However, newspapers are cited by date, page, and column. Columns
are lettered from left to right, beginning with column a. This follows
the practice of the *Index to the Times* and seemed appropriate for the
present work. Magazines are cited by date, volume, and page.

Acknowledgments: A number of individuals have supported and
cooperated with me to make this bibliography, and it is a pleasure to
be able to extend my thanks to all of them. In Great Britain Mary
Weston, Rosemary and Terrence Rix, the late Richard Jury, David
Cook, and M. Clift were especially helpful. In the United States Rod
Casper, Jeanne Tatro, Dennis Petticoffer, Ruth Bowen, Margaret
Foutch, Don McNamee, and Sophia Yen at Caltech provided willing
and courteous help; members of the reference department at USC including Dimity Berkner, Pat King, Kathy Fromberg, Kippy Gladish,
and others were equally helpful. I must also mention the courteous
service I received from the staffs in the reference department at UCLA
Research Library, the British Museum Newspaper Library in Colindale, the Library of Congress, the literature department of Los Angeles
Public Library Central Branch, and from the theatre curator and staff
of the theatre collection at the Victoria and Albert Museum, London.

I also want to thank my colleagues for their counsel and continued
interest over a long period: Dean Martha Boaz and Professors Raymond

Kilpela and Charles Metzger. Professor Mary Mahl, English Department, University of Southern California, lent special help by recommending me for the Winston Churchill Fellowship. Ed Hess and other colleagues gave valuable suggestions. Professor Mike Wheeler and Mick Gidly at the University of Exeter offered much encouragement. Mary Ann Gray and Keith Lassner, two former students, also contributed their labor to the project in an early stage. Finally Bill Emerson, Paul Farron, Bob Tamplin, and Frank Yanchulis provided sustained interest and support. I am also grateful for the labor of Maxine and Jean Pennington and to Marilyn Brownstein at Greenwood Press for many ideas.

Los Angeles
August 1977

Review Sources with Critics
Included in the Bibliography

These sources were searched for reviews from 1950 through 1975 with two exceptions. The *Daily Sketch* died in 1972 and is indexed here only through 1970. The *Daily Mirror* was added for the period 1971-1975.

DAILY EXPRESS   121-128 Fleet Street, London EC4A 2NJ.

John Barber	David Lewin
Clive Barnes	Judith Simons
Noel Goodwin	Cecil Smith
Ian Christie	Mary Steele
Ralph Hewins	John Thompson
Herbert Kretzmer	Michael Walsh
Bernard Levin	

DAILY HERALD   Became *SUN* in 1965. 30 Bouverie Street, London EC4Y 8EX.

Anthony Carthew	Ann Pacey
Fergus Cashin	Emery Pearce
Kenneth Eastaugh	Jack Piler
Paul Foster	Marjorie Proops
Paul Holt	Andrew Smith
Leslie Mallory	Michael Wall
P. L. Mannock	Harry Weaver
David Nathan	Alexandra Wells
Mike Nevard	

DAILY MAIL   Northcliffe House, London EC4.

E. C. Connolly	Eric Mason
Bernard Conolly	Robert Muller
Jane Gaskell	Barry Norman
Edward Goring	June Southworth
Julian Holland	Jack Tinker
Bernard Levin	Cecil W. Wilson
Peter Lewis	Maurice Wiltshire

DAILY MIRROR   33 Holborn, London EC1.
(Indexed only for 1971-1975)

Fergus Cashin	*Bill Haggerty*
Clifford Davis	*Arthur Thirkell*

DAILY SKETCH   Carmelite House, London EC4.
(Ceased publication, 1972. Indexed through 1970)

John Balfour	*Unity Hall*
H. E. C.	*Walter Hayes*
Fergus Cashin	*Paul Holt*
Sally Cline	*J. R.*
Harold Conway	*Ker Robertson*
H. B. D.	*Kenneth Tynan*
Angus Hall	

DAILY TELEGRAPH   135 Fleet Street, London EC4.

Harold Atkins	*R. P. M. G.*
John Barber	*Patrick Gibbs*
George W. Bishop	*Ronald Hastings*
A. V. Cotton	*L. L.*
W. A. Darlington	*A. E. P.*
Sean Day-Lewis	*Eric Shorter*

EVENING NEWS   Harmsworth House, London EC4.

Leslie Ayer	*Julian Holland*
Felix Barker	*Caren Meyer*
Bill Boorne	*H. J. Pankhurst*
Reg Cooper	*David Wainwright*
Colin Frame	*Stephen Williams*
James Green	

EVENING STANDARD   47 Shoe Lane, London EC4.

Beverly Baxter	*Stuart Griffiths*
Peter Carson	*Anthony Hern*
Harold Conway	*Milton Shulman*
Stan Gelber Davies	*J. W. M. Thompson*
Ronald Duncan	*Kenneth Tynan*
Sydney Edwards	*Alexander Walker*
F. G.	

FINANCIAL TIMES   Bracken House, 10 Cannon Street, London
EC4P 4BY.

Kenneth Adam	*Jenny Lewis*
Michael Coneney	*Garry O'Connor*

Anthony Curtis
Richard Findlater
Peter Forster
Derek Granger
John Higgins
Oleg Kerensky

David Pryce-Jones
D. W.
Gillian Widdicombe
T. C. Worsley
B. A. Young

ILLUSTRATED LONDON NEWS   Elm House, Elm Street, London WC1. (Became a monthly in 1972)

Wilfred De'ath

J. C. Trewin

THE GUARDIAN   (Formerly *THE MANCHESTER GUARDIAN*) 3 Cross Street, Manchester; 192 Gray's Inn Road, London WC 1X 5EY.

J. C. B.
Michael Billington
Caryl Barhmes
Terry Coleman
Christopher Driver
Gerard Fay
Peter Fiddick
David Gray
Edward Greenfield
Denis Hart
Philip Hope-Wallace
Eric Jacobs
Nicholas de Jongh
Michael Kenyon

Oleg Kerensky
Derek Malcolm
Benedict Nightingale
Roy Perrot
Peter Preston
Oliver Pritchett
J. R.
John Rosselli
John Russell
Norman Shrapnel
M. W. W.
Martin Walker
Michael Wall
W. J. Weatherby

THE NEW STATESMAN   Great Turnstile, High Holborn, WC 1V 7HJ.

A. Alvarez
Jeremy Brooks
Ronald Bryden
A. C. (Anthony Curtis?)
Michael Chamberlain
H. A. L. Craig
Carl Foreman
Philip French
Roger Gellert
D. A. N. Jones
J. A. L.

Naomi Lewis
Kingsley Martin
John Mortimer
Benedict Nightingale
J. N. B. R.
John Raymond
Robert Robinson
Desmond Shawe-Taylor
A. V.
Roy Walker
T. C. Worsley

THE OBSERVER   160 Queen Victoria Street, London EC4V 4DA.

David Benedictus
Ivor Brown
Robert Brustein

Mervyn Jones
John Mortimer
David Pryce-Jones

Ronald Bryden
Harold Clurman
Robert Cushman
Michael Davie
Helen Dawson
Bamber Gascoigne
Dane Gelly
Penelope Gilliatt
Benny Green

Victoria Radin
Robert Robinson
George Sedden
Hilary Spurling
Kenneth Tynan
John Wain
Irving Wardle
Angus Wilson

PUNCH   23-27 Tudor Street, London EC4Y OHR.

Alex Atkinson
D. C. B.
Gerald Barry
Basil Boothroyd
Bernard Braden
Alan Dent
Peter Dickinson

David Frost
Barry Humphries
Eric Keown
Jeremy Kingston
Sheridan Morley
B. A. Young

SPECTATOR   99 Gower Street, London WC1E 6AE.

Alan Brien
Anthony Burgess
A. V. C.
Martin Cooper
Robert Cushman
Gerard Fay
Peter Fleming
Bamber Gascoigne
Iain Hamilton
Anthony Hartley
John Higgins

Kenneth Hopkins
Kenneth Hurren
Brian Inglis
Rodney Milnes
Derek Monsey
David Pryce-Jones
Malcolm Rutherford
Hilary Spurling
Kenneth Tynan
D. W.
David Watt

SUNDAY TIMES   200 Gray's Inn Road, London WC 1X 8EZ.

Felix Aprahamian
Harold Hobson

J. W. Lambert
John Peter

THE TIMES   Printing House Square, London EC4P 4ED.
(Note: Reviews in *THE TIMES* were unsigned until 1965)

Michael Billington
Leonard Buckley
Ned Chaillet
John Higgins
Charles Lewsen

William Mann
John Peter
Henry Raynor
David Wade
Irving Wardle

Sketch of American Theatre
in London, 1950-1975

The exchange of theatrical works between London and New York has been an established pattern in our theatre life for well over a century and a half, yet historians generally agree that American theatre really came of age only after World War I. A group of serious and exciting new writers appeared then who won the respect of critics and audiences. Among these writers Maxwell Anderson, Eugene O'Neill, and Elmer Rice contributed notable works, and composers George Gershwin, Cole Porter, and Richard Rodgers added verve and sophistication to musical comedies. Well-made melodramas like *Broadway* by Philip Dunning and George Abbott and romantic comedies with wide popular appeal like *Abie's Irish Rose* by Anne Nichols continued to be staple items in New York's exports to London, but these new artists deepened the theatrical fare in the United States with works like *Anna Christie* by Eugene O'Neill and *Street Scene* by Elmer Rice and created a heightened interest in American theatre abroad.[1]

In the first decade following World War II American theatrical works continued to have a strong impact on London theatre life. Lawrence Kitchin, British theatre historian and critic, recognized American theatre as the most powerful foreign influence on the London stage during those years.[2] With the appearance of *Look Back in Anger*, first produced at the Royal Court in 1956, John Osborne turned British playwrights toward their own contemporary culture and helped to initiate a new era in British drama. After *Look Back in Anger* American influence as a cultural force in British theatre declined and provided little of interest until the mid-1960s, when the works of Edward Albee and experimental Off-off Broadway groups created a new stir.

Although the influence of American theatrical works was undoubtedly less significant after 1956, the flow of American works to London continued without any noticeable decline in the number or variety of productions. The chronological list that forms Part Two of this work offers evidence to support this view. A clearer impression of the scope of American theatre in London can be gained, perhaps, from a brief account of these London productions of American plays and musical comedies based upon the record compiled here from 1950 through 1975.

Miller, Williams, and Inge

From 1950 to 1960, three playwrights—Arthur Miller, Tennessee Williams, and William Inge—wrote plays that made them the leading playwrights of their generation. Miller and Williams came to prominence late in the 1940s with works that won enormous success. Broadway productions of plays by Inge began to appear during the 1950s. Of the three playwrights, only Arthur Miller achieved a success with critics and theatregoers in London that nearly matched his recognition in the United States.

All My Sons and *Death of a Salesman*, Miller's first two smash hits in New York, were produced in London in 1948 and 1949. These plays received mixed notices. The first failed; the second had a moderately successful run.[3]

In 1956 Miller's *The Crucible* and *A View From the Bridge* opened in London, and both plays made a substantial impact. *The Crucible*, a drama based on the Salem witch trials, had generated excitement in London theatre circles two years prior to the London staging when it had been presented by the Bristol Old Vic Company at the Theatre Royal, Bristol. Leading London critics representing the large daily newspapers and weekly periodicals reviewed the production, and in general, found it a strong and provocative work.[4] *The Crucible* opened on April 9, 1956, at the Royal Court, presented by the English Stage Company during its first season. The company was a newly formed avant garde theatre group that one month later, May 8, 1956, with Osborne's *Look Back in Anger* changed the course of contemporary British theatre. Miller's play was well-received, but since it was one of a series of plays, it ran for only thirty-six performances.

A View From the Bridge opened October 11, 1956, at the Comedy Theatre in the West End, sponsored by the New Watergate Theatre Club. The club was organized as a device to counter censorship by the Lord Chamberlain, who still licensed plays in London at that time.[5] This play has a homosexual theme, and for that reason it could not be presented by regular theatre management. Miller rewrote this play for the London production, changing the original one-act version, previously staged in New York with *A Memory of Two Mondays* in 1955, into a full-length work. Although some critics found *A View From the Bridge* less impressive than *The Crucible* and complained about aspects that struck them as sensational and sentimental, the production had a successful run of 220 performances.

In the next decade two additional plays by Miller were produced in

London, plus a revival of *The Crucible* by the National Theatre Company at the Old Vic, where it ran in repertory as part of the 1964-1965 season and received largely rave reviews. *Incident at Vichy* opened early in 1966, was found less favorable, and ran for only ninety-one performances. Although *After the Fall*, which opened in New York at Lincoln Center in 1964, attracted wide attention because several reviewers asserted it portrayed many episodes closely paralleling events in Miller's life, including his marriage to Marilyn Monroe, it was not presented in London. At the end of the decade *The Price* became Miller's most successful work in London for the entire twenty-five-year span from 1950 to 1975. *The Price* opened March 4, 1969, and closed February 14, 1970, completing 404 performances. Of serious American plays produced in London during this period, only Albee's *Who's Afraid of Virginia Woolf?* ran longer and received similar critical approval. The final Miller play produced during this period was a lackluster revival in 1972 of *All My Sons*, which closed after a short run.

Like Arthur Miller, Tennessee Williams had his first two successful plays produced in London at the end of the 1940s. *The Glass Menagerie*, starring Helen Hayes in her London debut, opened at the Haymarket Theatre July 28, 1948, and *A Streetcar Named Desire* with Vivien Leigh as Blanch DuBois opened at the Aldwych Theatre late in 1949.[6] Both Helen Hayes and Vivien Leigh won rave notices for their acting, but the plays were harshly attacked. *The Glass Menagerie* closed after a modest run, and in his recently issued *Memoirs* Williams commented on the London production that had been directed by Sir John Gielgud. "I saw a performance," he wrote, "and it was just as bad as I had expected. *Menagerie* can't be tricked. It has to be honestly and more than competently performed and directed."[7] Although *The Glass Menagerie* failed to attract a large audience, *A Streetcar Named Desire* managed to overcome the voluminous but sensational advance notoriety and an unprecedented outpouring of disgust and vituperation on its West End opening and achieved a successful run. With one or two exceptions, the influential critics found the play unworthy of its star and director, Sir Laurence Olivier. There was even a movement to have the play withdrawn because of elements considered obscene in spite of the fact that the Lord Chamberlain had had many passages deleted or altered before it could open. Frances Stephens, then editor of *Theatre World*, a publication that later merged with *Plays and Players*, described the tempest that surrounded the West End production in a succinct summary of that season:

> Then came *A Streetcar Named Desire* and the great controversy of the year. This time a section denounced the play (winner of the American Pulitzer Prize and the American Critics Circle A-

ward) as indecently sex-ridden and crude, thereby with typical
perversity, filling the Aldwych Theatre for months. A London
evening newspaper serialized the play, and no doubt reaped a fine
harvest in increased circulation.[8]

While this first London production of *A Streetcar Named Desire* had a
good run and undoubtedly acquainted a wide British public with Tennessee Williams's most famous work, it did little to enhance his reputation with British critics as a playwright in the front rank. Considered a
masterpiece during its initial engagement in New York in 1947, *A Streetcar Named Desire* finally received similar recognition by London theatre
critics in 1974, when it was, as Eric Johns, editor of *British Theatre Review* stated, "triumphantly revived at the Piccadilly, as alive and gripping
as ever."[9]

While plays by Tennessee Williams did not generally win full approval
from a majority of London theatre critics, his works were not roundly
denounced; but they did fail to attract large audiences and complete long
runs. From 1950 to 1975 ten major productions and three theatre club
productions of works by Williams appeared in London. Of these, two had
modest runs, one was a hit revival, and all the others ran less than one
hundred performances.

Cat on a Hot Tin Roof, a great critical and commercial success in New
York, opened in London in 1958 and received unenthusiastic notices.
Kim Stanley, an American star, played the role of Maggie, but the play
achieved only a moderate run of 132 performances. In 1962 *Period of
Adjustment* opened at the Royal Court, was warmly received, and trans-
ferred to the Wyndhams Theatre in the West End, where it proved to be
Williams's most successful work in London during the decade, comple-
ting 164 performances.

Plays by Williams that failed to attract sufficient audiences to achieve
successful runs included *Camino Real* (1957), *The Night of the Iguana*
(1965), *The Rose Tattoo* (1959), *Summer and Smoke* (1951), and a revival of *The Glass Menagerie* at the Haymarket in 1965.[10] In addition
to these commercial productions four plays were presented by noncom-
mercial companies. The Arts Theatre Club produced *Garden District* in
1955, and it ran for five weeks. *Orpheus Descending*, a failure in New
York, opened at the Royal Court in 1959, received mixed notices, and
ran for fifty-three performances. In the fall of 1967 the Hampstead Theatre Club presented twenty-four performances of *Two-Character Play*,
a work more recently entitled *Out Cry*. *Sweet Bird of Youth*, his last
great commercial success in New York, has yet to be performed in the
West End. Vivian Merchant starred in a production at the Palace Theatre,
Watford (1968). The reviews were favorable, but the production did not

transfer to a West End theatre. *Small Craft Warnings*, presented first by the Hampstead Theatre Club (1973) for twenty-six performances and later at the Comedy for two months, completed the record of plays by Williams produced in London from 1950 to 1975.

William Inge fared even less well than Williams in London. Only *A Loss of Roses* and *The Dark at the Top of the Stairs* received productions in the London area, but neither reached the West End. These plays appeared at the Pembroke Theatre, Croydon, and each ran for fourteen performances.

O'Neill and Others

Leading American dramatists known prior to World War II whose works continued to be performed in London from 1950 to 1975 included Lillian Hellman, Clifford Odets, Eugene O'Neill, Thornton Wilder, a minor work each by Maxwell Anderson, Philip Barry, Sidney Kingsley, and William Saroyan, and revivals by William Gillette and Robert Sherwood. Several writers of comedies and lighter entertainments belonging to the same generation also had plays presented in the West End during the period. Howard Lindsay and Russel Crouse, Sam and Bella Spewack, one work coauthored by George S. Kaufman, and two plays by Paul Osborn represented this group. London critics varied widely in their responses to American plays, but the majority of these works, whether praised or scorned, failed to attract substantial audiences.

Among the writers who were well-established prior to World War II, Eugene O'Neill consistently received the greatest praise in the postwar period. His later works attracted close and respectful attention. Two of these—*The Iceman Cometh* and *A Long Day's Journey Into Night*—the London critics generally agreed, surpassed O'Neill's previous achievements. Yet none of his later plays had a long run in the West End.

At the Arts, a theatre club of 347 seats, the London premier of *The Iceman Cometh* opened in January 1958 to rave notices. A month later it transferred to the Winter Garden, a much larger commercial house, where it played only thirty-one performances. The posthumous work, *A Long Day's Journey Into Night*, O'Neill's biting but compassionate portrayal of his parents, his brother, and his own youth, first appeared in Stockholm on February 10, 1956. The New York production in the fall of 1956 starring Frederick March, Florence Eldridge, and Jason Robards, Jr., directed by José Quintero, ran for 389 performances. In September 1958 the London premier of this work with a British cast directed by Quintero opened at the Globe Theatre. Although several critics considered it O'Neill's masterpiece and the notices generally were excellent, it closed after 108 performances. Lord Olivier produced a successful re-

vival in December 1971 for the National Theatre Company at the New
Theatre in London, where with an all-star cast that included Olivier as
James Tyrone, it ran in repertory.

Hughie, another posthumous work that had its world premier in
Stockholm, opened at the Duchess Theatre, London (1963) with Burgess Meredith in the title role. The bill had two other one-act plays by
O'Neill, but the production closed after fourteen performances. More
Stately Mansions, a play that has survived in a voluminous but unfin-
ished version despite O'Neill's attempt to destroy it, opened in an adapted version at the Greenwich Theatre (1974). The critics found it
well-produced but unsatisfactory, and it closed after twenty-five performances. The remaining productions of his plays in London from
1950 to 1975 did not appear in commercial West End houses.

O'Neill's monumental trilogy, Mourning Becomes Electra, had its original London production in 1938, and according to Audrey Williamson's
perceptive chronicle of British theatre, was "undoubtedly the most powerful and thought-provoking American play" performed in London during the 1930s.[11] This play continued to command the interest of distinguished companies and critics in the next two decades. The Arts Theatre
revived it in 1955 for a run of two months, and in 1967 the revival by
the Traverse Theatre of Edinburgh played at the Arts Theatre from June
27 to July 2. In November 1961 the Old Vic presented twenty-four performances in repertory.

Only two other O'Neill plays received productions in the London area
during this period. At the Arts A Moon for the Misbegotten (1960) received favorable notices but closed after a limited run. The Ashcroft Theatre, Croydon, presented fourteen performances of A Touch of the Poet
(1963), but no West End production of this posthumous play has occurred.

Of the several works by other members of the pre-World War II generation of American playwrights produced in London from 1950 to 1975,
few achieved success. Clifford Odets had two revivals of Awake and Sing
(1950 and 1971) that each ran less than a month; one solid hit, Winter
Journey (1952); and a modest run with The Big Knife (1954).[12]

Lillian Hellman's The Children's Hour was revived at the Arts Theatre
in 1956 and struck the critics as dated and unconvincing; Toys in the
Attic, which ran for 556 performances in New York and won the Drama
Critics Circle Award, opened at the Piccadilly Theatre on November 10,
1960, to decidedly unenthusiastic notices and closed after a run of
eighty-five performances. Hellman also wrote the book for Leonard
Bernstein's musical version of Candide (1959), which failed, and Hellman's contribution was roundly attacked by the critics. In 1952 Montserrat, Hellman's rendering of the French play by Emanuel Roblès,

opened at the Lyric Theatre in Hammersmith and ran for thirty-nine performances but did not transfer to the West End.
Theatre in Hammersmith and ran for thirty-nine performances but did not transfer to the West End.

Maxwell Anderson's adaptation of William March's novel, *The Bad Seed* (1955), had a successful run of 196 performances, but both Sidney Kingsley's *Detective Story* (1950) and Philip Barry's final play, *Second Threshold* (1952), ran less than 100 performances. In 1954 *The Matchmaker* by Thornton Wilder opened at the Haymarket Theatre for a run of 275 performances. Ten years later it became a super hit in a musical version, *Hello Dolly!* with a score by Jerry Herman.

William Saroyan collaborated with Henry Cecil, and English writer, on a thriller titled *Settled Out of Court* (1960), which was loathed by the critics but scored a successful run. In the same year Saroyan's *Sam, the Highest Jumper of Them All,* produced by Joan Littlewood at the Theatre Royal in the East End, failed. *Two Plays: Talking to You and Across the Board on Tomorrow Morning,* Saroyan's only solo effort produced in the West End during the decade, opened October 4, 1962, and closed after twelve performances.

Archibald Macleish won the Pulitzer Prize in 1959 for *J. B.*, his modern allegory based on Job, but in 1961 when the play appeared in London the reviews were full of reservations and it closed after nineteen performances. *Reunion in Vienna* by Robert Sherwood, revived successfully for the Chichester Festival in July 1971, ran briefly at the Picadilly in 1972.

Popular Dramatists Known Before World War II

Popular playwrights who belonged to the older generation scored some spectacular successes as well as several disastrous failures. Paul Osborn, known for his stageworthy adaptations of successful novels, represented both extremes equally well. His version of Richard Mason's best-selling novel, *The World of Suzie Wong* (1959), reaped an abundance of scorn from the critics but nevertheless became a super hit, achieving a run of 823 performances, lasting nearly a year longer than its New York production. Osborn's original play, *Morning's at Seven,* first staged in New York in 1939, had its London premier in 1953. The critics found it likeable, but it closed after forty-six performances.

Plays written by well-known teams had fates similar to Paul Osborn's works in London. *Remains To Be Seen* (1952), a thriller by Howard Lindsay and Russel Crouse, ran for a week. In 1952 they scored a success with Irving Berlin's *Call Me Madam,* for which they wrote the libretto. They shared a great success with Richard Rodgers and Oscar Hammerstein II's musical, *The Sound of Music,* for which they created the book.

The reviews were not raves, but the show ran nearly six years, from 1961 to 1967. They had another failure when Cole Porter's *Anything Goes*, a show with a libretto by them, was revived in 1961 and closed within two weeks.

Sam and Bella Spewack had a flop with *Spring Song* (1950), a modest hit with *My Three Angels* (1955), their version of Albert Husson's *Cusine des Anges*, and a smash hit with Cole Porter's *Kiss Me Kate* (1951), for which they contributed the book. Sam Spewack's *Under the Sycamore Tree* (1952) provided Alec Guinness with a successful vehicle that elicited good notices and played 189 performances.

George S. Kaufman and Howard Teichmann collaborated on *The Solid Gold Cadillac* (1965), a comedy that attacked executive authority in a large corporation. This was the only play of Kaufman's to appear in the West End during the years from 1950 to 1975. Margaret Rutherford starred as the lovable old lady who tackled the corporation giants and won, but the notices were far from glowing, and the play closed after a modest run of 142 performances.

Robert Anderson, Chayefsky, and Others of the 1950s

American playwrights who became well-known during the 1950s and had works produced in London included Robert Anderson, Paddy Chayefsky, William Gibson, Frank Gilroy, and Gore Vidal. Anderson made a strong impression with *Tea and Sympathy*, which had a successful run at the Comedy Theatre, London, in 1957. Two other productions, *You Know I Can't Hear You When the Water's Running* (1968) and *I Never Sang for My Father* (1970), failed. *The Tenth Man* by Paddy Chayefsky, produced in London in 1961, had a modest run of 132 performances, and his *The Latent Heterosexual*, staged at the Aldwych in 1968 by the Royal Shakespeare Company, ran in repertory. William Gibson had two hits, *The Miracle Worker*, which appeared in London in 1961, and *Two for the Seesaw* in 1958. Gibson also coauthored the book for a musical based on Odets's *Golden Boy* (1968), which ran about four months. Frank Gilroy's *Who'll Save the Ploughboy?* played thirty-seven performances at the Haymarket (1963), but his best known work, *The Subject Was Roses*, was not produced in London. Vidal's *Visit to a Small Planet* (1960) closed after two weeks.

Edward Albee and Others of the 1960s

During the 1960s, several new American writers of promise had plays presented in London, including Mart Crowley, Jules Feiffer, Jack Gelber, Arthur Kopit, Murray Schisgal, and most notably, Edward Albee. Crowley's slick but realistic study of New York homosexuals. *The Boys in the Band* (1969), ran for 396 performances at the Wyndham Theatre and was one of two substantial hits by this group of writers. In 1965 the Arts Theatre produced Feiffer's *Crawling Arnold* for a brief run; the Royal Shakespeare Company presented *Little Murders* (1967) and *God Bless* (1968). Jack Gelber's brutally candid view of drug addicts, *The Connection* (1961), had a short run at the Duke of York's Theatre, and Arthur Kopit's absurd comedy, *Oh Dad, Poor Dad, Mamma's Hung You in the Closet and I'm Feeling So Sad*, failed twice. In 1961 it opened at the Lyric in Hammersmith and closed after thirteen performances; revived in 1965 at the Piccadilly it ran for fifty-three performances. Kopit's most distinguished theatrical venture in London occurred in 1968, when the Royal Shakespeare Company presented the world premier of *Indians* that ran in repertory for thirty-four performances. Murray Schisgal had two plays produced by the Arts Theatre—*Ducks and Lovers* (1961) and *Luv* (1963)—for brief runs, and *The Tiger* and *The Typists*, two one-act plays performed together, failed at the Globe in 1964.

Edward Albee, unlike most of the other playwrights in this group from the 1960s, repeated his commercial success in London. His first Broadway play, *Who's Afraid of Virginia Woolf?* opened at the Globe in 1964, won acclaim from the critics, and ran for 489 performances, the longest run of any serious American play in London during the twenty-five years from 1950 to 1975. Albee's later Broadway works, however, were presented in repertory. The Royal Shakespeare Company produced *A Delicate Balance* (1969), *Tiny Alice* (1970), and *All Over* (1972), and all received largely favorable notices.

Three of Albee's shorter works which established his reputation before he began to have productions on Broadway also had stagings in the smaller, more experimental London theatres. In 1960 the Arts Theatre produced *The Zoo Story* with *This Property Is Condemned*, a one-act by Tennessee Williams. *The Zoo Story* was revived in 1965 and appeared with Molière's *George Dandin* at the Theatre Royal in the East End. The Royal Court Theatre presented *The American Dream* and *The Death of Bessie Smith* on a double bill in 1961 for twenty-three performances. Although only one of his plays was produced in a commercial West End house, Albee's work attracted considerable notice from influential critics, and he was generally recognized as the most important American playwright to be introduced to British audiences since Tennessee Williams.

From the middle of the 1960s onward a new group of American playwrights, who like Albee first had works presented in Off- and Off-off Broadway theatres, began to be produced in club, lunchtime, and other small theatres in London. Of these Robert Patrick has attracted the widest notice in London. His *Kennedy's Children* opened at the King's Theatre Club in 1974 and transferred to the Arts Theatre in 1975. Plays by

Ed Bullins, Michael McClure, and Jean Claude Van Itallie appeared in
London during the 1960s, and in the 1970s Peter Magdalamy, Terrence
McNally, Leonard Melfi, Perry Pontac, and Sam Shepard stand out a-
mong this group of experimental writers.

American Comedies

   Polished American comedies by Broadway craftsmen proved to be fa
more successful with London theatregoers than serious American plays.
Jean Kerr, Ira Levin, Liam O'Brien, John Patrick, Neil Simon, Samuel
Taylor, and the team of Joseph Fields and Peter DeVries all had outstanding successes. Several others, including George Axelrod, Abe Burrows, Thomas Heggen, Leonard Spigelgass, Leslie Stevens, Ira Wallich,
and the team of Jerome Lawrence and Robert E. Lee contributed substantial hits. John Patrick's *The Teahouse of the August Moon*, an ad-
aption of Vern Sneider's novel, ranked first in number of performances.
Not all the critics found it equally amusing, but the majority praised its
gentle spoofing of American military bureaucracy confronting Okina-
wan wiliness, and the play that opened at Her Majesty's Theatre on
April 22, 1954, closed August 11, 1956, after 954 performances.

Neil Simon

   Neil Simon, Broadway's master of comedies in the 1960s and 1970s,
was the most successful American playwright in London during the
1960s. Two plays by Simon—*Come Blow Your Horn* (1962) and *The
Odd Couple* (1966)— were enormous hits, and both *Barefoot in the
Park* (1965) and *Plaza Suite* (1969) had substantial runs. In addition
Simon contributed the book to three musicals: *Little Me* (1964),
Promises, Promises (1969), and *Sweet Charity* (1967). These were
all hits, and Simon's work received favorable notices.
   Later plays by Simon failed. Neither *Gingerbread Lady* (1974) nor
The Sunshine Boys (1975) won support, and both closed after brief
runs.
   Comedies that ran longer than a year included works by Jean Kerr,
Liam O'Brien, Samuel Taylor, and the team of Joseph Fields and Peter
DeVries. Two of these—*The Tunnel of Love* (1957) by Fields and De-
Vries and *No Time for Sergeants* by Ira Levin—were adaptations of best-
selling novels. *Mary, Mary* (1963) by Jean Kerr, *The Remarkable Mr.
Pennypacker* (1955) by Liam O'Brien, and *The Pleasure of His Compa-
ny* (1959) by Samuel Taylor were original plays. In 1973 Kerr's *Finishing Touches* failed, but Taylor's *A Touch of Spring* (1975) played
three hundred performances.

The Longest Running American Show in London—*Pyjama Tops*

Although American comedies produced in London seldom received unanimous praise, the reception was, on the whole, far more favorable than unfavorable with one notable exception. The longest running American show presented in London during the past twenty-five years was *Pyjama Tops*, a farce that opened at the Whitehall Theatre in 1969 and featured three nude women, one per act. This play by Mawby Green and Ed Feilbert, based on *Moumou* by Jean de Letraz, generated greater hostility from the critics than any other production covered in this study. The "nude scenes," John Barber wrote in the *Daily Telegraph*, "failed to save what proved to be an abysmal entertainment."[13] Herbert Kretzmer, critic for the *Daily Express*, found the play "indescribably dreadful" and the plot "a boring, brainless hotchpotch."[14] His reaction was shared by all the major critics. Nevertheless, the show ran for 2,498 performances.

In addition to *Pyjama Tops* a few other hit comedies reaped a number of bad and mixed notices. These included *Cactus Flower* (1967), adapted by Abe Burrows from *Fleur de Cactus* by Pierre Barillet and Jean-Pierre Grady; *Auntie Mame* (1960), a play by Jerome Lawrence and Robert E. Lee that was based on the successful book by Patrick Dennis; and *The Marriage-Go-Round* (1959) by Leslie Stevens.

Comedies That Failed

Several American comedies produced in London during this period achieved only modest runs ranging from 125 to 200 performances, and several others were outright flops. Both Ira Levin and Samuel Taylor, who had each scored an outstanding success, had works that ran modestly or failed, and John Patrick had both a critical and financial failure. Notable Broadway successes that ran less than one hundred performances in London included Herb Gardner's *A Thousand Clowns* (1964), Leonard Gershe's *Butterflies Are Free* (1970), and Hal Kurnitz's *Once More With Feeling* (1958). Among the flops, however, only three comedies received nearly unanimous condemnation from the critics. The first, *Mary Had a Little* (1951), by Arthur Hertzog, Muriel Herman, and Al Rosen, closed after fifteen performances; the second, *Everybody Loves Opal* (1964), had five performances; and the third, *The Impossible Years* (1966), by Bob Fisher and Arthur Marx, which ran for 670 performances in New York, closed in London after eighty-six.

American Musical Theatre

The most successful genre of American theatre produced in London during the past twenty-five years was musical comedy. British critics

and audiences found more to praise and to enjoy in this form than in
any other type of American theatre. Although several musical productions failed critically and financially, the record of outstanding successes is unmatched by other American efforts and clearly established
the musical comedy as the most popular American form.

A number of individual composers and teams of renowned musical
comedy creators contributed shows that helped to make the American musical a favorite with theatre audiences. Richard Rodgers and
Oscar Hammerstein II predominated, both in the number of productions and long-lasting popularity. They were closely followed by the
works of Alan Jay Lerner and Frederick Loewe. Outstanding hits were
also contributed by Burt Bacharach, Irving Berlin, Leonard Bernstein,
Jerry Bock, Cy Coleman, Jerry Herman, Eric Korngold, Frank Loesser,
Galt MacDermot, Cole Porter, Stephen Schwartz, Stephen Sondheim,
Meredith Wilson, and Robert Wright. All of these composers had shows
that ran well over a year.

Six musicals ran more than one thousand performances. These inclu-
ed *Fiddler on the Roof* (1967), which had 2,030; *Godspell* (1971),
1,128; *Hair* (1968), 1,998; *My Fair Lady* (1958), 2,281; *The Sound of
Music* (1961), 2,385; and *West Side Story* (1958), 1039. Both *West
Side Story*, with music by Leonard Bernstein, lyrics by Stephen Sondheim, and libretto by Arthur Laurents, and *My Fair Lady*, with music
by Frederick Loewe and lyrics and book by Alan Jay Lerner, received
nearly universal approval, but *The Sound of Music* by Rodgers and
Hammerstein, the longest running musical, was less pleasing to the
critics. *Fiddler on the Roof*, with music by Jerry Bock, lyrics by Sheldon Harnick, and book by Joseph Stein, and *Hair*, Composed by Galt
MacDermot with libretto and lyrics by Georme Ragni and James Rado,
and *Godspell*, by Stephen Schwartz and John-Michael Tebelak, received general approval.

Substantial musical hits which were not altogether welcomed by the
critics included *Camelot* (1964) by Lerner and Loewe, *Flower Drum
Song* (1960) by Rodgers and Hammerstein, and *Music Man* (1961) by
Meredith Wilson. Among musicals that failed, Bernstein's *Candide*
(1959), Bob Merrill's *Carnival* (1963), Mary Rodger's *Once Upon a
Mattress* (1960), and two works by Harvey Schmidt, *The Fantasticks*
(1961) and *I Do! I Do!* (1968), were all rigorously attacked by the
critics. Only three musical flops, however, won almost unanimous dis-
approval. Steve Allen's *Belle Starr* (1969) with Betty Grable as the
legendary Western saloonkeeper, Jerry Bock's *Fiorello* (1962), and
John Clifton's *Man With a Load of Mischief* (1968) attracted neither
critics nor audiences.

More than a dozen musical comedies were revived, including works by Vincent Youmans, Cole Porter, George Gershwin, and others. Only two met with outstanding success. *The Desert Song* by Sigmund Romberg appeared in 1967 to unenthusiastic critical response but achieved a run of 433 performances. *Show Boat* by Jerome Kern had a superb new production in 1971 and became a smash hit at the Adelphi, where it ran for 950 performances.

Revues

Only a handful of revues, the final category of theatrical works surveyed in this study, by American creators appeared in the West End from 1950 to 1975. Two—*Touch and Go* (1950), with music by Jay Gorney and sketches by Jean and Walter Kerr, and *The Premise* (1962), a series of improvised sketches under the direction of Theodore Flicker— found receptive audiences. Two others—*The Dirtiest Show in Town* (1971) by Tom Eyren and *Let My People Come* (1974) by Earl Wilson, Jr.—represent a recent theatrical trend: explicit sexual themes and casts who are naked for most of the performance.[15] The critics found these revues lacking both satirical punch and sexual appeal; nevertheless these shows became smash hits. None of the other revues met with success.

The number and variety of American theatrical works produced in London from 1950 to 1975, including those by commercial and subsidized theatres, indicated an abiding interest in American theatre by London producers. Critics and audiences often shared this interest. The fortunes of these American works in London offer a stimulating perspective from which to view American theatrical achievement by allowing us to "see ourselves as others see us."

1. *Broadway* opened at the Strand Theatre, London, December 22, 1926; transferred to the Adelphi, January 24, 1927, where it closed July 30, 1927, completing 251 performances; *Abie's Irish Rose* ran at the Apollo from April 10, 1923, to July 30, 1923, for 128 performances; *Anna Christie* opened at the Strand, April 10, 1923, and closed July 7, 1923, after 103 performances; *Street Scene* ran for 147 performances at the Globe from September 9, 1930 until January 17, 1931.

2. See Lawrence Kitchin, *Mid-Century Drama* (London: Faber and Faber, 1960), p. 56.

3. *All My Sons* opened at the Lyric in Hammersmith, May 11, 1948; it was transferred to the Globe in the West End June 15, 1948, where it closed September 18, 1948, after completing 110 performances. *Death of a Salesman* opened at the Phoenix July 28, 1949, and closed January 28, 1950, after a run of 204 performances.

4. For a detailed discussion of the reception of this production by London critics, see Lee Beltzer, "The Plays of Eugene O'Neill, Thornton Wilder, Arthur Miller and Tennessee Williams on the London Stage, 1945-1960" (Ph.D. dissertation, University of Wisconsin, 1965), pp. 443-471.

5. Censorship of plays by the Lord Chamberlain ended September 1968.

6. *The Glass Menagerie* closed October 30, 1948, after 109 performances; *A Streetcar Named Desire* ran from October 12, 1949, until August 19, 1950, completing 326 performances.

7. Tennessee Williams, *Memoirs* (New York: Doubleday, 1975), p. 150.

8. Frances Stephens, ed., *Theatre World Annual (London)* (London: Rockliff, 1950), p. 10.

9. Eric Johns, ed., *British Theatre Review 1974* (Eastbourne, England: Vance-Offord, 1975), p. 207. (Note: The revival ran from March 14, 1974, to October 12, 1974, completing 243 performances.)

10. Dates in parenthesis here and throughout the remainder of this discussion are dates of London productions.

11. Audrey Williamson, *Theatre of Two Decades* (London: Rockliff, 1951), p. 155.

12. *Winter Journey* appeared on Broadway with the title *A Country Girl.*

13. John Barber, *Daily Telegraph*, September 23, 1969, p. 21.

14. Herbert Kretzmer, *Daily Express*, September 23, 1969, p. 14.

15. *Oh! Calcutta!* a similar show and equally successful, is not included here because it is not primarily an American work.

BROADWAY

★ IN· THE WEST END ★

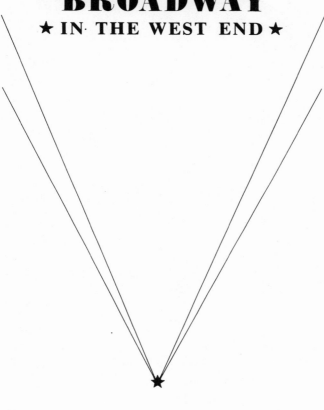

PART I

★ THE BIBLIOGRAPHY ★

ABBOTT, George
    The Boys from Syracuse. See: Rodgers, Richard
    Damn Yankees. See: Ross, Jerry
    Fiorello! See: Bock, Jerry
    The Pajama Game. See: Ross, Jerry

ADAMS, Lee
    Applause. See: Strouse, Charles
    Bye-Bye Birdie. See: Strouse, Charles
    Golden Boy. See: Strouse, Charles
    I and Albert. See: Strouse, Charles

ADLER, Richard
    Damn Yankees. See: Ross, Jerry
    The Pajama Game. See: Ross, Jerry

AIDMAN, Charles
    Spoon River. (A dramatic revue.) Originally conceived by Charles Aidman. (Based on Spoon River Anthology by Edgar Lee Masters.) Royal Court: February 13, 1954-March 14, 1954 (36)

        Barker, Felix. Evening News, February 14, 1964, p. 5f.
        Gascoigne, Bamber. Observer, February 16, 1964, p. 5b.
        Gellert, Roger. New Statesman, February 21, 1964, p. 306.
        Hobson, Harold. Sunday Times, February 16, 1964, p. 33b.
        Hope-Wallace, Philip. Manchester Guardian, February 14, 1964, p. 11e.
        Kretzmer, Herbert. Daily Express, February 14, 1964, p. 4e.
        Nathan, David. Daily Herald, February 14, 1964, p. 7c.
        Pryce-Jones, David. Spectator, February 28, 1964, p. 279.
        Shulman, Milton. Evening Standard, February 14, 1964, p. 4d.
        The Times, February 14, 1964, p. 15a.
        Trewin, J. C. Illustrated London News, February 29, 1964, p. 328.
        Young, B. A. Punch, February 19, 1964, p. 283-284.

ALBEE, Edward
   All Over.
   Aldwych: Produced by The Royal Shakespeare Company as
   part of the 1972 season. Opening performance was
   January 31, 1972. (26 performances in repertory)

        Barber, John. Daily Telegraph, February 1, 1972,
            p. 9a.
        Barker, Felix. Evening News, February 1, 1972,
            p. 3c.
        Billington, Michael. The Guardian, February 1,
            1972, p. 10c.
        Dawson, Helen. The Observer, February 6, 1972,
            p. 31f.
        Hobson, Harold. Sunday Times, February 6, 1972,
            p. 29b.
        Hurren, Kenneth. Spectator, February 12, 1972,
            p. 245.
        Kingston, Jeremy. Punch, February 9, 1972, p. 194.
        Kretzmer, Herbert. Daily Express, February 1, 1972,
            p. 10a.
        Lewis, Peter. Daily Mail, February 2, 1972, p. 27f.
        Nightingale, Benedict. New Statesman, February 4,
            1972, p. 152.
        O'Connor, Garry. Financial Times, February 1, 1972,
            p. 3a.
        Shulman, Milton. Evening Standard, February 1,
            1972, p. 13e.
        Trewin, J. C. Illustrated London News, April 1972,
            p. 57.
        Wardle, Irving. The Times, February 1, 1972, p. 10a.

   The American Dream and Death of Bessie Smith.
   Royal Court: October 24, 1961-November 11, 1961 (23)

        Barker, Felix. Evening News, October 25, 1961,
            p. 11e.
        Gascoigne, Bamber. Spectator, November 3, 1961,
            p. 623.
        Gellert, Roger. New Statesman, November 3, 1961,
            p. 667.
        Hobson, Harold. Sunday Times, October 29, 1961,
            p. 41c.
        Keown, Eric. Punch, November 1, 1961, p. 657.
        Levin, Bernard. Daily Express, October 25, 1961,
            p. 6f.
        Muller, Robert. Daily Mail, October 25, 1961, p. 3a.
        Nathan, David. Daily Herald, October 25, 1961,
            p. 5g.
        Shrapnel, Norman. Manchester Guardian, October 25,
            1961, p. 9a.
        Shorter, Eric. Daily Telegraph, October 25, 1961,
            p. 14e.
        Shulman, Milton. Evening Standard, October 25,
            1961, p. 20b.
        The Times, October 25, 1961, p. 13e.

Trewin, J. C. Illustrated London News, November 11,
     1961, p. 836.
Tynan, Kenneth. Observer, October 29, 1961, p. 27e.
Worsley, T. C. Financial Times, October 25, 1961,
     p. 29c.

A Delicate Balance.
Aldwych: January 14, 1969 (48 performances in repertory)

Barber, John. Daily Telegraph, January 15, 1969,
     p. 17a.
Barker, Felix. Evening News, January 15, 1969, p.
     11g.
Bryden, Ronald. Observer, January 19, 1969, p. 27a.
Hobson, Harold. Sunday Times, January 19, 1969, p.
     57a.
Hope-Wallace, Philip. Manchester Guardian, January
     15, 1969, p. 6e.
Kingston, Jeremy. Punch, January 22, 1969, p. 138.
Nathan, David. Sun, January 15, 1969, p. 9d.
Nightingale, Benedict. New Statesman, January 22,
     1969, p. 128.
Spurling, Hilary. Spectator, January 24, 1969, pp.
     116-117.
Trewin, J. C. Illustrated London News, January 25,
     1969, p. 28.
Walker, Alexander. Evening Standard, January 15,
     1969, p. 19a.
Wardle, Irving. The Times, January 15, 1969, p. 6b.
Young, B. A. Financial Times, January 15, 1969, p.
     3a.

Tiny Alice.
Aldwych: January 15, 1970 (34 performances in repertory)

Barber, John. Daily Telegraph, January 17, 1970,
     p. 10a.
Barker, Felix. Evening News, January 16, 1970,
     p. 2g.
Bryden, Ronald. Observer, January 18, 1970, p. 32a.
Griffiths, Stuart. Evening Standard, January 16,
     1970, p. 21d.
Hobson, Harold. Sunday Times, January 18, 1970,
     p. 57a.
Hope-Wallace, Philip. Manchester Guardian, January
     16, 1970, p. 8e.
Kingston, Jeremy. Punch, January 21, 1970, p. 116.
Kretzmer, Herbert. Daily Express, January 16, 1970,
     p. 14a.
Nightingale, Benedict. New Statesman, January 23,
     1970, p. 125.
Spurling, Hilary. Spectator, January 24, 1970,
     p. 115.
Trewin, J. C. Illustrated London News, January 31,
     1970, p. 31.

Wardle, Irving. The Times, January 16, 1970, p. 13b.
Young, B. A. Financial Times, January 16, 1970, p.
   3a.

Who's Afraid of Virginia Woolf?
Piccadilly: February 6, 1964-July 18, 1964 (trans-
ferred to Globe, then to Garrick)
Globe: July 29, 1964-January 23, 1965
Garrick: January 25, 1965-June 12, 1965 (489)

   Barker, Felix. Evening News, February 7, 1964,
      p. 7g.
   Darlington, W. A. Daily Telegraph, February 7,
      1964, p. 18d.
   Financial Times, February 7, 1964, p. 24d.
   Gascoigne, Bamber. Observer, February 9, 1964,
      p. 25c.
   Gellert, Roger. New Statesman, February 14, 1964,
      p. 262.
   Hobson, Harold. Sunday Times, February 9, 1964,
      p. 33b.
   Hope-Wallace, Philip. Manchester Guardian, February
      7, 1964, p. 11e.
   Kretzmer, Herbert. Daily Express, February 7, 1964,
      p. 4e.
   Nathan, David. Daily Herald, February 7, 1964, p.
      5d.
   Pryce-Jones, David. Spectator, February 14, 1964,
      pp. 213-214.
   Shulman, Milton. Evening Standard, February 7,
      1964, p. 4a.
   The Times, February 7, 1964, p. 15b.
   Trewin, J. C. Illustrated London News, February
      22, 1964, p. 288.
   Young, B. A. Punch, February 12, 1964, p. 245.

The Zoo Story. With This Property Is Condemned by
Tennessee Williams.
Arts: August 25, 1960-September 28, 1960 (40)*

   Barker, Felix. Evening News, August 26, 1960, p.
      8a.
   Brooks, Jeremy. New Statesman, September 3, 1960,
      p. 304.
   Findlater, Richard. Financial Times, August 26,
      1960, p. 19a.
   Hastings, Ronald. Daily Telegraph, August 26, 1960,
      p. 14e.
   Lambert, J. W. Sunday Times, August 28, 1960, p.
      33f.
   Levin, Bernard. Daily Express, August 26, 1960,
      p. 7a.
   Muller, Robert. Daily Mail, August 26, 1960, p. 3b.
   Rosselli, John. Manchester Guardian, August 27,
      1960, p. 3e.
   Shulman, Milton. Evening Standard, August 26, 1960,
      p. 4e.

Smith, Andrew. <u>Daily Herald</u>, August 26, 1960, p. 3h.
<u>The Times</u>, August 26, 1960, p. 5d.
Wardle, Irving. <u>Observer</u>, August 28, 1960, p. 24c.
Young, B. A. <u>Punch</u>, August 31, 1960, p. 318.

<u>The Zoo Story</u>. Revival, performed with <u>George Dandin</u>
by Moliere.
Royal Stratford: February 8, 1965-February 27, 1965
(28)

Barker, Felix. <u>Evening News</u>, February 9, 1965, p.
    5h.
Bryden, Ronald. <u>New Statesman</u>, February 12, 1965,
    p. 253.
Darlington, W. A. <u>Daily Telegraph</u>, February 9,
    1965, p. 18c.
Gilliatt, Penelope. <u>Observer</u>, February 14, 1965,
    p. 25a.
Hobson, Harold. <u>Sunday Times</u>, February 14, 1965,
    p. 45c.
Hope-Wallace, Philip. <u>Manchester Guardian</u>, February
    9, 1965, p. 9a.
Kingston, Jeremy. <u>Punch</u>, February 17, 1965, p. 253.
Nathan, David. <u>Sun</u>, February 9, 1965, p. 5c.
Rutherford, Malcolm. <u>Spectator</u>, February 12, 1965,
    p. 200.
<u>The Times</u>, February 9, 1965, p. 8e.
Young, B. A. <u>Financial Times</u>, February 9, 1965,
    p. 22d.

ALLEN, Jay
   <u>I and Albert</u>. See: Strouse, Charles

ALLEN, Steve
   <u>Belle Starr</u>. Music by Steve Allen and Warren Douglas;
   book and lyrics by Jerry Schafer.
   Palace: April 30, 1969-May 17, 1969 (21)

Bryden, Ronald. <u>Observer</u>, May 4, 1969, p. 27e.
Hobson, Harold. <u>Sunday Times</u>, May 4, 1969, p. 53d.
Kingston, Jeremy. <u>Punch</u>, May 7, 1969, p. 688.
Malcolm, Derek. <u>Manchester Guardian</u>, May 2, 1969,
    p. 10e.
Nathan, David. <u>Sun</u>, May 2, 1969, p. 12h.
Nightingale, Benedict. <u>New Statesman</u>, May 9, 1969,
    p. 669.
Norman, Barry. <u>Daily Mail</u>, May 2, 1969, p. 12d.
Shorter, Eric. <u>Daily Telegraph</u>, May 2, 1969, p. 21f.
Shulman, Milton. <u>Evening Standard</u>, May 2, 1969, p.
    23d.
Wardle, Irving. <u>The Times</u>, May 2, 1969, p. 9b.
Young, B. A. <u>Financial Times</u>, May 2, 1969, p. 3g.

ALLEN, Woody
   <u>Play It Again, Sam</u>
   Globe: September 11, 1969-August 24, 1970 (355)

Barber, John. Daily Telegraph, September 12, 1969,
     p. 21a.
Barker, Felix. Evening News, September 12, 1969,
     p. 2f.
Braden, Bernard. Punch, September 24, 1969, p. 510.
Bryden, Ronald. Observer, September 14, 1969, p.
     26h.
Lambert, J. W. Sunday Times, September 14, 1969,
     p. 58g.
Nathan, David. Sun, September 12, 1969, p. 7a.
Nightingale, Benedict. New Statesman, September 19,
     1969, p. 390.
Preston, Peter. Manchester Guardian, September 12,
     1969, p. 8e.
Shulman, Milton. Evening Standard, September 12,
     1969, p. 17a.
Spurling, Hilary. Spectator, September 20, 1969,
     p. 382.
Trewin, J. C. Illustrated London News, September
     27, 1969, p. 35.
Wardle, Irving. The Times, September 12, 1969,
     p. 8d.
Young, B. A. Financial Times, September 12, 1969,
     p. 3c.

ANDERSON, Maxwell
  The Bad Seed. Based on a novel by William March.
  Aldwych: April 14, 1955-October 1, 1955 (196)

     Darlington, W. A. Daily Telegraph, April 21, 1955,
          p. 6d.
     Granger, Derek. Financial Times, April 21, 1955,
          p. 7d.
     Hartley, Anthony. Spectator, April 22, 1955, p. 502.
     Hope-Wallace, Philip. Manchester Guardian, April
          16, 1955, p. 3a.
     Keown, Eric. Punch, April 20, 1955, p. 507.
     Lambert, J. W. Sunday Times, April 24, 1955, p. 7b.
     Shulman, Milton. Evening Standard, April 21, 1955,
          p. 6c.
     The Times, April 22, 1955, p. 16g.
     Trewin, J. C. Illustrated London News, April 30,
          1955, p. 794.
     Williams, Stephen. Evening News, April 21, 1955,
          p. 9c.
     Worsley, T. C. New Statesman, April 23, 1955, p.
          576.

ANDERSON, Robert
  I Never Sang for My Father.
  Duke of York: May 27, 1970-July 4, 1970 (45)

     Barber, John. Daily Telegraph, May 29, 1970, p. 16g.
     Barker, Felix. Evening News, May 28, 1970, p. 13e.
     Bryden, Ronald. Observer, May 31, 1970, p. 28f.
     Hobson, Harold. Sunday Times, May 31, 1970, p. 29f.

Hope-Wallace, Philip. <u>Manchester Guardian</u>, May 28,
     1970, p. 10e.
Kretzmer, Herbert. <u>Daily Express</u>, May 28, 1970,
     p. 12f.
Lewis, Peter. <u>Daily Mail</u>, May 29, 1970, p. 14b.
Nightingale, Benedict. <u>New Statesman</u>, June 5, 1970,
     p. 815.
Shulman, Milton. <u>Evening Standard</u>, May 28, 1970,
     p. 25d.
Trewin, J. C. <u>Illustrated London News</u>, June 6, 1970,
     p. 33.
Wardle, Irving. <u>The Times</u>, May 28, 1970, p. 16a.
Young, B. A. <u>Financial Times</u>, May 28, 1970, p. 3c.

<u>Tea and Sympathy</u>.
Comedy: April 25, 1957-September 21, 1957 (172)

Barber, John. <u>Daily Express</u>, April 26, 1957, p. 3h.
Boorne, Bill. <u>Evening News</u>, April 26, 1957, p. 3e.
Darlington, W. A. <u>Daily Telegraph</u>, April 26, 1957,
     p. 10f.
Granger, Derek. <u>Financial Times</u>, April 26, 1957,
     p. 2g.
Hobson, Harold. <u>Sunday Times</u>, April 28, 1957, p.
     19c.
Keown, Eric. <u>Punch</u>, May 1, 1957, p. 574.
R., J. <u>Manchester Guardian</u>, April 27, 1957, p. 3b.
<u>The Times</u>, April 26, 1957, p. 3a.
Trewin, J. C. <u>Illustrated London News</u>, May 11,
     1957, p. 786.
Tynan, Kenneth. <u>Observer</u>, April 28, 1957, p. 11b.
Watt, David. <u>Spectator</u>, May 3, 1957, p. 587.
Wilson, Cecil W. <u>Daily Mail</u>, April 26, 1957, p. 3d.
Worsley, T. C. <u>New Statesman</u>, May 4, 1957, pp. 570-
     572.

<u>You Know I Can't Hear You When the Water's Running</u>.
New: June 26, 1968-July 27, 1968 (37)

Barker, Felix. <u>Evening News</u>, June 26, 1968, p. 3a.
Bryden, Ronald. <u>Observer</u>, June 30, 1968, p. 27b.
Darlington, W. A. <u>Daily Telegraph</u>, June 27, 1968,
     p. 19a.
Higgins, John. <u>Spectator</u>, July 5, 1968, p. 27.
Hobson, Harold. <u>Sunday Times</u>, June 30, 1968, p. 49c.
Hope-Wallace, Philip. <u>Manchester Guardian</u>, June 27,
     1968, p. 6e.
Kingston, Jeremy. <u>Punch</u>, July 3, 1968, p. 26.
Kretzmer, Herbert. <u>Daily Express</u>, June 27, 1968,
     p. 4h.
Nathan, David. <u>Sun</u>, June 27, 1968, p. 5a.
Trewin, J. C. <u>Illustrated London News</u>, July 6,
     1968, p. 32.
Wardle, Irving. <u>The Times</u>, June 27, 1968, p. 8g.

APOLINAR, Danny
     <u>Your Own Thing</u>. See: Hester, Hal

ARCHIBALD, William
    The Innocents. (Based on The Turn of the Screw by Henry
    James.)
    Her Majesty's: July 3, 1952-December 13, 1952 (188)

        Barber, John. Daily Express, July 4, 1952, p. 6c.
        Brown, Ivor. Observer, July 6, 1952, p. 6a.
        Darlington, W. A. Daily Telegraph, July 4, 1952,
           p. 7e.
        Fay, Gerald. Spectator, July 11, 1952, p. 65.
        Hayes, Walter. Daily Sketch, July 4, 1952, p. 3a.
        Hobson, Harold. Sunday Times, July 6, 1952, p. 4b.
        Hope-Wallace, Philip. Manchester Guardian, July 5,
           1952, p. 5a.
        Keown, Eric. Punch, July 16, 1952, p. 127.
        Mannock, P. L. Daily Herald, July 4, 1952, p. 3a.
        The Times, July 4, 1952, p. 9a.
        Trewin, J. C. Illustrated London News, July 19,
           1952, p. 108.
        Tynan, Kenneth. Evening Standard, July 4, 1952,
           p. 2f.
        Williams, Stephen. Evening News, July 4, 1952, p.
           6e.
        Wiltshire, Maurice. Daily Mail, July 4, 1952, p. 6e.
        Worsley, T. C. New Statesman, July 12, 1952, pp.
           39-40.

ARDREY, Robert
    Shadow of Heroes.
    Piccadilly: October 7, 1958-November 15, 1958 (47)

        Barber, John. Daily Express, October 8, 1958, p. 7d.
        Barker, Felix. Evening News, October 8, 1958, p. 4e.
        Brien, Alan. Spectator, October 17, 1958, p. 514.
        Carthew, Anthony. Daily Herald, October 8, 1958,
           p. 2h.
        Darlington, W. A. Daily Telegraph, October 8, 1958,
           p. 12d.
        Goring, Edward. Daily Mail, October 9, 1958, p. 3h.
        G., F. Evening Standard, October 8, 1958, p. 14c.
        Hobson, Harold. Sunday Times, October 12, 1958,
           p. 21a.
        Keown, Eric. Punch, October 15, 1958, p. 513.
        Shrapnel, Norman. Manchester Guardian, October 9,
           1958, p. 5a.
        The Times, October 8, 1958, p. 6b.
        Trewin, J. C. Illustrated London News, October 18,
           1958, p. 662.
        Tynan, Kenneth. Observer, October 12, 1958, p. 19a.
        Worsley, T. C. Financial Times, October 8, 1958,
           p. 15f.
        Worsley, T. C. New Statesman, October 18, 1958,
           p. 520.

AXELROD, George
    Seven Year Itch.
    Aldwych: May 14, 1953-February 27, 1954 (331).

Barber, John. Daily Express, May 15, 1953, p. 3h.
Brown, Ivor. Observer, May 17, 1953, p. 15a.
C., E. Daily Mail, May 15, 1953, p. 5f.
Curtis, Anthony. New Statesman, May 23, 1953, p.
    613.
Darlington, W. A. Daily Telegraph, May 15, 1953, p.
    10f.
Granger, Derek. Financial Times, May 15, 1953, p.
    7g.
Hamilton, Iain. Spectator, May 22, 1953, p. 671.
Hayes, Walter. Daily Sketch, May 15, 1953, p. 5c.
Hobson, Harold. Sunday Times, May 17, 1953, p. 11a.
Holt, Paul. Daily Herald, May 15, 1953, p. 3e.
Keown, Eric. Punch, May 27, 1953, p. 643.
The Times, May 15, 1953, p. 2f.
Trewin, J. C. Illustrated London News, June 13,
    1953, p. 1002.
Tynan, Kenneth. Evening Standard, May 15, 1953,
    p. 10d.
Williams, Stephen. Evening News, May 15, 1953,
    p. 6d.
Wiltshire, Maurice. Daily Mail, May 15, 1953, p. 5f.

BACHARACH, Burt
    Promises, Promises. Book by Neil Simon; lyrics by Hal
    David.
    Prince of Wales: October 2, 1969-February 13, 1971 (569)

Barber, John. Daily Telegraph, October 3, 1969, p.
    21a.
Barker, Felix. Evening News, October 2, 1969, p. 3a.
Billington, Michael. The Times, October 3, 1969,
    p. 13b.
Cushman, Robert. Spectator, October 11, 1969, p.
    488.
Dawson, Helen. Observer, October 5, 1969, p. 31f.
Higgins, John. Financial Times, October 3, 1969,
    p. 3b.
Hobson, Harold. Sunday Times, October 5, 1969, p.
    53c.
Hope-Wallace, Philip. Manchester Guardian, October
    3, 1969, p. 10e.
Kingston, Jeremy. Punch, October 15, 1969, pp.
    639-640.
Nathan, David. Sun, October 3, 1969, p. 7a.
Nightingale, Benedict. New Statesman, October 10,
    1969, p. 507.
Shulman, Milton. Evening Standard, October 3, 1969,
    p. 26a.
Trewin, J. C. Illustrated London News, October 11,
    1969, p. 28.

BAKER, Dorothy & Howard
    Two Loves I Have . . .
    Arts: September 24, 1952--Next production began October
    14, 1952 (30)*

Barker, Felix. Evening News, September 25, 1952,
    p. 3b.
Fay, Gerard. Manchester Guardian, September 27,
    1952, p. 5a.
Hamilton, Iain. Spectator, October 3, 1952, p. 424.
Hobson, Harold. Sunday Times, September 28, 1952,
    p. 9b.
L., L. Daily Telegraph, September 25, 1952, p. 8f.
Proops, Marjorie. Daily Herald, September 25, 1952,
    p. 3a.
The Times, September 25, 1952, p. 9c.
Worsley, T. C. New Statesman, October 4, 1952, p.
    376.

BAKER, Marshall
    Once Upon a Mattress. See: Rodgers, Mary

BALDWIN, James
    The Amen Corner.
    Saville: October 12, 1965-December 4, 1965, limited
    engagement of 6 weeks (54)

Boothroyd, Basil. Punch, October 20, 1965, p. 583.
Gilliatt, Penelope. Observer, October 17, 1965,
    p. 24e.
Hobson, Harold. Sunday Times, October 17, 1965,
    p. 49f.
Kretzmer, Herbert. Daily Express, October 13, 1965,
    p. 4b.
Lewis, Jenny. Financial Times, October 14, 1965,
    p. 28c.
Shorter, Eric. Daily Telegraph, October 13, 1965,
    p. 18e.
Shulman, Milton. Evening Standard, October 13,
    1965, p. 4e.
The Times, October 13, 1965, p. 13d.
Trewin, J. C. Illustrated London News, October 23,
    1965, p. 42.

Blues for Mr. Charlie.
Aldwych: May 3, 1965-May 22, 1965 (36 performances in
repertory)

Barker, Felix. Evening News, May 4, 1965, p. 5f.
Bryden, Ronald. New Statesman, May 7, 1965, p. 737.
Burgess, Anthony. Spectator, May 14, 1965, p. 632.
Cline, Sally. Daily Sketch, May 4, 1965, p. 9f.
Coleman, Terry. Manchester Guardian, May 4, 1965,
    p. 9a.
Darlington, W. A. Daily Telegraph, May 4, 1965,
    p. 18d.
Gilliatt, Penelope. Observer, May 9, 1965, p. 25e.
Hobson, Harold. Sunday Times, May 9, 1965, p. 45a.
Kingston, Jeremy. Punch, May 12, 1965, p. 711.
Kretzmer, Herbert. Daily Express, May 4, 1965,
    p. 4b.
Nathan, David. Sun, May 4, 1965, p. 8e.

Shulman, Milton. Evening Standard, May 4, 1965,
    p. 4c.
The Times, May 4, 1965, p. 15a.
Trewin, J. C. Illustrated London News, May 15,
    1965, p. 34.

BARKENTIN, Marjorie
    Ulysses in Nighttime.
    Arts: May 21, 1959-July 9, 1959 (53)*

Alvarez, A. New Statesman, May 30, 1959, p. 759.
Atkinson, Alex. Punch, June 3, 1959, pp. 757-758.
Brien, Alan. Spectator, May 29, 1959, p. 766.
Hope-Wallace, Philip. Manchester Guardian, May 22,
    1959, p. 7c.
Lambert, J. W. Sunday Times, May 24, 1959, p. 23b.
The Times, May 22, 1959, p. 16a.
Trewin, J. C. Illustrated London News, June 6,
    1959, p. 984.
Wain, John. Observer, May 24, 1959, p. 19c.

BARNES, Billy
    Billy Barnes Revue.
    Lyric, Hammersmith: April 4, 1960-April 23, 1960 (23)

Alvarez, A. New Statesman, April 9, 1960, p. 518.
Barker, Felix. Evening News, April 5, 1960, p. 5c.
Barnes, Clive. Daily Express, April 5, 1960, p. 17c.
Keown, Eric. Punch, April 13, 1960, p. 533.
L., L. Daily Telegraph, April 5, 1960, p. 14d.
Lambert, J. W. Sunday Times, April 10, 1960, p. 25c.
Nathan, David. Daily Herald, April 5, 1960, p. 3e.
Shulman, Milton. Evening Standard, April 5, 1960,
    p. 11d.
The Times, April 5, 1960, p. 7a.
Wall, Michael. Manchester Guardian, April 6, 1960,
    p. 7b.
Worsley, T. C. Financial Times, April 5, 1960, p.
    17g.

BARRY, Julian
    Lenny. Music by Tom O'Horgan; based on the life and
    words of Lenny Bruce.
    Criterion: April 14, 1975-May 24, 1975 (48)

Barber, John. Daily Telegraph, April 15, 1975,
    p. 13a.
Barker, Felix. Evening News, April 15, 1975, p. 4c.
Billington, Michael. The Guardian, April 15, 1975,
    p. 12d.
Coveney, Michael. Financial Times, April 15, 1975,
    p. 3g.
Cushman, Robert. The Observer, April 20, 1975, p.
    28f.
Hurren, Kenneth. Spectator, April 26, 1975, p. 518.
Kretzmer, Herbert. Daily Express, April 15, 1975,
    p. 12e.

Morley, Sheridan. Punch, April 23, 1975, p. 731.
Nightingale, Benedict. New Statesman, April 25,
     1975, p. 560.
Shulman, Milton. Evening Standard, April 15, 1975,
     p. 15e.
Thirkell, Arthur. Daily Mirror, April 15, 1975,
     p. 16b.
Tinker, Jack. Daily Mail, April 15, 1975, p. 24e.
Trewin, J. C. Illustrated London News, June 1975,
     p. 93.
Wardle, Irving. The Times, April 15, 1975, p. 9c.

BARRY, Philip
   Second Threshold.
   Vaudeville: September 24, 1952-November 22, 1952 (69)

     Barber, John. Daily Express, September 25, 1952,
          p. 3f.
     Brown, Ivor. Observer, September 28, 1952, p. 11a.
     Conway, Harold. Evening Standard, September 25,
          1952, p. 5d.
     Darlington, W. A. Daily Telegraph, September 25,
          1952, p. 8f.
     Fay, Gerard. Manchester Guardian, September 26,
          1952, p. 5d.
     Hamilton, Iain. Spectator, October 3, 1952, p. 424.
     Hayes, Walter. Daily Sketch, September 25, 1952,
          p. 3a.
     Hobson, Harold. Sunday Times, October 5, 1952, p.
          9a.
     Keown, Eric. Punch, October 8, 1952, p. 463.
     Mannock, P. L. Daily Herald, September 25, 1952,
          p. 3a.
     The Times, September 25, 1952, p. 9c.
     Trewin, J. C. Illustrated London News, October 11,
          1952, p. 598.
     Williams, Stephen. Evening News, September 25,
          1952, p. 4e.
     Wilson, Cecil. Daily Mail, September 25, 1952,
          p. 6d.
     Worsley, T. C. New Statesman, October 4, 1952,
          pp. 375-376.

BEHRMAN, S. N.
   Fanny. See: Rome, Harold

BELLAK, George
   The Trouble-Makers.
   Strand (later transferred to the Comedy): September
   16, 1952-November 15, 1952 (71)

     B., J. C. Manchester Guardian, September 18, 1952,
          p. 5e.
     Barber, John. Daily Express, September 17, 1952,
          p. 3g.
     Brown, Ivor. Observer, September 21, 1952, p. 10a.

Conway, Harold. <u>Evening Standard</u>, September 17,
    1952, p. 5c.
Darlington, W. A. <u>Daily Telegraph</u>, September 17,
    1952, p. 8f.
Hamilton, Iain. <u>Spectator</u>, September 26, 1952,
    p. 392.
Hayes, Walter. <u>Daily Sketch</u>, September 17, 1952,
    p. 3a.
Hobson, Harold. <u>Sunday Times</u>, September 21, 1952,
    p. 9b.
Keown, Eric. <u>Punch</u>, October 1, 1952, p. 433.
Mannock, P. L. <u>Daily Herald</u>, September 7, 1952,
    p. 3b.
<u>The Times</u>, September 17, 1952, p. 2d.
Trewin, J. C. <u>Illustrated London News</u>, CCXXI (n.d.),
    598.
Williams, Stephen. <u>Evening News</u>, September 17,
    1952, p. 4f.
Wilson, Cecil. <u>Daily Mail</u>, September 17, 1952, p.
    6d.
Worsley, T. C. <u>New Statesman</u>, September 27, 1952,
    p. 346.

BELLOW, Saul
   The Bellow Plays: <u>Out From Under</u>, <u>Orange Souffle</u>, <u>The
   Wen</u>.
   Jeannetta Cochrane: May 26, 1966-June 25, 1966, trans-
   ferred to the Fortune: June 28, 1966-August 3, 1966
   (79)

        Jeannetta Cochrane:
        Bryden, Ronald. <u>Observer</u>, May 29, 1966, p. 20h.
        Frame, Colin. <u>Evening News</u>, May 27, 1966, p. 7c.
        Higgins, John. <u>Financial Times</u>, May 28, 1966, p.
            7a.
        Higgins, John. <u>Spectator</u>, June 3, 1966, pp. 693-
            694.
        Jones, D. A. N. <u>New Statesman</u>, June 3, 1966, p.
            819.
        Kretzmer, Herbert. <u>Daily Express</u>, May 27, 1966,
            p. 4f.
        Lambert, J. W. <u>Sunday Times</u>, May 29, 1966, p. 29.
        Nathan, David. <u>Sun</u>, May 27, 1966, p. 7c.
        Shorter, Eric. <u>Daily Telegraph</u>, May 27, 1966,
            p. 19a.
        Shulman, Milton. <u>Evening Standard</u>, June 29, 1966,
            p. 10e.
        <u>The Times</u>, May 27, 1966, p. 7a.
        Trewin, J. C. <u>Illustrated London News</u>, June 11,
            1966, p. 31.

        Fortune:
        Shulman, Milton. <u>The Times</u>, June 29, 1966, p. 7d.

BEMBERG, George
   Someone To Talk To.
   Duchess: July 18, 1956-July 21, 1956 (5)

       Barber, John. Daily Express, July 19, 1956, p. 3h.
       Darlington, W. A. Daily Telegraph, July 19, 1956,
           p. 8d.
       Granger, Derek. Financial Times, July 19, 1956,
           p. 2g.
       Hobson, Harold. Sunday Times, July 22, 1956, p. 4a.
       Hope-Wallace, Philip. Manchester Guardian, July 20,
           1956, p. 5e.
       Keown, Eric. Punch, July 25, 1956, p. 112.
       Shulman, Milton. Evening Standard, July 19, 1956,
           p. 6c.
       The Times, July 19, 1956, p. 4g.
       Trewin, J. C. Illustrated London News, August 4,
           1956, p. 200.
       Walker, Roy. Observer, July 22, 1956, p. 10d.
       Wilson, Cecil. Daily Mail, July 19, 1956, p. 3h.

BENSON, Sally
   The Young and the Beautiful.
   Arts: August 15, 1956-September 18, 1956 (40)*

       Carthew, Anthony. Daily Herald, August 16, 1956,
           p. 5h.
       Gibbs, Patrick. Daily Telegraph, August 16, 1956,
           p. 6d.
       Granger, Derek. Financial Times, August 16, 1956,
           p. 2g.
       Hartley, Anthony. Spectator, August 24, 1956, p.
           262.
       Hobson, Harold. Sunday Times, August 19, 1956,
           p. 4.
       Hope-Wallace, Philip. Manchester Guardian, August
           17, 1956, p. 5c.
       Keown, Eric. Punch, August 12, 1956, p. 226.
       Lambert, John. Daily Express, August 16, 1956,
           p. 3a.
       Shulman, Milton. Evening Standard, August 16, 1956,
           p. 5b.
       The Times, August 16, 1956, p. 10d.
       Trewin, J. C. Illustrated London News, September
           1, 1956, p. 354.
       Tynan, Kenneth. Observer, August 19, 1956, p. 10c.
       Wilson, Cecil. Daily Mail, August 16, 1956, p. 3h.
       Worsley, T. C. New Statesman, September 1, 1956,
           p. 242.

BERGMAN, Ingmar
   Smiles in a Summer Night. See: Sondheim, Stephen, A
   Little Night Music

BERLIN, Irving
    Call Me Madam. Libretto by Howard Lindsay and Russel
    Crouse.
    Coliseum: March 15, 1952-May 16, 1953 (485)

        Barber, John. Daily Express, March 17, 1952, p. 3c.
        Conway, Harold. Evening Standard, March 17, 1952,
           p. 6d.
        Darlington, W. A. Daily Telegraph, March 17, 1952,
           p. 7d.
        Fleming, Peter. Spectator, March 21, 1952, p. 365.
        Hayes, Walter. Daily Sketch, March 17, 1952, p. 5e.
        Hope-Wallace, Philip. Manchester Guardian, March
           17, 1952, p. 3c.
        Keown, Eric. Punch, April 2, 1952, p. 436.
        L., J. W. Sunday Times, March 16, 1952, p. 5e.
        Mannock, P. L. Daily Herald, March 17, 1952, p. 3d.
        The Times, March 17, 1952, p. 8c.
        Trewin, J. C. Illustrated London News, March 29,
           1952, p. 556.
        Wilson, Cecil. Daily Mail, March 17, 1952, p. 4c.
        Worsley, T. C. New Statesman, March 29, 1952, p.
           372.

BERNSTEIN, Leonard
    Candide. Music by Leonard Bernstein; lyrics by Richard
    Wilbur; other lyrics by John Latouche and Dorothy
    Parker; play by Lillian Hellman.
    Saville: April 29, 1959-June 20, 1959 (60)

        Alvarez, A. New Statesman, May 9, 1959, p. 642.
        Atkinson, Alex. Punch, May 13, 1959, p. 661.
        Barker, Felix. Evening News, May 1, 1959, p. 7d.
        Brien, Alan. Spectator, May 8, 1959, p. 649.
        Carthew, Anthony. Daily Herald, May 1, 1959, p. 3a.
        Clurman, Harold. Observer, May 3, 1959, p. 21b.
        Gibbs, Patrick. Daily Telegraph, May 1, 1959, p.
           14f.
        Hobson, Harold. Sunday Times, May 3, 1959, p. 25d.
        Hope-Wallace, Philip. Manchester Guardian, May 2,
           1959, p. 5f.
        Shulman, Milton. Evening Standard, May 1, 1959,
           p. 15e.
        Thompson, John. Daily Express, May 1, 1959, p. 11e.
        The Times, May 1, 1959, p. 6c.
        Trewin, J. C. Illustrated London News, May 16,
           1959, p. 852.
        Wilson, Cecil. Daily Mail, May 1, 1959, p. 5e.
        Worsley, T. C. Financial Times, May 1, 1959, p.
           19f.

    On the Town. Book and lyrics by Betty Comden and Adolph
    Green.
    Prince of Wales: May 30, 1963-July 13, 1963 (53)

Barker, Felix. Evening News, May 31, 1963, p. 9c.
Darlington, W. A. Daily Telegraph, May 31, 1963,
    p. 18f.
Dent, Alan. Punch, June 12, 1963, pp. 862-863.
Fay, Gerard. Manchester Guardian, May 31, 1963,
    p. 9a.
Gascoigne, Bamber. Spectator, June 14, 1963, p.
    779.
Gellert, Roger. New Statesman, June 14, 1963, p.
    913.
Kretzmer, Herbert. Daily Express, May 31, 1963,
    p. 4e.
Lambert, J. W. Sunday Times, June 2, 1963, p. 39c.
Levin, Bernard. Daily Mail, May 31, 1963, p. 3f.
Nathan, David. Daily Herald, May 31, 1963, p. 6d.
Shulman, Milton. Evening Standard, May 31, 1963,
    p. 4a.
The Times, May 31, 1963, p. 15e.
Trewin, J. C. Illustrated London News, June 15,
    1963, p. 940.

West Side Story. Music by Leonard Bernstein; lyrics by
Stephen Sondheim; book by Arthur Laurents.
Her Majesty's: December 12, 1958-June 10, 1961 (1,039)

Barker, Felix. Evening News, December 13, 1958,
    p. 3a.
Brien, Alan. Spectator, December 19, 1958, pp. 887-
    888.
Carthew, Anthony. Daily Herald, December 13, 1958,
    p. 2e.
Conway, Harold. Daily Sketch, December 13, 1958,
    p. 9a.
Darlington, W. A. Daily Telegraph, December 13,
    1958, p. 8c.
Hobson, Harold. Sunday Times, December 14, 1958,
    p. 15b.
Keown, Eric. Punch, December 24, 1958, p. 846.
R., J. Manchester Guardian, December 15, 1958,
    p. 5a.
Shulman, Milton. Evening Standard, December 13,
    1958, p. 3a.
Thompson, John. Daily Express, December 13, 1958,
    p. 5a.
The Times, December 13, 1958, p. 3e.
Trewin, J. C. Illustrated London News, December
    27, 1958, pp. 1150-1151.
Wilson, Angus. Observer, December 14, 1958, p. 15c.
Wilson, Cecil. Daily Mail, December 13, 1958, p.
    3a.
Worsley, T. C. Financial Times, December 13, 1958,
    p. 9f.
Worsley, T. C. New Statesman, December 20, 1958,
    pp. 880-881.

West Side Story (Revival).
Shaftesbury: December 19, 1974-July 19, 1975   (252)*

    Cooper, Reg. Evening News, December 27, 1974, p.
       18g.
    Lewsen, Charles. The Times, December 20, 1974,
       p. 7b.
    Thirkell, Arthur. Daily Mirror, December 20, 1974,
       p. 16d.
    Young, B. A. Financial Times, December 21, 1974,
       p. 20e.

Wonderful Town. Music by Leonard Bernstein; lyrics by
Betty Comden and Adolph Green; book by Joseph Fields
and Jerome Chodorov.
Princess: February 23, 1955-August 20, 1955   (207)

    Barber, John. Daily Express, February 24, 1955,
       p. 3b.
    Darlington, W. A. Daily Telegraph, February 24,
       1955, p. 8e.
    Granger, Derek. Financial Times, February 24, 1955,
       p. 7d.
    Hartley, Anthony. Spectator, March 4, 1955, p. 256.
    Hobson, Harold. Sunday Times, February 27, 1955,
       p. 13a.
    Holt, Paul. Daily Herald, February 24, 1955, p. 3d.
    Hope-Wallace, Philip. Manchester Guardian, February
       25, 1955, p. 7f.
    Keown, Eric. Punch, March 2, 1955, p. 300.
    Shulman, Milton. Evening Standard, February 24,
       1955, p. 6d.
    The Times, February 24, 1955, p. 13a.
    Trewin, J. C. Illustrated London News, March 12,
       1955, p. 468.
    Tynan, Kenneth. Observer, February 27, 1955, p. 11a.
    Williams, Stephen. Evening News, February 24, 1955,
       p. 5g.
    Wilson, Cecil. Daily Mail, February 24, 1955, p. 3d.

BESOYAN, Rick
    Little Mary Sunshine.
    Comedy: May 17, 1962-June 23, 1962   (44)

    Gellert, Roger. New Statesman, June 1, 1962, p. 808.
    Hobson, Harold. Sunday Times, May 20, 1962, p. 41b.
    Holland, Julian. Evening News, May 18, 1962, p. 3c.
    Kretzmer, Herbert. Daily Express, May 18, 1962,
       p. 6h.
    Lewis, Peter. Daily Mail, May 18, 1962, p. 3.
    Pacey, Ann. Daily Herald, May 18, 1962, p. 5h.
    Shorter, Eric. Daily Telegraph, May 18, 1962, p.
       16d.
    Shulman, Milton. Evening Standard, May 18, 1962,
       p. 16c.
    The Times, May 18, 1962, p. 15c.

Trewin, J. C. Illustrated London News, June 2,
    1962, p. 906.
Wardle, Irving. Observer, May 20, 1962, p. 26g.
Weatherby, W. J. Manchester Guardian, May 18, 1962,
    p. 13a.
Young, B. A. Punch, May 23, 1962, p. 803.

BEVAN, Donald J. and TRZCINSKI, Edmund
    Stalag 17.
    Princess: April 4, 1953-April 11, 1953 (11)

    Barber, John. Daily Express, April 6, 1953, p. 3c.
    Gibbs, Patrick. Daily Telegraph, April 6, 1953,
        p. 7f.
    Hobson, Harold. Sunday Times, April 5, 1953, p. 4b.
    Keown, Eric. Punch, April 15, 1953, p. 475.
    R., J. Daily Sketch, April 6, 1953, p. 8e.
    The Times, April 6, 1953, p. 9b.
    Trewin, J. C. Illustrated London News, April 18,
        1953, p. 618.
    Williams, Stephen. Evening News, April 6, 1953,
        p. 3d.
    Wilson, Cecil. Daily Mail, April 6, 1953, p. 3b.

BISSELL, Richard
    The Pajama Game. See: Adler, Richard

BOBRICK, Sam
    Norman, Is That You? See: Clark, Ronald

BOCK, Jerry
    Fiddler on the Roof. Music by Jerry Bock; book by
    Joseph Stein; lyrics by Sheldon Harnick.
    Her Majesty's: February 16, 1967-October 2, 1971 (2,030)

    Barker, Felix. Evening News, February 17, 1967, p.
        9a.
    Bryden, Ronald. Observer, February 19, 1967, p. 25e.
    Darlington, W. A. Daily Telegraph, February 17,
        1967, p. 19c.
    Hobson, Harold. Sunday Times, February 19, 1967,
        p. 27f.
    Hope-Wallace, Philip. Manchester Guardian, February
        17, 1967, p. 11e.
    Jones, D. A. N. New Statesman, February 24, 1967,
        p. 270.
    Kingston, Jeremy. Punch, February 22, 1967, p. 279.
    Kretzmer, Herbert. Daily Express, February 17, 1967,
        p. 4f.
    Nathan, David. Sun, February 17, 1967, p. 3c.
    Shulman, Milton. Evening Standard, February 17,
        1967, p. 4e.
    Spurling, Hilary. Spectator, February 24, 1967,
        p. 225.
    Trewin, J. C. Illustrated London News, February 25,
        1967, p. 34.
    Wardle, Irving. The Times, February 17, 1967, p.
        10d.

Young, B. A. Financial Times, February 18, 1967,
     p. 7d.

Fiorello! Music by Jerry Bock; lyrics by Sheldon
Harnick; book by Jerome Weidman and George Abbott.
Piccadilly: October 8, 1962-November 24, 1962 (56)

     Barker, Felix. Evening News, October 9, 1962, p. 7c.
     Gellert, Roger. New Statesman, October 19, 1962,
          p. 543.
     Hobson, Harold. Sunday Times, October 14, 1962, p.
          41a.
     Hope-Wallace, Philip. Manchester Guardian, October
          9, 1962, p. 7a.
     Keown, Eric. Punch, October 17, 1962, pp. 572-573.
     Kretzmer, Herbert. Daily Express, October 9, 1962,
          p. 4g.
     Levin, Bernard. Daily Mail, October 9, 1962, p. 3e.
     Nathan, David. Daily Herald, October 9, 1962, p. 5c.
     Shulman, Milton. Evening Standard, October 9, 1962,
          p. 4b.
     The Times, October 9, 1962, p. 13d.
     Trewin, J. C. Illustrated London News, October 20,
          1962, p. 622.
     Tynan, Kenneth. Observer, October 14, 1962, p. 28c.
     Worsley, T. C. Financial Times, October 10, 1962,
          p. 20c.

She Loves Me. Music by Jerry Bock; lyrics by Sheldon
Harnick; book by Joe Masteroff.
Lyric: April 29, 1964-August 22, 1964 (189)

     Boothroyd, Basil. Punch, May 6, 1964, p. 687.
     Bryden, Ronald. New Statesman, May 8, 1964, p. 738.
     Frame, Colin. Evening News, April 30, 1964, p. 5a.
     Gascoigne, Bamber. Observer, May 3, 1964, p. 25b.
     Hobson, Harold. Sunday Times, May 3, 1964, p. 33b.
     Hope-Wallace, Philip. Manchester Guardian, April
          30, 1964, p. 9e.
     Kretzmer, Herbert. Daily Express, April 30, 1964,
          p. 4f.
     Levin, Bernard. Daily Mail, May 1, 1964, p. 18f.
     Nathan, David. Daily Herald, April 30, 1964, p. 4h.
     Pryce-Jones, David. Spectator, May 8, 1964, p. 632.
     The Times, April 30, 1964, p. 8a.
     Trewin, J. C. Illustrated London News, May 16,
          1964, p. 792.

BOLTON, Guy
     Lady Be Good. See: Gershwin, George
     Oh, Kay! See: Gershwin, George

BRODERICK, Patricia
     Admiration of Life.
     Arts: March 30, 1960-April 26, 1960 (31)*

Brien, Alan. Spectator, April 8, 1960, p. 506.
Cotton, A. V. Daily Telegraph, March 31, 1960, p.
    14e.
Craig, H. A. L. New Statesman, April 9, 1960, p.
    520.
Keown, Eric. Punch, March 30, 1960, p. 496.
Lambert, J. W. Sunday Times, April 3, 1960, p.
    25c.
Levin, Bernard. Daily Express, March 31, 1960, p.
    11e.
Perrot, Roy. Manchester Guardian, April 1, 1960,
    p. 9g.
Thompson, J. W. M. Evening Standard, March 31, 1960,
    p. 16c.
The Times, March 31, 1960, p. 5a.
Trewin, J. C. Illustrated London News, April 16,
    1960, p. 660.
Wardle, Irving. Observer, April 3, 1960, p. 23a.
Worsley, T. C. Financial Times, March 31, 1960,
    p. 19g.

BROWN, Kenneth H.
    The Brig.
    Mermaid: September 2, 1964-September 26, 1964 (43)

Barker, Felix. Evening News, September 3, 1964,
    p. 8c.
Bryden, Ronald. New Statesman, September 11, 1964,
    p. 368.
Darlington, W. A. Daily Telegraph, September 3,
    1964, p. 18d.
Frost, David. Punch, September 9, 1964, p. 393.
Gascoigne, Bamber. Observer, September 6, 1964,
    p. 27f.
Hobson, Harold. Sunday Times, September 6, 1964,
    p. 33h.
Hope-Wallace, Philip. Manchester Guardian, September
    3, 1964, p. 7c.
Kretzmer, Herbert. Daily Express, September 3, 1964,
    p. 4f.
Levin, Bernard. Daily Mail, September 4, 1964, p.
    12b.
Nathan, David. Daily Herald, September 3, 1964, p.
    7c.
Rutherford, Malcolm. Spectator, September 11, 1964,
    p. 340.
Shulman, Milton. Evening Standard, September 3,
    1964, p. 4b.
The Times, September 3, 1964, p. 14a.

BURROWS, Abe
    Cactus Flower. (Based on Fleur de Cactus by Pierre
    Barrillet and Jean-Pierre Gredy.)
    Lyric: March 6, 1967-September 16, 1967 (223)

Barker, Felix. <u>Evening News</u>, March 7, 1967, p. 5a.
Bryden, Ronald. <u>Observer</u>, March 12, 1967, p. 25c.
Darlington, W. A. <u>Daily Telegraph</u>, March 7, 1967,
    p. 17a.
Hobson, Harold. <u>Sunday Times</u>, March 12, 1967, p.
    49b.
Hope-Wallace, Philip. <u>Manchester Guardian</u>, March 7,
    1967, p. 5e.
Jones, D. A. N. <u>New Statesman</u>, April 7, 1967, p.
    482.
Kingston, Jeremy. <u>Punch</u>, March 15, 1967, pp. 389-
    390.
Kretzmer, Herbert. <u>Daily Express</u>, March 7, 1967,
    p. 4d.
Trewin, J. C. <u>Illustrated London News</u>, March 18,
    1967, p. 30.
Wardle, Irving. <u>The Times</u>, March 7, 1967, p. 8c.
Young, B. A. <u>Financial Times</u>, March 8, 1967, p. 25b.

<u>Can-Can</u>. See: Porter, Cole

<u>Guys and Dolls</u>. See: Loesser, Frank

<u>How to Succeed in Business Without Really Trying</u>. See:
Loesser, Frank

CAESAR, Irving
    <u>No, No Nanette</u>. See: Youmans, Vincent

CASEY, Warren
    <u>Grease</u>. See: Jacobs, Jim

CECIL, Henry
    <u>Settled Out of Court</u>. See: Saroyan, William

CHASE, Mary
    <u>Harvey</u> (Revival).
    Prince of Wales: April 9, 1975-September 27, 1975 (204)

    Barber, John. <u>Daily Telegraph</u>, April 10, 1975, p.
        15b.
    Barker, Felix. <u>Evening News</u>, April 10, 1975, p. 13a.
    Billington, Michael. <u>Manchester Guardian</u>, April 10,
        1975, p. 8f.
    Cashin, Fergus. <u>Daily Mirror</u>, April 10, 1975, p.
        22b.
    Cushman, Robert. <u>Observer</u>, April 13, 1975, p. 28c.
    Hobson, Harold. <u>Sunday Times</u>, April 13, 1975, p.
        39f.
    Hurren, Kenneth. <u>Spectator</u>, April 19, 1975, p. 481.
    Kretzmer, Herbert. <u>Daily Express</u>, April 10, 1975,
        p. 12e.
    Morley, Sheridan. <u>Punch</u>, April 16, 1975, p. 685.
    Nightingale, Benedict. <u>New Statesman</u>, April 18,
        1975, p. 521.

Shulman, Milton. Evening Standard, April 10, 1975,
     p. 11a.
Thirkell, Arthur. Daily Mirror, April 10, 1975, p.
     18b.
Tinker, Jack. Daily Mail, April 10, 1975, p. 20e.
Trewin, J. C. Illustrated London News, June 1975,
     p. 93.
Wardle, Irving. The Times, April 10, 1975, p. 15g.
Young, B. A. Financial Times, April 10, 1975, p. 3a.

CHAYEFSKY, Paddy
   The Latent Heterosexual.
   Aldwych: September 16, 1968 (36 performances in reper-
   tory)

       Barker, Felix. Evening News, September 16, 1968,
            p. 3d.
       Bryden, Ronald. Observer, September 22, 1968, p.
            29b.
       French, Philip. New Statesman, September 20, 1968,
            p. 371.
       Hobson, Harold. Sunday Times, September 22, 1968,
            p. 59b.
       Hope-Wallace, Philip. Manchester Guardian, September
            17, 1968, p. 6d.
       Kingston, Jeremy. Punch, September 25, 1968, p. 448.
       Kretzmer, Herbert. Daily Express, September 17,
            1968, p. 4f.
       Lewis, Peter. Daily Mail, September 18, 1968, p. 8d.
       Nathan, David. Sun, September 17, 1968, p. 7b.
       Shulman, Milton. Evening Standard, September 17,
            1968, p. 4a.
       Spurling, Hilary. Spectator, September 17, 1968,
            p. 440.
       Trewin, J. C. Illustrated London News, September
            28, 1968, p. 32.
       Wardle, Irving. The Times, September 17, 1968, p.
            8c.

   The Tenth Man.
   Comedy: April 13, 1961-August 5, 1961 (132)

       Barker, Felix. Evening News, April 14, 1961, p. 4d.
       Craig, H. A. L. New Statesman, April 21, 1961, p.
            639.
       Darlington, W. A. Daily Telegraph, April 14, 1961,
            p. 16e.
       Gascoigne, Bamber. Spectator, April 21, 1961, p.
            557.
       Hobson, Harold. Sunday Times, April 16, 1969, p.
            41f.
       Hope-Wallace, Philip. Manchester Guardian, April
            15, 1961, p. 5e.
       Keown, Eric. Punch, April 25, 1961, pp. 658-659.
       Levin, Bernard. Daily Express, April 14, 1961, p.
            11d.

Muller, Robert. Daily Mail, April 14, 1961, p. 11d.
Nathan, David. Daily Herald, April 14, 1961, p. 3g.
Shulman, Milton. Evening Standard, April 14, 1961,
     p. 14f.
The Times, April 14, 1961, p. 20e.
Trewin, J. C. Illustrated London News, April 29,
     1961, p. 726.
Tynan, Kenneth. Observer, April 16, 1961, p. 27b.
Worsley, T. C. Financial Times, April 14, 1961,
     p. 20g.

CHODOROV, Jerome
     Anniversary Waltz. By Jerome Chodorov and Joseph Fields.
     Lyric: November 30, 1955-February 11, 1956 (85)

     Barber, John. Daily Express, December 1, 1955, p.
          3d.
     Carthew, Anthony. Daily Herald, December 1, 1955,
          p. 3a.
     Darlington, W. A. Daily Telegraph, December 1,
          1955, p. 8d.
     Granger, Derek. Financial Times, December 1, 1955,
          p. 2g.
     Hartley, Anthony. Spectator, December 9, 1955, p.
          804.
     Hobson, Harold. Sunday Times, December 4, 1955, p.
          7a.
     Hope-Wallace, Philip. Manchester Guardian, December
          2, 1955, p. 5d.
     Keown, Eric. Punch, December 7, 1955, p. 676.
     Shulman, Milton. Evening Standard, December 1, 1955,
          p. 17a.
     The Times, December 1, 1955, p. 3c.
     Trewin, J. C. Illustrated London News, December 10,
          1955, p. 1026.
     Tynan, Kenneth. Observer, December 4, 1955, p. 9a.
     Williams, Stephen. Evening News, December 1, 1955,
          p. 5c.
     Wilson, Cecil. Daily Mail, December 1, 1955, p. 3h.

     The Great Waltz. See: Korngold, Eric

     Wonderful Town. See: Bernstein, Leonard

CLARK, Ronald
     Norman, Is That You? By Ronald Clark and Sam Bobrick.
     Phoenix: April 16, 1975-May 24, 1975 (47)

     Barber, John. Daily Telegraph, April 17, 1975, p.
          13d.
     Barker, Felix. Evening News, April 17, 1975, p. 14c.
     Billington, Michael. The Guardian, April 17, 1975,
          p. 10b.
     Hurren, Kenneth. Spectator, April 26, 1975, p. 518.
     Kretzmer, Herbert. Daily Express, April 17, 1975,
          p. 12d.

Morley, Sheridan. Punch, April 23, 1975, p. 731.
Shulman, Milton. Evening Standard, April 17, 1975,
     p. 18b.
Thirkell, Arthur. Daily Mirror, April 17, 1975, p.
     16b.
Tinker, Jack. Daily Mail, April 17, 1975, p. 24e.
Wardle, Irving. The Times, April 17, 1975, p. 15e.
Young, B. A. Financial Times, April 17, 1975, p. 3g.

CLIFTON, John
     Man with a Load of Mischief. Music by John Clifton;
     book by Ben Traver.
     Comedy: December 9, 1968-December 28, 1968 (26)

     Barber, John. Daily Telegraph, December 10, 1968,
          p. 19a.
     Barker, Felix. Evening News, December 10, 1968,
          p. 3c.
     Bryden, Ronald. Observer, December 15, 1968, p. 23f.
     Hobson, Harold. Sunday Times, December 15, 1968, p.
          29d.
     Hope-Wallace, Philip. Manchester Guardian, December
          10, 1968, p. 6g.
     Kingston, Jeremy. Punch, December 18, 1968, p. 894.
     Kretzmer, Herbert. Daily Express, December 10, 1968,
          p. 11g.
     Lewis, Peter. Daily Mail, December 11, 1968, p. 11b.
     Nathan, David. Sun, December 11, 1968, p. 3b.
     Raynor, Henry. The Times, December 10, 1968, p. 7a.
     Shulman, Milton. Evening Standard, December 10,
          1968, p. 17a.
     Trewin, J. C. Illustrated London News, December 21,
          1968, p. 33.
     Young, B. A. Financial Times, December 11, 1968,
          p. 3a.

COLEMAN, Cy
     Little Me. Music by Cy Coleman; lyrics by Carolyn
     Leigh; book by Neil Simon. Based on a novel by Patrick
     Dennis.
     Cambridge: November 18, 1964-September 4, 1965 (334)

     Barker, Felix. Evening News, November 19, 1964, p.
          8e.
     Barnes, Clive. Daily Express, November 19, 1964,
          p. 10a.
     Bryden, Ronald. New Statesman, November 27, 1964,
          p. 850.
     Darlington, W. A. Daily Telegraph, November 19,
          1964, p. 18f.
     Gilliatt, Penelope. Observer, November 22, 1964,
          p. 25c.
     Hobson, Harold. Sunday Times, November 22, 1964,
          p. 43e.
     Hope-Wallace, Philip. Manchester Guardian, November
          19, 1964, p. 9a.

Kingston, Jeremy. Punch, November 25, 1964, p. 815.
Nathan, David. Sun, November 19, 1964, p. 10e.
Shulman, Milton. Evening Standard, November 19,
    1964, p. 4a.
The Times, November 19, 1964, p. 15a.
Trewin, J. C. Illustrated London News, November 28,
    1964, p. 852.

Sweet Charity. Music by Cy Coleman; lyrics by Dorothy
Fields; book by Neil Simon.
Prince of Wales: October 11, 1967-November 30, 1968
(484)

Barker, Felix. Evening News, October 12, 1967, p.
    3a.
Bryden, Ronald. Observer, October 15, 1967, p. 24h.
Day-Lewis, Sean. Daily Telegraph, October 12, 1967,
    p. 19a.
French, Philip. New Statesman, October 20, 1967,
    p. 518.
Hobson, Harold. Sunday Times, October 15, 1967, p.
    29b.
Hope-Wallace, Philip. Manchester Guardian, October
    12, 1967, p. 8e.
Kingston, Jeremy. Punch, October 18, 1967, p. 594.
Kretzmer, Herbert. Daily Express, October 12, 1967,
    p. 8d.
Nathan, David. Sun, October 12, 1967, p. 7e.
Peter, John. The Times, October 12, 1967, p. 7c.
Shulman, Milton. Evening Standard, October 12,
    1967, p. 17d.
Spurling, Hilary. Spectator, October 20, 1967, p.
    467.
Trewin, J. C. Illustrated London News, October 21,
    1967, p. 48.
Young, B. A. Financial Times, October 13, 1967, p.
    30a.

COMDEN, Betty
    Applause. See: Styne, Jule
    Bells Are Ringing. See: Styne, Jule
    Do Re Mi. See: Styne, Jule
    On the Town. See: Bernstein, Leonard
    Wonderful Town. See: Bernstein, Leonard

CONNELLY, Marcus
    Hunter's Moon.
    Winter Garden: February 26, 1958-March 10, 1958 (13)

Barber, John. Daily Express, February 27, 1958,
    p. 9h.
Barker, Felix. Evening News, February 27, 1958,
    p. 5c.
Darlington, W. A. Daily Telegraph, February 27,
    1958, p. 10d.
Granger, Derek. Financial Times, February 27, 1958,
    p. 11h.

Hope-Wallace, Philip. Manchester Guardian, February
     28, 1958, p. 9e.
Keown, Eric. Punch, March 5, 1958, p. 330.
Shulman, Milton. Evening Standard, February 27,
     1958, p. 6a.
The Times, February 27, 1958, p. 3e.
Trewin, J. C. Illustrated London News, March 15,
     1958, p. 442.
Tynan, Kenneth. Observer, March 2, 1958, p. 15c.
Weaver, Harry. Daily Herald, February 27, 1958,
     p. 3g.
Wilson, Cecil. Daily Mail, February 27, 1958, p.
     3d.

CRICHTON, Kyle
     The Happiest Millionaire.
     Cambridge: November 15, 1957-March 22, 1958 (147)

     Barber, John. Daily Express, November 16, 1957, p.
          5a.
     Barker, Felix. Evening News, November 16, 1957, p.
          7c.
     Darlington, W. A. Daily Telegraph, November 16,
          1957, p. 8e.
     Granger, Derek. Financial Times, November 18, 1957,
          p. 9d.
     Hobson, Harold. Sunday Times, November 24, 1957,
          p. 25c.
     Keown, Eric. Punch, November 5, 1957, p. 640.
     Shulman, Milton. Evening Standard, November 16,
          1957, p. 5a.
     The Times, November 16, 1957, p. 10c.
     Trewin, J. C. Illustrated London News, November
          30, 1957, p. 946.
     Tynan, Kenneth. Observer, November 17, 1957, p. 15b
     Wilson, Cecil. Daily Mail, November 16, 1957, p. 3d
     Worsley, T. C. New Statesman, November 23, 1957, p.
          692.

CROSS, Beverly
     Hans Anderson. See: Loesser, Frank

CROUSE, Russel
     Anything Goes. See: Porter, Cole
     Remains to be Seen. See: Lindsay, Howard
     The Sound of Music. See: Rodgers, Richard

CROWLEY, Mart
     The Boys in the Band.
     Wyndham's: February 11, 1969-January 10, 1970 (396)

     Barber, John. Daily Telegraph, February 12, 1969,
          p. 21a.
     Barker, Felix. Evening News, February 12, 1969,
          p. 6g.
     Bryden, Ronald. Observer, February 16, 1969, p. 27d

Hobson, Harold. Sunday Times, February 16, 1969,
    p. 55b.
Hope-Wallace, Philip. Manchester Guardian, February
    12, 1969, p. 6f.
Kingston, Jeremy. Punch, February 19, 1969, p. 282.
Nathan, David. Sun, February 12, 1969, p. 7b.
Nightingale, Benedict. New Statesman, February 21,
    1969, p. 267.
Shulman, Milton. Evening Standard, February 12,
    1969, p. 5f.
Spurling, Hilary. Spectator, February 21, 1969, p.
    249.
Trewin, J. C. Illustrated London News, February 22,
    1969, p. 26.
Wardle, Irving. The Times, February 12, 1969, p. 8a.
Young, B. A. Financial Times, February 12, 1969, p.
    3b.

CRYER, Gretchen and FORD, Nancy
    Grass Roots.
    Leatherhead Theater Club: October 15, 1968

    Billington, Michael. The Times, October 16, 1968,
        p. 16d.
    Bryden, Ronald. Observer, October 20, 1968, p. 26f.

DAVID, Hal
    Promises, Promises. See: Bacharach, Burt

DAVIS, Luther
    Kismet. See: Wright, Robert

DE VRIES, Peter
    Tunnel of Love. See: Fields, Joseph

DINELLI, Mel
    The Man.
    Her Majesty's: December 30, 1952-March 28, 1953 (95)

    Barber, John. Daily Express, December 31, 1952,
        p. 3b.
    Darlington, W. A. Daily Telegraph, December 31,
        1952, p. 8d.
    Hamilton, Iain. Spectator, January 9, 1953, p. 35.
    Hayes, Walter. Daily Sketch, December 31, 1952,
        p. 8a.
    Hobson, Harold. Sunday Times, January 4, 1953, p.
        9h.
    Mannock, P. L. Daily Herald, December 31, 1952,
        p. 3a.
    The Times, December 31, 1952, p. 4c.
    Trewin, J. C. Illustrated London News, January 17,
        1953, p. 100.
    Trewin, J. C. Punch, January 14, 1953, p. 106.
    Williams, Stephen. Evening News, December 31, 1952,
        p. 4e.

Wilson, Cecil. Daily Mail, December 31, 1952, p. 4
Worsley, T. C. New Statesman, January 10, 1953, p.
    39.

DONLEAVY, J. P.
  Fairy Tales of New York.
  Pembroke, Croydon: December 6, 1960-December 18, 1960
  (13)

    Barker, Felix. Evening News, December 7, 1960, p.
      4g.
    Brien, Alan. Spectator, December 9, 1960, pp. 939-
      941.
    Craig, H. A. L. New Statesman, December 17, 1960,
      pp. 968-969.
    Levin, Bernard. Daily Express, December 7, 1960,
      p. 11g.
    Muller, Robert. Daily Mail, December 7, 1960, p. 3
    Nathan, David. Daily Herald, December 7, 1960, p.
      3f.
    Rosselli, John. Manchester Guardian, December 8,
      1960, p. 9g.
    Shorter, Eric. Daily Telegraph, December 7, 1960,
      p. 14d.
    Shulman, Milton. Evening Standard, December 7, 1960
      p. 20c.
    The Times, December 7, 1960, p. 15a.
    Tynan, Kenneth. Observer, December 11, 1960, p. 26

  Fairy Tales of New York.
  Comedy: January 24, 1961-April 8, 1961 (86)

    Barker, Felix. Evening News, January 25, 1961, p.
      9c.
    Craig, H. A. L. New Statesman, February 3, 1961,
      p. 191.
    Gascoigne, Bamber. Spectator, February 3, 1961,
      p. 148.
    Hobson, Harold. Sunday Times, January 29, 1961,
      p. 37a.
    Hope-Wallace, Philip. Manchester Guardian, January
      26, 1961, p. 11c.
    Keown, Eric. Punch, February 1, 1961, p. 222.
    Levin, Bernard. Daily Express, January 25, 1961,
      p. 11f.
    Muller, Robert. Daily Mail, January 25, 1961, p.
      5f.
    Nathan, David. Daily Herald, January 25, 1961, p.
      4g.
    Shorter, Eric. Daily Telegraph, January 25, 1961,
      p. 12d.
    Shulman, Milton. Evening Standard, January 25,
      1961, p. 14e.
    The Times, January 25, 1961, p. 13a.
    Trewin, J. C. Illustrated London News, February 4,
      1961, p. 192.

Wardle, Irving. Observer, January 29, 1961, p. 30d.
Worsley, T. C. Financial Times, January 25, 1961,
    p. 21d.

The Ginger Man.
Fortune: September 15, 1959-October 24, 1959 (23)

Alvarez, A. New Statesman, September 26, 1959, p.
    388.
Barker, Felix. Evening News, September 16, 1959,
    p. 7b.
Brien, Alan. Spectator, September 25, 1959, p. 401.
Carthew, Anthony. Daily Herald, September 16, 1959,
    p. 5h.
Darlington, W. A. Daily Telegraph, September 16,
    1959, p. 12d.
Hobson, Harold. Sunday Times, September 20, 1959,
    p. 25b.
Hope-Wallace, Philip. Manchester Guardian, September
    17, 1959, p. 9a.
Keown, Eric. Punch, September 13, 1959, p. 220.
Levin, Bernard. Daily Express, September 16, 1959,
    p. 13d.
Pryce-Jones, Alan. Observer, September 20, 1959,
    p. 25b.
Shulman, Milton. Evening Standard, September 16,
    1959, p. 14b.
The Times, September 16, 1959, p. 14c.
Trewin, J. C. Illustrated London News, October 3,
    1959, p. 374.
Wilson, Cecil. Daily Mail, September 16, 1959, p.
    3f.

The Ginger Man.
Royal Court: November 20, 1963-January 4, 1964 (52)

Barker, Felix. Evening News, November 21, 1963, p.
    4g.
Darlington, W. A. Daily Telegraph, November 21,
    1963, p. 18e.
Gascoigne, Bamber. Observer, November 24, 1963,
    p. 27a.
Gellert, Roger. New Statesman, November 29, 1963,
    pp. 804-805.
Hobson, Harold. Sunday Times, November 10, 1963,
    p. 33a.
Hobson, Harold. Sunday Times, reviewed again Novem-
    ber 24, 1963, p. 33b.
Pryce-Jones, David. Spectator, November 15, 1963,
    p. 629.
Shulman, Milton. Evening Standard, November 21,
    1963, p. 4c.
The Times, November 21, 1963, p. 17c.
Trewin, J. C. Illustrated London News, December 7,
    1963, p. 962.

Worsley, T. C. Financial Times, November 7, 1963,
     p. 26g.
Young, B. A. Punch, November 13, 1963, p. 720.
Young, B. A. Punch, reviewed again November 27,
     1963, p. 790.

A Singular Man.
Comedy: October 21, 1964-November 28, 1964 (45)

Barker, Felix. Evening News, October 22, 1964, p.
     9a.
Bryden, Ronald. New Statesman, October 29, 1964,
     p. 670.
Darlington, W. A. Daily Telegraph, October 22,
     1964, p. 18d.
Frost, David. Punch, October 28, 1964, pp. 655-656.
Gilliatt, Penelope. Observer, October 25, 1964, p.
     25a.
Hobson, Harold. Sunday Times, October 25, 1964, p.
     44a.
Hope-Wallace, Philip. Manchester Guardian, October
     22, 1964, p. 7a.
Kretzmer, Herbert. Daily Express, October 22, 1964,
     p. 15a.
Levin, Bernard. Daily Mail, October 23, 1964, p.
     22b.
Shulman, Milton. Evening Standard, October 22, 1964,
     p. 4a.
The Times, October 22, 1964, p. 16g.
Trewin, J. C. Illustrated London News, October 31,
     1964, p. 708.
Young, B. A. Financial Times, October 22, 1964, p.
     24d.

DOUGLAS, Warren
     Belle Starr. See: Allen, Steve

DOWLING, Jennette
     The Young Elizabeth. By Jennette Dowling and Francis
     Letton.
     New: April 2, 1952-June 30, 1953 (498)

Barber, John. Daily Express, April 3, 1952, p. 3f.
Brown, Ivor. Observer, April 6, 1952, p. 6a.
Conway, Harold. Evening Standard, April 3, 1952,
     p. 5c.
Darlington, W. A. Daily Telegraph, April 3, 1952,
     p. 6e.
Hayes, Walter. Daily Sketch, April 3, 1952, p. 3a.
Hobson, Harold. Sunday Times, April 6, 1952, p. 2f.
Hope-Wallace, Philip. Manchester Guardian, April
     4, 1952, p. 11c.
Keown, Eric. Punch, April 16, 1952, p. 492.
M., K. New Statesman, April 12, 1952, p. 435.
Mannock, P. L. Daily Herald, April 3, 1952, p. 5b.
The Times, April 3, 1952, p. 8e.

Trewin, J. C. Illustrated London News, April 25,
    1952, p. 722.
Tynan, Kenneth. Spectator, April 11, 1952, p. 481.
Williams, Stephen. Evening News, April 3, 1952, p.
    3b.
Wiltshire, Maurice. Daily Mail, April 3, 1952, p.
    4f.

DOYLE, Arthur Conan
    Sherlock Holmes. See: Gillette, William

DRIVER, Donald
    Your Own Thing. See: Hester, Hal

DUBERMAN, Martin B.
    In White America. A documentary play.
    Arts: November 16, 1964-December 12, 1964 (28)

        Barnes, Clive. Daily Express, November 17, 1964,
            p. 8a.
        Bryden, Ronald. New Statesman, November 20, 1964,
            p. 799.
        Darlington, W. A. Daily Telegraph, November 17,
            1964, p. 18e.
        Frame, Colin. Evening News, November 17, 1964, p.
            7f.
        Gilliatt, Penelope. Observer, November 22, 1964,
            p. 25b.
        Hobson, Harold. Sunday Times, November 22, 1964,
            p. 13.
        Hope-Wallace, Philip. Manchester Guardian, November
            17, 1964, p. 9a.
        Kingston, Jeremy. Punch, November 25, 1964, p. 815.
        Levin, Bernard. Daily Mail, November 18, 1964, p.
            18b.
        Rutherford, Malcolm. Spectator, November 20, 1964,
            p. 679.
        The Times, November 17, 1964, p. 5b.
        Trewin, J. C. Illustrated London News, December 5,
            1964, p. 912.
        Wall, Michael. Sun, November 17, 1964, p. 9a.
        Young, B. A. Financial Times, November 17, 1964,
            p. 24a.

DUMARES, William
    Isabel's a Jezebel. See: MacDermot, Galt

EBB, Fred
    Cabaret. See: Kander, John
    Zorba. See: Kander, John

EDWARDS, Sherman
    1776. See: Stone, Peter

El Coca-Cola Grande.
    Hampstead Theatre Club: July 15, 1971-August 3, 1971
    (18)*

Billington, Michael. <u>The Times</u>, July 16, 1971, p.
9d.
Brahms, Caryl. <u>Manchester Guardian</u>, July 16, 1971,
p. 8c.
Curtis, Anthony. <u>Financial Times</u>, July 17, 1971,
p. 8e.

ELLIOTT, Don
<u>Thurber Carnival</u>. See: Thurber, James

ETTINGER, Don.
<u>Ambassador</u>. See: Gohman, Don

EYREN, Tom
<u>The Dirtiest Show in Town</u>.
Duchess: May 11, 1971-March 31, 1973 (795)

Barber, John. <u>Daily Telegraph</u>, May 12, 1971, p. 14d.
Barker, Felix. <u>Evening News</u>, May 12, 1971, p. 3c.
Bryden, Ronald. <u>The Observer</u>, May 16, 1971, p. 30a.
Hope-Wallace, Philip. <u>Manchester Guardian</u>, May 12,
1971, p. 10b.
Hurren, Kenneth. <u>Spectator</u>, May 22, 1971, p. 709.
Kingston, Jeremy. <u>Punch</u>, May 19, 1971, p. 683.
Kretzmer, Herbert. <u>Daily Express</u>, May 12, 1971,
p. 17a.
Lambert, J. W. <u>Sunday Times</u>, May 16, 1971, p. 30b.
Lewis, Peter. <u>Daily Mail</u>, May 12, 1971, p. 25a.
Shulman, Milton. <u>Evening Standard</u>, May 12, 1971,
p. 23d.
Trewin, J. C. <u>Illustrated London News</u>, July 1971,
p. 48.
Wardle, Irving. <u>The Times</u>, May 12, 1971, p. 9c.
Young, B. A. <u>Financial Times</u>, May 12, 1971, p. 3a.

<u>Sarah B. Divine</u>.
Jeannetta Cochrane: March 19, 1973-March 31, 1973 (16)

Billington, Michael. <u>Manchester Guardian</u>, March 20,
1973, p. 12e.
Coveney, Michael. <u>Financial Times</u>, March 20, 1973,
p. 3a.
Kretzmer, Herbert. <u>Daily Express</u>, March 20, 1973,
p. 10d.
Tinker, Jack. <u>Daily Mail</u>, March 20, 1973, p. 4f.

FAULKNER, William
<u>Requiem for a Nun</u>.
Royal Court: November 26, 1957-December 21, 1957 (29)

Barber, John. <u>Daily Express</u>, November 27, 1957, p.
3h.
Barker, Felix. <u>Evening News</u>, November 27, 1957, p.
5c.
Darlington, W. A. <u>Daily Telegraph</u>, November 27,
1957, p. 10d.

Granger, Derek. Financial Times, November 27, 1957,
    p. 2g.
Hobson, Harold. Sunday Times, December 1, 1957, p.
    25a.
Hope-Wallace, Philip. Manchester Guardian, November
    28, 1957, p. 5c.
Keown, Eric. Punch, December 4, 1957, pp. 671-672.
Shulman, Milton. Evening Standard, November 27,
    1957, p. 6a.
The Times, November 27, 1957, p. 3b.
Trewin, J. C. Illustrated London News, December 14,
    1957, p. 1046.
Tynan, Kenneth. Observer, December 1, 1957, p. 15a.
Watt, David. Spectator, December 6, 1957, p. 793.
Wilson, Cecil. Daily Mail, November 27, 1957, p. 3d.
Worsley, T. C. New Statesman, December 7, 1957, p.
    773.

FEIFFER, Jules
    Crawling Arnold. Presented with Miss Julie by Johan
    August Strindberg.
    Arts: February 17, 1965-March 13, 1965 (26)

    Bryden, Ronald. New Statesman, February 26, 1965,
        p. 332.
    Frame, Colin. Evening News, February 18, 1965, p.
        8g.
    Gilliatt, Penelope. Observer, February 21, 1965,
        p. 25g.
    Hobson, Harold. Sunday Times, February 21, 1965,
        p. 45d.
    Kingston, Jeremy. Punch, March 3, 1965, p. 327.
    Kretzmer, Herbert. Daily Express, February 19, 1965,
        p. 4c.
    Nathan, David. Sun, February 18, 1965, p. 9c.
    Shorter, Eric. Daily Telegraph, February 18, 1965,
        p. 19a.
    Shulman, Milton. Evening Standard, February 18,
        1965, p. 4b.
    The Times, February 18, 1965, p. 16f.
    Young, B. A. Financial Times, February 19, 1965,
        p. 28d.

    God Bless.
    Aldwych: October 23, 1968 (19 performances in reper-
    tory)

    Barker, Felix. Evening News, October 24, 1968, p.
        11e.
    Bryden, Ronald. Observer, October 27, 1968, p. 27a.
    Hobson, Harold. Sunday Times, October 27, 1968, p.
        59c.
    Kingston, Jeremy. Punch, October 30, 1968, p. 629.
    Kretzmer, Herbert. Daily Express, October 24, 1968,
        p. 15d.
    Nathan, David. Sun, October 24, 1968, p. 9a.

Nightingale, Benedict. New Statesman, November 1,
     1968, p. 602.
Pritchett, Oliver. Manchester Guardian, October 24,
     1968, p. 6d.
Shulman, Milton. Evening Standard, October 24, 1968,
     p. 21a.
Spurling, Hilary. Spectator, November 1, 1968, p.
     635.
Trewin, J. C. Illustrated London News, November 2,
     1968, p. 31.
Wardle, Irving. The Times, October 24, 1968, p. 17e.

Little Murders. Part of Royal Shakespeare Company Season,
1967/68.
Aldwych: July 3, 1967 (44 performances in repertory)

Bryden, Ronald. Observer, July 9, 1967, p. 19c.
Darlington, W. A. Daily Telegraph, July 4, 1967,
     p. 17a.
Hobson, Harold. Sunday Times, July 9, 1967, p. 3b.
Hope-Wallace, Philip. Manchester Guardian, July 4,
     1967, p. 5e.
Kingston, Jeremy. Punch, July 2, 1967, p. 69.
Kretzmer, Herbert. Daily Express, July 4, 1967, p.
     4g.
Mortimer, John. New Statesman, July 7, 1967, p. 28.
Nathan, David. Sun, July 4, 1967, p. 6f.
Shulman, Milton. Evening Standard, July 4, 1967,
     p. 4e.
Spurling, Hilary. Spectator, July 14, 1967, p. 54.
Trewin, J. C. Illustrated London News, July 15,
     1967, p. 36.
Wardle, Irving. The Times, July 4, 1967, p. 8c.
Young, B. A. Financial Times, July 5, 1967, p. 26a.

FEILBERT, Ed
   Pyjama Tops. See: Green, Maubry

FERBER, Edna
   Show Boat. See: Kern, Jerome

FEUER, Cy
   Guys and Dolls. See: Loesser, Frank

FIELDS, Dorothy
   Sweet Charity. See: Coleman, Cy

FIELDS, Joseph
   Anniversary Waltz. See: Chodorov, Jerome
   Flower Drum Song. See: Rodgers, Richard

   The Tunnel of Love. By Joseph Fields and Peter DeVries.
   Her Majesty's: December 3, 1957-February 14, 1959
   (transferred to Apollo December 8, 1957) (563)

Barber, John. Daily Express, December 4, 1957, p.
     7d.

Barker, Felix. <u>Evening News</u>, December 4, 1957, p.
   5d.
Darlington, W. A. <u>Daily Telegraph</u>, December 4, 1957,
   p. 10e.
Granger, Derek. <u>Financial Times</u>, December 4, 1957,
   p. 2g.
Hobson, Harold. <u>Sunday Times</u>, December 8, 1957, p.
   23c.
Hope-Wallace, Philip. <u>Manchester Guardian</u>, December
   5, 1957, p. 7b.
Keown, Eric. <u>Punch</u>, December 11, 1957, p. 708.
Shulman, Milton. <u>Evening Standard</u>, December 4, 1957,
   p. 6a.
<u>The Times</u>, December 4, 1957, p. 3c.
Trewin, J. C. <u>Illustrated London News</u>, December 21,
   1957, p. 1096.
Tynan, Kenneth. <u>Observer</u>, December 8, 1957, p. 15b.
Watt, David. <u>Spectator</u>, December 13, 1957, p. 837.
Wilson, Cecil. <u>Daily Mail</u>, December 4, 1957, p. 3a.
Worsley, T. C. <u>New Statesman</u>, December 14, 1957,
   p. 815.

<u>Wonderful Town</u>. See: Bernstein, Leonard

FISHER, Bob
   <u>The Impossible Years</u>. By Bob Fisher and Arthur Marx.
   Cambridge: November 24, 1966-February 4, 1967 (86)

Barker, Felix. <u>Evening News</u>, November 25, 1966, p.
   5e.
Bryden, Ronald. <u>Observer</u>, November 27, 1966, p. 24e.
Darlington, W. A. <u>Daily Telegraph</u>, November 25,
   1966, p. 19a.
Higgins, John. <u>Financial Times</u>, November 25, 1966,
   p. 28c.
Hobson, Harold. <u>Sunday Times</u>, November 27, 1966,
   p. 49e.
Hope-Wallace, Philip. <u>Manchester Guardian</u>, November
   25, 1966, p. 9e.
Jones, D. A. N. <u>New Statesman</u>, December 2, 1966,
   pp. 850-852.
Kingston, Jeremy. <u>Punch</u>, November 30, 1966, p. 823.
Kretzmer, Herbert. <u>Daily Express</u>, November 25, 1966,
   p. 4d.
Nathan, David. <u>Sun</u>, November 25, 1966, p. 8g.
Shulman, Milton. <u>Evening Standard</u>, November 25,
   1966, p. 4a.
<u>The Times</u>, November 25, 1966, p. 17a.
Trewin, J. C. <u>Illustrated London News</u>, December 3,
   1966, p. 39.

FLICKER, Theodore
   <u>The Premise</u> (a revue). By Theodore Flicker and The
   Company.
   Comedy: July 26, 1962-January 12, 1963 (194)

Barker, Felix. Evening News, July 27, 1962, p. 3c.
Fay, Gerard. Manchester Guardian, July 27, 1962, p.
    9a.
Gascoigne, Bamber. Spectator, August 3, 1962, p.
    159.
Gellert, Robert. New Statesman, August 3, 1962, p.
    154.
Hobson, Harold. Sunday Times, July 29, 1962, p. 25b.
Keown, Eric. Punch, August 8, 1962, p. 209.
Kretzmer, Herbert. Daily Express, July 27, 1962,
    p. 6d.
Muller, Robert. Daily Mail, July 27, 1962, p. 3b.
Pacey, Ann. Daily Herald, July 27, 1962, p. 7a.
Shorter, Eric. Daily Telegraph, July 27, 1962, p.
    14e.
Shulman, Milton. Evening Standard, July 27, 1962,
    p. 8b.
The Times, July 27, 1962, p. 15a.
Trewin, J. C. Illustrated London News, August 11,
    1962, p. 226.
Tynan, Kenneth. Observer, July 29, 1962, p. 21b.

FOOTE, Horton
    Gone With the Wind. See: Rome, Harold

    The Trip to Bountiful.
    Arts: July 4, 1956-August 14, 1956 (48)*

Barber, John. Daily Express, July 5, 1956, p. 7d.
Carthew, Anthony. Daily Herald, July 5, 1956, p. 3e.
Darlington, W. A. Daily Telegraph, July 5, 1956, p.
    8d.
Forster, Peter. Financial Times, July 5, 1956, p.
    2g.
Hobson, Harold. Sunday Times, July 8, 1956, p. 4b.
Hope-Wallace, Philip. Manchester Guardian, July 6,
    1956, p. 9f.
Keown, Eric. Punch, July 11, 1956, p. 54.
Shulman, Milton. Evening Standard, July 5, 1956,
    p. 7f.
The Times, July 5, 1956, p. 7c.
Trewin, J. C. Illustrated London News, July 21,
    1956, p. 116.
Tynan, Kenneth. Observer, July 8, 1956, p. 8d.
Williams, Stephen. Evening News, July 5, 1956,
    p. 5c.
Wilson, Cecil. Daily Mail, July 5, 1956, p. 3b.

FORD, Nancy
    Grass Roots. See: Cryer, Gretchen

FORREST, George
    The Great Waltz. See: Korngold, Eric
    Kismet. See: Wright, Robert

FOSTER, Paul
   Tom Paine.
   Vaudeville: October 17, 1967-November 18, 1967   (34)
   Limited season.

      Barker, Felix. Evening News, October 18, 1967, p.
        3b.
      Bryden, Ronald. Observer, October 22, 1967, p. 29b.
      French, Philip. New Statesman, October 27, 1967,
        p. 564.
      Higgins, John. Spectator, October 27, 1967, p. 507.
      Hobson, Harold. Sunday Times, October 22, 1967, p.
        53f (not a review).
      Kretzmer, Herbert. Daily Express, October 18, 1967,
        p. 4b.
      Lewis, Peter. Daily Mail, October 19, 1967, p. 14b.
      Nathan, David. Sun, October 17, 1967, p. 5d.
      Shorter, Eric. Daily Telegraph, October 18, 1967,
        p. 21a.
      Shulman, Milton. Evening Standard, October 18, 1967,
        p. 12f.
      Trewin, J. C. Illustrated London News, October 28,
        1967, p. 36.
      Wardle, Irving. The Times, October 18, 1967, p. 8g.

FRIML, Rudolf
   Rose Marie. Music by Rudolf Friml and Herbert Stothart;
   book and lyrics by Otto Harbach and Oscar Hammerstein
   II. (Revival)
   Victoria Palace: August 22, 1960-December 17, 1960   (135)

      Barker, Felix. Evening News, August 23, 1960, p. 5e.
      Barnes, Clive. Daily Express, August 23, 1960, p.
        4f.
      Findlater, Richard. Financial Times, August 23,
        1960, p. 13b.
      Grunfield, Edward. Manchester Guardian, August 24,
        1960, p. 5f.
      Hastings, Ronald. Daily Telegraph, August 23, 1960,
        p. 14e.
      Lewis, Naomi. New Statesman, September 3, 1960, p.
        304.
      Muller, Robert. Daily Mail, August 23, 1960, p. 3a.
      Shulman, Milton. Evening Standard, August 23, 1960,
        p. 4f.
      Smith, Andrew. Daily Herald, August 23, 1960, p. 3e.
      The Times, August 23, 1960, p. 11d.

FRINGS, Ketti
   Look Homeward Angel.
   Pembroke, Croydon: October 10, 1960-October 22, 1960
   (16)

      Barker, Felix. Evening News, October 11, 1960, p.
        5a.
      Brooks, Jeremy. New Statesman, October 22, 1960,
        p. 602.

Hope-Wallace, Philip. <u>Manchester Guardian</u>, October
    12, 1960, p. 7d.
Lewis, Peter. <u>Daily Mail</u>, October 11, 1960, p. 3b.
Shorter, Eric. <u>Daily Telegraph</u>, October 11, 1960,
    p. 16e.
<u>The Times</u>, October 11, 1960, p. 16c.
Wardle, Irving. <u>Observer</u>, October 16, 1960, p. 26d.

<u>Look Homeward Angel</u>.
Phoenix: April 3, 1962-May 12, 1962   (45)

Darlington, W. A. <u>Daily Telegraph</u>, April 4, 1962,
    p. 16e.
Gellert, Roger. <u>New Statesman</u>, April 20, 1962, p.
    573.
Hobson, Harold. <u>Sunday Times</u>, April 8, 1962, p. 41d.
Hope-Wallace, Philip. <u>Manchester Guardian</u>, April 4,
    1962, p. 7a.
Keown, Eric. <u>Punch</u>, April 11, 1962, p. 584.
Levin, Bernard. <u>Daily Express</u>, April 4, 1962, p. 4e.
Muller, Robert. <u>Daily Mail</u>, April 4, 1962, p. 3b.
Nathan, David. <u>Daily Herald</u>, April 4, 1962, p. 5f.
Shulman, Milton. <u>Evening Standard</u>, April 4, 1962,
    p. 14a.
<u>The Times</u>, April 4, 1962, p. 6c.
Trewin, J. C. <u>Illustrated London News</u>, April 14,
    1962, p. 594.
Wardle, Irving. <u>Observer</u>, April 8, 1962, p. 28h.

FULLER, Dean
   <u>Once Upon a Mattress</u>. See: Rodgers, Mary

FURTH, George
   <u>Company</u>. See: Sondheim, Stephen

GARDNER, Herb
   <u>A Thousand Clowns</u>.
   Comedy: June 2, 1964-July 11, 1964   (46)

Barker, Felix. <u>Evening News</u>, June 3, 1964, p. 6a.
Bryden, Ronald. <u>New Statesman</u>, June 12, 1964, p.
    924.
Gascoigne, Bamber. <u>Observer</u>, June 7, 1964, p. 24d.
Hobson, Harold. <u>Sunday Times</u>, June 7, 1964, p. 33b.
Kingston, Jeremy. <u>Punch</u>, June 10, 1964, p. 869.
Kretzmer, Herbert. <u>Daily Express</u>, June 3, 1964, p.
    4f.
Levin, Bernard. <u>Daily Mail</u>, June 4, 1964, p. 18b.
Nathan, David. <u>Daily Herald</u>, June 3, 1964, p. 3b.
Pryce-Jones, David. <u>Spectator</u>, June 12, 1964, p.
    797.
Shulman, Milton. <u>Evening Standard</u>, June 3, 1964,
    p. 4e.
<u>The Times</u>, June 3, 1964, p. 5a.
Trewin, J. C. <u>Illustrated London News</u>, June 20,
    1964, p. 1006.

Wall, Michael. <u>Manchester Guardian</u>, June 3, 1964,
    p. 9a.
Young, B. A. <u>Financial Times</u>, June 3, 1964, p. 26a.

GARSON, Barbara
    <u>Macbird</u>!
    Royal Stratford East: April 10, 1967-May 20, 1967 (43)

    Bryden, Ronald. <u>Observer</u>, April 16, 1967, p. 24e.
    Higgins, John. <u>Financial Times</u>, April 12, 1967, p.
        30a.
    Hobson, Harold. <u>Sunday Times</u>, April 16, 1967, p.
        49g.
    Jones, D. A. N. <u>New Statesman</u>, April 21, 1967, p.
        553.
    Kingston, Jeremy. <u>Punch</u>, April 19, 1967, p. 578.
    Kretzmer, Herbert. <u>Daily Express</u>, April 11, 1967,
        p. 4f.
    Lewis, Peter. <u>Daily Mail</u>, April 12, 1967, p. 12b.
    Nathan, David. <u>Sun</u>, April 11, 1967, p. 4e.
    Preston, Peter. <u>Manchester Guardian</u>, April 11, 1967,
        p. 5d.
    Shorter, Eric. <u>Daily Telegraph</u>, April 11, 1967, p.
        17a.
    Shulman, Milton. <u>Evening Standard</u>, April 11, 1967,
        p. 4f.
    Spurling, Hilary. <u>Spectator</u>, April 21, 1967, p. 465.
    <u>The Times</u>, April 11, 1967, p. 8c.

GAZZO, Michael
    <u>A Hatful of Rain</u>.
    Princess: March 7, 1957-May 25, 1957 (92)

    Barber, John. <u>Daily Express</u>, March 8, 1957, p. 3h.
    Barker, Felix. <u>Evening News</u>, March 8, 1957, p. 5a.
    Darlington, W. A. <u>Daily Telegraph</u>, March 8, 1957,
        p. 11d.
    Granger, Derek. <u>Financial Times</u>, March 8, 1957, p.
        2g.
    Hobson, Harold. <u>Sunday Times</u>, March 10, 1957, p. 19b.
    Hope-Wallace, Philip. <u>Manchester Guardian</u>, March 9,
        1957, p. 5e.
    Keown, Eric. <u>Punch</u>, March 13, 1957, p. 370.
    Shulman, Milton. <u>Evening Standard</u>, March 8, 1957,
        p. 6a.
    <u>The Times</u>, March 8, 1957, p. 3c.
    Trewin, J. C. <u>Illustrated London News</u>, March 23,
        1957, p. 470.
    Tynan, Kenneth. <u>Observer</u>, March 10, 1957, p. 15c.
    Watt, David. <u>Spectator</u>, March 22, 1957, p. 378.
    Wilson, Cecil. <u>Daily Mail</u>, March 8, 1957, p. 10c.
    Worsley, T. C. <u>New Statesman</u>, March 16, 1957, p.
        336.

GELBART, Larry
    <u>A Funny Thing Happened on the Way to the Forum</u>. See:
    Sondheim, Stephen

Jump
Queen's: August 31, 1971-October 9, 1971   (53)

     Adam, Kenneth. Financial Times, September 1, 1971,
        p. 3c.
     Baxter, Felix. Evening News, September 1, 1971, p.
        3a.
     Bryden, Ronald. The Observer, September 5, 1971,
        p. 26g.
     Cashin, Fergus. Sun, September 1, 1971, p. 13f.
     Hurren, Kenneth. Spectator, September 11, 1971, p.
        380.
     Kerensky, Oleg. Manchester Guardian, September 1,
        1971, p. 8d.
     Kretzmer, Herbert. Daily Express, September 1, 1971,
        p. 8f.
     Lambert, J. W. Sunday Times, September 5, 1971, p.
        27a.
     Lewis, Peter. Daily Mail, September 2, 1971, p. 15c.
     Shorter, Eric. Daily Telegraph, September 1, 1971,
        p. 9c.
     Shulman, Milton. Evening Standard, September 1,
        1971, p. 11d.

GELBER, Jack
   The Connection.
   Duke of York's: February 22, 1961-April 1, 1961   (42)

     Barker, Felix. Evening News, February 23, 1961, p.
        11e.
     Craig, H. A. L. New Statesman, March 3, 1961, pp.
        357-358.
     Darlington, W. A. Daily Telegraph, February 23,
        1961, p. 16d.
     Gascoigne, Bamber. Spectator, March 3, 1961, p. 296.
     Hobson, Harold. Sunday Times, February 26, 1961, p.
        41a.
     Hope-Wallace, Philip. Manchester Guardian, February
        24, 1961, p. 11b.
     Keown, Eric. Punch, March 1, 1961, p. 367.
     Levin, Bernard. Daily Express, February 23, 1961,
        p. 11f.
     Muller, Robert. Daily Mail, February 23, 1961, p.
        3a.
     Nathan, David. Daily Herald, February 23, 1961, p.
        3a.
     Shulman, Milton. Evening Standard, February 22,
        1961, p. 17a.
     The Times, February 23, 1961, p. 8a.
     Trewin, J. C. Illustrated London News, March 11,
        1961, p. 408.
     Tynan, Kenneth. Observer, February 26, 1961, p. 27a.
     Worsley, T. C. Financial Times, February 23, 1961,
        p. 20d.

GERSHE, Leonard
   Butterflies Are Free.
   Apollo: November 4, 1970-December 5, 1970   (37)

      Barber, John. Daily Telegraph, November 5, 1970,
         p. 16a.
      Billington, Michael. The Times, November 5, 1970,
         p. 16a.
      Bryden, Ronald. Observer, November 8, 1970, p. 28g.
      Hobson, Harold. Sunday Times, November 8, 1970, p.
         26h.
      Hope-Wallace, Philip. Manchester Guardian, November
         5, 1970, p. 10a.
      Hurren, Kenneth. Spectator, November 14, 1970, p.
         609.
      Kingston, Jeremy. Punch, November 11, 1970, pp.
         696-697.
      Kretzmer, Herbert. Daily Express, November 5, 1970,
         p. 16e.
      Shulman, Milton. Evening Standard, November 5, 1970,
         p. 19a.
      Trewin, J. C. Illustrated London News, November 14,
         1970, p. 28.
      Young, B. A. Financial Times, November 5, 1970, p.
         3a.

   Miss Pell Is Missing.
   Criterion: September 12, 1962-January 26, 1963   (187)

      Darlington, W. A. Daily Telegraph, September 13,
         1962, p. 14d.
      Hobson, Harold. Sunday Times, September 16, 1962,
         p. 33b.
      Hope-Wallace, Philip. Manchester Guardian, September
         13, 1962, p. 7b.
      Kerensky, Oleg. Financial Times, September 14, 1962,
         p. 20g.
      Kretzmer, Herbert. Daily Express, September 13,
         1962, p. 4d.
      Levin, Bernard. Daily Mail, September 13, 1962, p.
         3a.
      Meyer, Caren. Evening News, September 13, 1962, p.
         2b.
      Nathan, David. Daily Herald, September 13, 1962,
         p. 9c.
      Shulman, Milton. Evening Standard, September 13,
         1962, p. 4a.
      The Times, September 13, 1962, p. 12c.
      Trewin, J. C. Illustrated London News, September
         29, 1962, p. 494.
      Wardle, Irving. Observer, September 16, 1962, p.
         20h.
      Young, B. A. Punch, September 19, 1962, pp. 428-
         429.

GERSHWIN, George
  Lady Be Good (Revival). Music by George Gershwin; lyrics
  by Ira Gershwin; book by Guy Bolton and Fred Thompson.
  Saville: July 25, 1968-December 7, 1968 (156)

      Barker, Felix. Evening News, July 26, 1968, p. 3a.
      Darlington, W. A. Daily Telegraph, July 26, 1968,
         p. 19d.
      French, Philip. New Statesman, August 2, 1968, p.
         149.
      Green, Benny. Observer, July 28, 1968, p. 21c.
      Hobson, Harold. Sunday Times, July 28, 1968, p. 45d.
      Hope-Wallace, Philip. Manchester Guardian, July 26,
         1968, p. 6a.
      Kingston, Jeremy. Punch, August 7, 1968, pp. 202-
         203.
      Kretzmer, Herbert. Daily Express, July 26, 1968,
         p. 4g.
      Pacey, Ann. Sun, July 26, 1968, p. 7b.
      Shulman, Milton. Evening Standard, July 26, 1968,
         p. 4f.
      Spurling, Hilary. Spectator, August 2, 1968, p. 172.
      Trewin, J. C. Illustrated London News, August 3,
         1968, pp. 32-33.
      Wardle, Irving. The Times, July 26, 1968, p. 11b.

  Oh, Kay! (Revival) Book by P. G. Wodehouse and Guy
  Bolton; lyrics by Ira Gershwin; music by George Gershwin.
  Westminster: March 7, 1974-September 21, 1974 (228)

      Barber, John. Daily Telegraph, March 8, 1974, p.
         13f.
      Barker, Felix. Evening News, March 8, 1974, p. 8g.
      Billington, Michael. Manchester Guardian, March 8,
         1974, p. 12e.
      Cushman, Robert. The Observer, March 10, 1974, p.
         31c.
      Hobson, Harold. Sunday Times, March 10, 1974, p.
         37c.
      Hurren, Kenneth. Spectator, March 16, 1974, p. 337.
      Kingston, Jeremy. Punch, March 20, 1974, p. 477.
      Kretzmer, Herbert. Daily Express, March 8, 1974,
         p. 12e.
      Shulman, Milton. Evening Standard, March 8, 1974,
         p. 26a.
      Southworth, June. Daily Mail, March 8, 1974, p. 3f.
      Thirkell, Arthur. Daily Mirror, March 8, 1974, p.
         18d.
      Wardle, Irving. The Times, March 8, 1974, p. 12d.
      Young, B. A. Financial Times, March 8, 1974, p. 3c.

  Porgy and Bess. Lyrics by Ira Gershwin; book by Dubose
  Heyward.
  Stoll: October 9, 1952-February 10, 1953 (142)

      Aprahamian, Felix. Sunday Times, October 12, 1952,
         p. 9d.

B., D. C. Punch, October 22, 1952, p. 523.
Brown, Ivor. Observer, October 12, 1952, p. 18a.
Cooper, Martin. Spectator, October 17, 1952, p. 502.
Darlington, W. A. Daily Telegraph, October 10, 1952,
     p. 9d.
Hayes, Walter. Daily Sketch, October 10, 1952, p.
     5e.
Hope-Wallace, Philip. Manchester Guardian, October
     11, 1952, p. 3a.
Mannock, P. L. Daily Herald, October 10, 1952, p.
     3a.
Shawe-Taylor, Desmond. New Statesman, October 18,
     1952, p. 448.
Smith, Cecil. Daily Express, October 10, 1952, p.
     6a.
The Times, October 10, 1952, p. 2d.
Trewin, J. C. Illustrated London News, October 25,
     1952, p. 688.
Tynan, Kenneth. Evening Standard, October 10, 1952,
     p. 11d.
Williams, Stephen. Evening News, October 10, 1952,
     p. 4e.
Wiltshire, Maurice. Daily Mail, October 10, 1952,
     p. 6e.

GERSHWIN, Ira
     Lady Be Good. See: Gershwin, George
     Oh, Kay! See: Gershwin, George
     Porgy and Bess. See: Gershwin, George

GESNER, Clark
     You're a Good Man, Charlie Brown. Music and lyrics by
     Clark Gesner; book by John Gordon. (Based on comic
     strip "Peanuts" by Charles Schulz.)
     Fortune: February 1, 1968-May 11, 1968 (117)

     Barker, Felix. Evening News, February 1, 1968, p.
          3d.
     Bryden, Ronald. Observer, February 4, 1968, p. 25a.
     French, Philip. New Statesman, February 9, 1968,
          p. 182.
     Hobson, Harold. Sunday Times, February 4, 1968, p.
          49f.
     Hope-Wallace, Philip. Manchester Guardian, February
          2, 1968, p. 11c.
     Kingston, Jeremy. Punch, February 7, 1968, p. 207.
     Kretzmer, Herbert. Daily Express, February 2, 1968,
          p. 4g.
     Nathan, David. Sun, February 2, 1968, p. 7f.
     Raynor, Henry. The Times, February 2, 1968, p. 7e.
     Shorter, Eric. Daily Telegraph, February 2, 1968,
          p. 19c.
     Shulman, Milton. Evening Standard, February 2,
          1968, p. 4e.
     Trewin, J. C. Illustrated London News, February 10,
          1968, p. 31.

GIBSON, William
    Golden Boy. See: Strouse, Charles

    Miracle Worker.
    Royalty: March 9, 1961-May 6, 1961, transferred to
    Wyndham's: May 8, 1961-October 28, 1961 (267)

        Barker, Felix. Evening News, March 10, 1961, p. 4d.
        Craig, H. A. L. New Statesman, March 17, 1961, p.
            448.
        Gascoigne, Bamber. Spectator, March 17, 1961, p.
            364.
        Hastings, Ronald. Daily Telegraph, March 10, 1961,
            p. 16d.
        Hobson, Harold. Sunday Times, March 12, 1961, p.
            41c.
        Hope-Wallace, Philip. Manchester Guardian, March
            11, 1961, p. 5c.
        Keown, Eric. Punch, March 15, 1961, p. 438.
        Levin, Bernard. Daily Express, March 10, 1961, p.
            15f.
        Muller, Robert. Daily Mail, March 10, 1961, p. 3f.
        Nathan, David. Daily Herald, March 10, 1961, p. 3h.
        Shulman, Milton. Evening Standard, March 10, 1961,
            p. 19a.
        The Times, March 10, 1961, p. 19f.
        Trewin, J. C. Illustrated London News, March 25,
            1961, p. 514.
        Tynan, Kenneth. Observer, March 12, 1961, p. 27b.
        Worsley, T. C. Financial Times, March 10, 1961, p.
            22f.

    Two for the Seesaw.
    Haymarket: December 17, 1958-April 18, 1959 (140)

        Brien, Alan. Spectator, December 26, 1958, pp. 912-
            913.
        Carthew, Anthony. Daily Herald, December 18, 1958,
            p. 3e.
        Darlington, W. A. Daily Telegraph, December 18,
            1958, p. 8d.
        Hobson, Harold. Sunday Times, December 21, 1958,
            p. 13e.
        Hope-Wallace, Philip. Manchester Guardian, December
            19, 1958, p. 5a.
        Keown, Eric. Punch, December 24, 1958, p. 846.
        Robinson, Robert. New Statesman, December 27, 1958,
            p. 906.
        Shulman, Milton. Evening Standard, December 18,
            1958, p. 11e.
        Thompson, John. Daily Express, December 18, 1958,
            p. 9f.
        The Times, December 18, 1958, p. 14a.
        Trewin, J. C. Illustrated London News, January 3,
            1958, p. 34.
        Wainwright, David. Evening News, December 18, 1958,
            p. 3c.

Wilson, Angus. Observer, December 21, 1958, p. 11b.
Wilson, Cecil. Daily Mail, December 18, 1958, p. 3c.
Worsley, T. C. Financial Times, December 18, 1958,
   p. 15e.

GILBERT, Willie
  How to Succeed in Business Without Really Trying. See:
Loesser, Frank

GILLETTE, William
  Sherlock Holmes. Based on stories by A. Conan Doyle.
Produced by the Royal Shakespeare Company for the 1974
season.
Aldwych: January 1, 1974-August 10, 1974   (71 in
repertory)

    Barker, Felix. Evening News, January 2, 1974, p. 9e.
    Billington, Michael. Manchester Guardian, January 2,
      1974, p. 8c.
    Christie, Ian. Daily Express, January 2, 1974, p.
      10d.
    Cushman, Robert. The Observer, January 6, 1974, p.
      24c.
    Gaskell, Jane. Daily Mail, January 2, 1974, p. 3f.
    Hobson, Harold. Sunday Times, January 6, 1974, p.
      27a.
    Hurren, Kenneth. Spectator, January 12, 1974, p.
      48.
    Kingston, Jeremy. Punch, January 16, 1974, p. 102.
    Nightingale, Benedict. New Statesman, January 11,
      1974, p. 56.
    Shulman, Milton. Evening Standard, January 2, 1974,
      p. 19d.
    Trewin, J. C. Illustrated London News, March 1974,
      p. 87.
    Wardle, Irving. The Times, January 2, 1974, p. 7c.
    Young, B. A. Financial Times, January 2, 1974, p.
      3c.

GILROY, Frank
  Who'll Save the Plowboy?
Haymarket: April 2, 1963-May 4, 1963   (37)

    Barker, Felix. Evening News, April 3, 1963, p. 9c.
    Darlington, W. A. Daily Telegraph, April 3, 1963,
      p. 16d.
    Driver, Christopher. Manchester Guardian, April 3,
      1963, p. 7d.
    Kretzmer, Herbert. Daily Express, April 3, 1963,
      p. 4a.
    Lambert, J. W. Sunday Times, April 7, 1963, p. 41c.
    Lewis, Peter. Daily Mail, April 3, 1963, p. 3b.
    Pacey, Ann. Daily Herald, April 3, 1963, p. 3g.
    Sedden, George. Observer, April 7, 1963, p. 26d.
    Shulman, Milton. Evening Standard, April 3, 1963,
      p. 4c.

The Times, April 3, 1963, p. 17b.
Young, B. A. Punch, April 17, 1963, p. 570.

GLICKMAN, William
    Plain and Fancy. See: Stein, Joseph

GOELL, Kermit
    Pocahontas.
    Lyric: November 14, 1963-November 23, 1963 (14)

        Barker, Felix. Evening News, November 15, 1963, p.
            8h.
        Darlington, W. A. Daily Telegraph, November 15,
            1963, p. 18.
        Gascoigne, Bamber. Observer, November 17, 1963,
            p. 27c.
        Hobson, Harold. Sunday Times, November 17, 1963,
            p. 33c.
        Kenyon, Michael. Manchester Guardian, November 15,
            1963, p. 11a.
        Kretzmer, Herbert. Daily Express, November 15,
            1963, p. 9g.
        Lewis, Jenny. Financial Times, November 16, 1963,
            p. 6e.
        Nathan, David. Daily Herald, November 15, 1963, p.
            9f.
        Pryce-Jones, David. Spectator, November 22, 1963,
            p. 200.
        Shulman, Milton. Evening Standard, November 15,
            1963, p. 4a.
        The Times, November 15, 1963, p. 17d.
        Trewin, J. C. Illustrated London News, November 30,
            1963, p. 916.
        Young, B. A. Punch, November 20, 1963, p. 755.

GOETZ, Ruth
    The Immoralist. By Ruth and Augustus Goetz. (Based on
    the novel by Andrebide.)
    Arts: November 3, 1954-December 4, 1954* (37)*

        Barber, John. Daily Express, November 4, 1954, p.
            3b.
        Darlington, W. A. Daily Telegraph, November 4,
            1954, p. 6e.
        Granger, Derek. Financial Times, November 4, 1954,
            p. 5d.
        Hartley, Anthony. Spectator, November 12, 1954, p.
            573.
        Hobson, Harold. Sunday Times, November 7, 1954, p.
            11a.
        Hope-Wallace, Philip. Manchester Guardian, November
            5, 1954, p. 3c.
        Keown, Eric. Punch, November 10, 1954, pp. 609-610.
        Shulman, Milton. Evening Standard, November 4, 1954,
            p. 10a.
        The Times, November 4, 1961, p. 7f.

Trewin, J. C. Illustrated London News, November 20,
    1954, p. 901.
Tynan, Kenneth. Observer, November 7, 1954, p. 11a.
Wilson, Cecil. Daily Mail, November 4, 1961, p. 3d.
Worsley, T. C. New Statesman, November 13, 1954,
    p. 610.

GOHMAN, Don
    Ambassador. Book by Don Ettinger, based on The Ambas-
    sadors by Henry James. Lyrics by Hal Hackady; music by
    Don Gohman.
    Her Majesty's: October 19, 1971-January 15, 1972 (97)

        Barber, John. Daily Telegraph, October 20, 1971,
            p. 12a.
        Barker, Felix. Evening News, October 20, 1971, p.
            3c.
        Billington, Michael. Manchester Guardian, October
            20, 1971, p. 8e.
        Bryden, Ronald. The Observer, October 24, 1971, p.
            35b.
        Eastaugh, Kenneth. Sun, October 20, 1971, p. 5c.
        Hobson, Harold. Sunday Times, October 24, 1971, p.
            34f.
        Hurren, Kenneth. Spectator, October 30, 1971, p.
            626.
        Kretzmer, Herbert. Daily Express, October 20, 1971,
            p. 17f.
        Shulman, Milton. Evening Standard, October 20, 1971,
            p. 22b.
        Trewin, J. C. Illustrated London News, October 19,
            1971, p. 68.
        Young, B. A. Financial Times, October 20, 1971, p.
            3a.

GOLDMAN, James
    They Might Be Giants.
    Theatre Royal, Stratford East: June 28, 1961-July 29,
    1961 (33)

        Barker, Felix. Evening News, June 29, 1961, p. 5d.
        Gellert, Roger. New Statesman, July 14, 1961, p.
            64.
        Hastings, Ronald. Daily Telegraph, June 29, 1961,
            p. 14e.
        Hobson, Harold. Sunday Times, July 2, 1961, p. 35c.
        Muller, Robert. Daily Mail, June 29, 1961, p. 3a.
        Nathan, David. Daily Herald, June 29, 1961, p. 5h.
        Shulman, Milton. Evening Standard, June 29, 1961,
            p. 16c.
        The Times, June 29, 1961, p. 5b.
        Trewin, J. C. Illustrated London News, July 15,
            1961, p. 106.
        Tynan, Kenneth. Observer, July 2, 1961, p. 22g.
        Worsley, T. C. Financial Times, June 29, 1961, p.
            20a.

GOOD, Jack
Catch My Soul; a rock version of Othello. Book by Jack
Good; music by Ray Pohlman and Emil Dean Zoghby.
Round House; transferred to Prince of Wales: December
21, 1970-July 24, 1971 (248)

    Barber, John. Daily Telegraph, December 22, 1970,
        p. 6c.
    Barker, Felix. Evening News, December 22, 1970, p.
        7c.
    Fiddick, Peter. Manchester Guardian, December 22,
        1970, p. 8e.
    Higgins, John. The Times, December 22, 1970, p. 11c.
    Hobson, Harold. Sunday Times, January 3, 1971, p.
        41a.
    Kingston, Jeremy. Punch, December 30, 1970, p. 943.
    Shulman, Milton. Evening Standard, December 22,
        1970, p. 21c.
    Thirkell, Arthur. Daily Mirror, December 22, 1970,
        p. 14c.
    Trewin, J. C. Illustrated London News, January 16,
        1971, p. 29.
    Young, B. A. Financial Times, December 22, 1970,
        p. 3a.

GOODRICH, Frances
The Diary of Anne Frank. By Frances Goodrich and Albert
Hackett.
Phoenix: November 29, 1956-March 30, 1957 (141)

    Barber, John. Daily Express, November 30, 1956, p.
        3a.
    Carthew, Anthony. Daily Herald, November 30, 1956,
        p. 3c.
    Darlington, W. A. Daily Telegraph, November 30,
        1956, p. 10d.
    Granger, Derek. Financial Times, November 30, 1956,
        p. 2g.
    Hobson, Harold. Sunday Times, December 2, 1956, p.
        13a.
    Hope-Wallace, Philip. Manchester Guardian, December
        1, 1956, p. 4d.
    Keown, Eric. Punch, December 5, 1956, p. 692.
    Martin, Kingsley. New Statesman, December 8, 1956,
        pp. 742-743.
    Shulman, Milton. Evening Standard, November 30,
        1956, p. 6c.
    The Times, November 30, 1956, p. 5a.
    Trewin, J. C. Illustrated London News, December
        15, 1956, p. 1050.
    Tynan, Kenneth. Observer, December 2, 1956, p. 11a.
    Watt, David. Spectator, December 7, 1956, p. 834.
    Williams, Stephen. Evening News, November 30, 1956,
        p. 5d.
    Wilson, Cecil. Daily Mail, November 30, 1956, p.
        12h.

GORDON, John
    You're a Good Man, Charlie Brown. See: Gesner, Clark

GORNEY, Jay
    Touch and Go. Revue sketches by Jean and Walter Kerr.
    Music by Jay Gorney.
    Prince of Wales: May 19, 1950-December 16, 1951 (348)

        Bishop, George W. Daily Telegraph, May 20, 1950,
            p. 6c.
        Brown, Ivor. Observer, May 21, 1950, p. 6a.
        Evening Standard Night Reporting Corps. Evening
            Standard, May 20, 1950, p. 5a.
        Hayes, Walter. Daily Sketch, May 20, 1950, p. 3c.
        Hobson, Harold. Sunday Times, May 21, 1950, p. 4d.
        Mannock, P. L. Daily Herald, May 20, 1950, p. 3d.
        Steel, Mary. Daily Express, May 20, 1950, p. 3g.
        The Times, May 20, 1950, p. 6d.
        Trewin, J. C. Illustrated London News, June 3, 1950,
            p. 872.
        Wilson, Cecil. Daily Mail, May 20, 1950, p. 5b.

GREEN, Adolph
    Applause. See: Strouse, Charles
    Bells Are Ringing. See: Styne, Jule
    Do Re Mi. See: Styne, Jule
    On the Town. See: Bernstein, Leonard
    Wonderful Town. See: Bernstein, Leonard

GREEN, Carolyn
    Janus.
    Aldwych: April 24, 1957-July 20, 1957 (101)

        Barber, John. Daily Express. April 25, 1957, p.
            3g.
        Barker, Felix. Evening News, April 25, 1957, p. 3c.
        Darlington, W. A. Daily Telegraph, April 25, 1957,
            p. 10d.
        Granger, Derek. Financial Times, April 25, 1957,
            p. 2g.
        Hobson, Harold. Sunday Times, April 28, 1957, p.
            19c.
        Hope-Wallace, Philip. Manchester Guardian, April
            26, 1957, p. 7f.
        Keown, Eric. Punch, May 1, 1957, p. 574.
        L., J. A. New Statesman, May 11, 1957, p. 608.
        Shulman, Milton. Evening Standard, April 25, 1957,
            p. 6a.
        The Times, April 25, 1957, p. 3a.
        Trewin, J. C. Illustrated London News, May 11,
            1957, p. 786.
        Tynan, Kenneth. Observer, April 28, 1957, p. 11c.
        Watt, David. Spectator, May 3, 1957, p. 587.
        Wilson, Cecil. Daily Mail, April 25, 1957, p. 3h.

GREEN, Maubry
    Pyjama Tops. By Maubry Green and Ed Feilbert.
    Whitehall Theatre: September 22, 1969-May 3, 1975
    (2,498)

        Barber, John. Daily Telegraph, September 23, 1969,
            p. 21a.
        Barker, Felix. Evening News, September 23, 1969,
            p. 2a.
        Bryden, Ronald. Observer, September 28, 1969, p.
            27g.
        Buckley, Leonard. The Times, September 23, 1969,
            p. 9e.
        Hobson, Harold. Sunday Times, September 28, 1969,
            p. 59d.
        Hope-Wallace, Philip. Manchester Guardian, September
            23, 1969, p. 8f.
        Kretzmer, Herbert. Daily Express, September 23,
            1969, p. 14c.
        Nathan, David. Sun, September 23, 1969, p. 3a.
        Norman, Barry. Daily Mail, September 24, 1969, p.
            12b.
        Shulman, Milton. Evening Standard, September 23,
            1969, p. 21a.
        Trewin, J. C. Illustrated London News, October 4,
            1969, p. 27.
        Young, B. A. Financial Times, September 23, 1969,
            p. 3a.

GREER, Herb
    Po' Miss Julie.
    Hampstead Theatre Club: June 26, 1972-July 15, 1972
    (25)

        Hobson, Harold. Sunday Times, July 2, 1972, p. 37a.
        Kingston, Jeremy. Punch, July 5, 1972, p. 29.
        Kretzmer, Herbert. Daily Express, June 27, 1972,
            p. 9a.
        Lewis, Peter. Daily Mail, June 28, 1972, p. 26d.
        O'Connor, Garry. Financial Times, June 27, 1972,
            p. 3a.
        Shorter, Eric. Daily Telegraph, June 27, 1972, p.
            13c.
        Shulman, Milton. Evening Standard, June 27, 1972,
            p. 21f.
        Wardle, Irving. The Times, June 27, 1972, p. 10g.

GUARE, John
    A Day for Surprises. On a double bill with Impossible
    Lovers by Arrabal at lunchtime.
    Basement: October 18, 1971-October 22, 1971 (5)

        Wardle, Irving. The Times, October 19, 1971, p. 17c.
        Young, B. A. Financial Times, October 20, 1971, p.
            3g.

Two Gentlemen of Verona. See: MacDermot, Galt

GURNEY, A. R., Jr.
    Children.
    Mermaid: April 8, 1974-May 11, 1974 (29)

        Barber, John. Daily Telegraph, April 9, 1974, p.
            13e.
        Barker, Felix. Evening News, April 9, 1974, p. 4g.
        Billington, Michael. Manchester Guardian, April 9,
            1974, p. 10e.
        Cushman, Robert. Observer, April 14, 1974, p. 30e.
        Hurren, Kenneth. Spectator, April 20, 1974, p. 490.
        Kingston, Jeremy. Punch, April 17, 1974, p. 653.
        Lambert, J. W. Sunday Times, April 14, 1974, p. 34c.
        Nightingale, Benedict. New Statesman, April 26,
            1974, pp. 595-596.
        Thirkell, Arthur. Daily Mirror, April 9, 1974, p.
            22c.
        Tinker, Jack. Daily Mail, April 10, 1974, p. 27a.
        Trewin, J. C. Illustrated London News, June 1974,
            p. 77.
        Wardle, Irving. The Times, April 9, 1974, p. 13c.
        Young, B. A. Financial Times, April 9, 1974, p. 3a.

HACKADY, Hal
    Ambassador. See: Gohman, Don

HACKETT, Albert
    Diary of Anne Frank. See: Goodrich, Frances

HAGUE, Albert
    Plain and Fancy. Book by Joseph Stein and Will Glickman;
    lyrics by Arnold Howitt; music by Albert Hague.
    Drury Lane: January 25, 1956-October 27, 1956 (217)

        Barber, John. Daily Express, January 26, 1956, p.
            6a.
        Carthew, Anthony. Daily Herald, January 26, 1956,
            p. 3d.
        Darlington, W. A. Daily Telegraph, January 26,
            1956, p. 8e.
        Granger, Derek. Financial Times, January 26, 1956,
            p. 2g.
        Hartley, Anthony. Spectator, February 3, 1956, p.
            154.
        Hobson, Harold. Sunday Times, January 29, 1956, p.
            4a.
        Keown, Eric. Punch, February 1, 1956, pp. 185-186.
        Shulman, Milton. Evening Standard, January 26, 1956,
            p. 5a.
        The Times, January 26, 1956, p. 10d.
        Trewin, J. C. Illustrated London News, February 11,
            1956, p. 212.
        Tynan, Kenneth. Observer, January 29, 1956, p. 8a.

Williams, Stephen. *Evening News*, January 26, 1956,
    p. 5b.
Worsley, T. C. *New Statesman*, February 11, 1956,
    p. 151.

HAIMSOHN, George
    Dames at Sea. See: Wise, Jim

HAMMERSTEIN, Oscar, II
    Carousel. See: Rodgers, Richard
    Cinderella. See: Rodgers, Richard
    Desert Song. See: Romberg, Sigmund
    Flower Drum Song. See: Rodgers, Richard
    The King and I. See: Rodgers, Richard
    Rose Marie. See: Friml, Rudolf
    Show Boat. See: Kern, Jerome
    The Sound of Music. See: Rodgers, Richard
    South Pacific. See: Rodgers, Richard

HANSBERRY, Lorraine
    A Raisin in the Sun.
    Adelphi: August 4, 1959-October 10, 1959 (78)

        Alvarez, A. *New Statesman*, August 15, 1959, p. 190.
        Barker, Felix. *Evening News*, August 5, 1959, p. 3b.
        Brien, Alan. *Spectator*, August 14, 1959, p. 191.
        Darlington, W. A. *Daily Telegraph*, August 5, 1959,
            p. 8e.
        Hobson, Harold. *Sunday Times*, August 9, 1959, p.
            17b.
        Hope-Wallace, Philip. *Manchester Guardian*, August
            6, 1959, p. 3a.
        Keown, Eric. *Punch*, August 12, 1959, p. 27.
        Levin, Bernard. *Daily Express*, August 5, 1959, p.
            6f.
        Nathan, David. *Daily Herald*, August 5, 1959, p. 3c.
        Pryce-Jones, Alan. *Observer*, August 9, 1959, p. 11c.
        Shulman, Milton. *Evening Standard*, August 5, 1959,
            p. 10e.
        The Times, August 5, 1959, p. 11a.
        Trewin, J. C. *Illustrated London News*, September
            12, 1959, p. 240.
        Wilson, Cecil. *Daily Mail*, August 5, 1959, p. 3c.
        Worsley, T. C. *Financial Times*, August 5, 1959, p.
            12f.

HARBACH, Otto
    Desert Song. See: Romberg, Sigmund
    No, No Nanette. See: Youmans, Vincent
    Rose Marie. See: Friml, Rudolf

HARNICK, Sheldon
    Fiddler on the Roof. See: Bock, Jerry
    Fiorello! See: Bock, Jerry
    She Loves Me. See: Bock, Jerry

HART, Lorenz
    The Boys from Syracuse. See: Rodgers, Richard
    Pal Joey. See: Rodgers, Richard

HARTOG, Jan de
    The Fourposter. See: Rodgers, Richard

HAYES, Alfred
    The Girl on the Via Flaminia.
    New Lindsay: October 12, 1954-November 1, 1954 (22)

        Darlington, W. A. Daily Telegraph, October 13, 1954,
            p. 8c.
        The Times, October 13, 1954, p. 9d.
        Tynan, Kenneth. Observer, October 17, 1954, p. 11a.
        Wiltshire, Maurice. Daily Mail, October 13, 1954,
            p. 6b.

HAYES, Joseph
    The Desperate Hours.
    Hippodrome: April 19, 1955-September 10, 1955 (167)

        Boothroyd, J. B. Punch, April 27, 1955, p. 538.
        Darlington, W. A. Daily Telegraph, April 21, 1955,
            p. 6d.
        Granger, Derek. Financial Times, April 21, 1955,
            p. 7d.
        Hartley, Anthony. Spectator, April 29, 1955, p.
            538.
        Holt, Paul. Daily Herald, April 21, 1955, p. 3f.
        Hope-Wallace, Philip. Manchester Guardian, April
            21, 1955, p. 5c.
        Lambert, J. W. Sunday Times, April 24, 1955, p. 7b.
        Shulman, Milton. Evening Standard, April 21, 1955,
            p. 6c.
        The Times, April 22, 1955, p. 16f.
        Trewin, J. C. Illustrated London News, April 30,
            1955, p. 794.
        Williams, Stephen. Evening News, April 21, 1955,
            p. 9c.

HECHT, Ben
    The Front Page. By Ben Hecht and Charles MacArthur.
    Produced by the National Theatre for the 1972 season.
    Old Vic: July 6, 1972-January 31, 1973 (110 perform-
    ances in repertory)

        Billington, Michael. Manchester Guardian, July 7,
            1972, p. 10b.
        Dawson, Helen. Observer, July 9, 1972, p. 31a.
        Hobson, Harold. Sunday Times, July 9, 1972, p. 29d.
        Hurren, Kenneth. Spectator, July 15, 1972, p. 100.
        Kingston, Jeremy. Punch, July 19, 1972, p. 90.
        Kretzmer, Herbert. Daily Express, July 7, 1972,
            p. 13a.
        Nightingale, Benedict. New Statesman, July 14,
            1972, p. 64.

O'Connor, Garry. Financial Times, July 7, 1972, p.
    3a.
Shorter, Eric. Daily Telegraph, July 7, 1972, p.
    11g.
Shulman, Milton. Evening News, June 7, 1972, p. 25c.
Trewin, J. C. Illustrated London News, September
    1972, p. 65.
Wardle, Irving. The Times, July 7, 1972, p. 9d.

HEGGEN, Thomas
    Mister Roberts.
    Coliseum: July 19, 1950-January 20, 1951 (214)

        Barber, John. Daily Express, July 29, 1950, p. 3a.
        Brown, Ivor. Observer, July 23, 1950, p. 6a.
        Conway, Harold. Evening Standard, July 20, 1950,
            p. 5d.
        Darlington, W. A. Daily Telegraph, July 20, 1950,
            p. 6e.
        Fleming, Peter. Spectator, July 28, 1950, p. 113.
        Hayes, Walter. Daily Sketch, July 20, 1950, p. 3a.
        Hobson, Harold. Sunday Times, July 23, 1950, p. 2d.
        Hope-Wallace, Philip. Manchester Guardian, July 22,
            1950, p. 5c.
        Keown, Eric. Punch, August 2, 1950, p. 132.
        Mannock, P. L. Daily Herald, July 20, 1950, p. 3d.
        The Times, July 20, 1950, p. 8f.
        Trewin, J. C. Illustrated London News, August 12,
            1950, p. 254.
        Williams, Stephen. Evening News, July 21, 1950, p.
            2f.
        Wilson, Cecil. Daily Mail, July 20, 1950, p. 5f.
        Worsley, T. C. New Statesman, July 29, 1950, p. 123.

HELLMAN, Lillian
    Candide. See: Bernstein, Leonard

    The Children's Hour (Revival).
    Arts: September 19, 1956-November 5, 1956 (53)*

        Barber, John. Daily Express, September 20, 1956,
            p. 3f.
        Darlington, W. A. Daily Telegraph, September 20,
            1956, p. 8d.
        Granger, Derek. Financial Times, September 20,
            1956, p. 2g.
        Hartley, Anthony. Spectator, September 28, 1956,
            p. 418.
        Hobson, Harold. Sunday Times, September 22, 1956,
            p. 13b.
        Hope-Wallace, Philip. Manchester Guardian, September
            21, 1956, p. 7g.
        Keown, Eric. Punch, September 26, 1956, p. 386.
        Raymond, John. New Statesman, September 29, 1956,
            p. 372.
        Shulman, Milton. Evening Standard, September 20,
            1956, p. 7e.

Trewin, J. C. Illustrated London News, October 6,
    1956, p. 566.
Unsigned. The Times, September 20, 1956, p. 5f.
Williams, Stephen. Evening News, September 20, 1956,
    p. 5d.
Wilson, Cecil. Daily Mail, September 20, 1956, p.
    3e.

Montserrat.
Lyric, Hammersmith: April 8, 1952-May 10, 1952 (39)

Barber, John. Daily Express, April 9, 1952, p. 3f.
Brown, Ivor. Observer, April 13, 1952, p. 6a.
Conway, Harold. Evening Standard, April 9, 1952,
    p. 5c.
Darlington, W. A. Daily Telegraph, April 9, 1952,
    p. 6e.
Hayes, Walter. Daily Sketch, April 9, 1952, p. 3b.
Hobson, Harold. Sunday Times, April 13, 1952, p. 2c.
Hope-Wallace, Philip. Manchester Guardian, April 10,
    1952, p. 5d.
Mannock, P. L. Daily Herald, April 9, 1952, p. 3d.
The Times, April 9, 1952, p. 6d.
Trewin, J. C. Illustrated London News, April 26,
    1952, p. 723.
Tynan, Kenneth. Spectator, April 18, 1952, p. 512.
Wilson, Cecil. Daily Mail, April 9, 1952, p. 4c.
Worsley, T. C. New Statesman, April 19, 1952, p.
    463.

Toys in the Attic.
Piccadilly: November 10, 1960-January 28, 1961 (85)

Barker, Felix. Evening News, November 11, 1960, p.
    19d.
Brien, Alan. Spectator, November 18, 1960, p. 782.
Craig, H. A. L. New Statesman, November 19, 1960,
    p. 782.
Darlington, W. A. Daily Telegraph, November 11,
    1960, p. 16e.
Hobson, Harold. Sunday Times, November 13, 1960,
    p. 35b.
Hope-Wallace, Philip. Manchester Guardian, November
    12, 1960, p. 5c.
Keown, Eric. Punch, November 16, 1960, pp. 716-717.
Levin, Bernard. Daily Express, November 11, 1960,
    p. 15g.
Muller, Robert. Daily Mail, November 11, 1960, p.
    3b.
Nathan, David. Daily Herald, November 11, 1960, p.
    3f.
Shulman, Milton. Evening Standard, November 11,
    1960, p. 4d.
The Times, November 11, 1960, p. 16a.
Trewin, J. C. Illustrated London News, November
    26, 1960, p. 964.

Tynan, Kenneth. Observer, November 13, 1960, p. 30b.
Worsley, T. C. Financial Times, November 11, 1960,
    p. 19d.

HERBERT, Frederick Hugh
    The Moon Is Blue.
    Duke of York's: July 7, 1953-December 5, 1953 (175)

    Barber, John. Daily Express, July 8, 1953, p. 3f.
    Brown, Ivor. Observer, July 12, 1953, p. 6a.
    Darlington, W. A. Daily Telegraph, July 8, 1953,
        p. 8e.
    Granger, Derek. Financial Times, July 8, 1953, p.
        7g.
    Hayes, Walter. Daily Sketch, July 8, 1953, p. 5b.
    Hobson, Harold. Sunday Times, July 12, 1953, p. 9a.
    Holt, Paul. Daily Herald, July 8, 1953, p. 3h.
    Hope-Wallace, Philip. Manchester Guardian, July 9,
        1953, p. 3c.
    Keown, Eric. Punch, July 22, 1953, p. 130.
    Monsey, Derek. Spectator, July 17, 1953, p. 83.
    R., J. N. B. New Statesman, July 18, 1953, p. 73.
    The Times, July 8, 1953, p. 3d.
    Trewin, J. C. Illustrated London News, July 18,
        1953, p. 106.
    Tynan, Kenneth. Evening Standard, July 10, 1953,
        p. 9c.
    Williams, Stephen. Evening News, July 8, 1953, p.
        4e.
    Wilson, Cecil. Daily Mail, July 9, 1953, p. 9d.

HERMAN, Jerry
    Hello, Dolly! Music and lyrics by Jerry Herman; book
    by Michael Stewart. (Based on The Matchmaker by
    Thornton Wilder.)
    Drury Lane: December 2, 1965-October 28, 1967 (794)

    Barker, Felix. Evening News, December 3, 1965, p.
        7d.
    Benedictus, David. Observer, December 5, 1965, p.
        24c.
    Bryden, Ronald. New Statesman, December 10, 1965,
        p. 945.
    Darlington, W. A. Daily Telegraph, December 3, 1965,
        p. 19a.
    Fay, Gerard. Manchester Guardian, December 3, 1965,
        p. 11e.
    Hobson, Harold. Sunday Times, December 5, 1965, p.
        45g.
    Kingston, Jeremy. Punch, December 8, 1965, p. 855.
    Kretzmer, Herbert. Daily Express, December 3, 1965,
        p. 7e.
    Nathan, David. Sun, December 3, 1965, p. 15d.
    Shulman, Milton. Evening Standard, December 3, 1965,
        p. 5a.
    The Times, December 3, 1965, p. 15d.

Trewin, J. C. Illustrated London News, December 11,
      1965, p. 9c.
Young, B. A. Financial Times, December 4, 1965, p.
      9c.

Mame. Book by Jerome Laurence and Robert E. Lee. Music
and lyrics by Jerry Herman.
Drury Lane: February 20, 1969-March 14, 1970 (430)

Barber, John. Daily Telegraph, February 21, 1969,
      p. 21a.
Barker, Felix. Evening News, February 21, 1961, p.
      13f.
Bryden, Ronald. Observer, February 23, 1969, p. 24f.
Hobson, Harold. Sunday Times, February 23, 1969,
      p. 57a.
Hope-Wallace, Philip. Manchester Guardian, February
      21, 1969, p. 8f.
Kingston, Jeremy. Punch, February 26, 1969, p. 320.
Nathan, David. Sun, February 21, 1969, p. 5a.
Nightingale, Benedict. New Statesman, February 28,
      1969, p. 307.
Shulman, Milton. Evening Standard, February 21,
      1969, p. 19a.
Spurling, Hilary. Spectator, February 28, 1969, p.
      279.
Trewin, J. C. Illustrated London News, March 8,
      1969, p. 30.
Wardle, Irving. The Times, February 21, 1969, p.
      11e.
Young, B. A. Financial Times, February 21, 1969,
      p. 3g.

HERMAN, Muriel
   Mary Had a Little. See: Hertzog, Arthur

HERTZOG, Arthur
   Mary Had a Little. By Arthur Hertzog, Muriel Herman,
   and Al Rosen.
   Strand: November 27, 1951-December 8, 1951 (15)

Barber, John. Daily Express, November 28, 1951,
      p. 3b.
Darlington, W. A. Daily Telegraph, November 28,
      1951, p. 6f.
Hayes, Walter. Daily Sketch, November 28, 1951,
      p. 7b.
Keown, Eric. Punch, December 12, 1951, p. 682.
Mannock, P. L. Daily Herald, November 28, 1951,
      p. 3c.
The Times, November 28, 1951, p. 6e.

HESTER, Hal
   Your Own Thing. Libretto by Donald Driver. Music and
   lyrics by Hal Hester and Danny Apolinar.
   Comedy: February 6, 1969-March 22, 1969 (57)

Barber, John. <u>Daily Telegraph</u>, February 7, 1969,
    p. 21f.
Barker, Felix. <u>Evening News</u>, February 7, 1969, p.
    11h.
Bryden, Ronald. <u>Observer</u>, February 9, 1969, p. 28c.
Hobson, Harold. <u>Sunday Times</u>, February 9, 1969, p.
    57a.
Hope-Wallace, Philip. <u>Manchester Guardian</u>, February
    7, 1969, p. 8d.
Kingston, Jeremy. <u>Punch</u>, February 12, 1969, p. 246.
Nathan, David. <u>Sun</u>, February 7, 1969, p. 7c.
Nightingale, Benedict. <u>New Statesman</u>, February 14,
    1969, p. 234.
Shulman, Milton. <u>Evening Standard</u>, February 7, 1969,
    p. 19a.
Spurling, Hilary. <u>Spectator</u>, February 14, 1969, p.
    216.
Trewin, J. C. <u>Illustrated London News</u>, February 22,
    1969, p. 26.
Wardle, Irving. <u>The Times</u>, February 7, 1969, p. 9a.
Young, B. A. <u>Financial Times</u>, February 7, 1969, p.
    3a.

HEYWARD, Dubose
    <u>Porgy and Bess</u>. See: Gershwin, George

HILLIER, Robert P.
    <u>Jamie Jackson</u>.
    New: July 29, 1968-August 17, 1968 (24)

Bryden, Ronald. <u>Observer</u>, August 4, 1968, p. 21e.
Frame, Colin. <u>Evening News</u>, July 30, 1968, p. 3b.
Hope-Wallace, Philip. <u>Manchester Guardian</u>, July 30,
    1968, p. 4c.
Kingston, Jeremy. <u>Punch</u>, August 7, 1968, p. 203.
Kretzmer, Herbert. <u>Daily Express</u>, July 31, 1968,
    p. 5c.
Nathan, David. <u>Sun</u>, July 30, 1968, p. 3f.
Nightingale, Benedict. <u>New Statesman</u>, August 9,
    1968, p. 181.
Shorter, Eric. <u>Daily Telegraph</u>, July 30, 1968, p.
    17d.
Shulman, Milton. <u>Evening Standard</u>, July 30, 1968,
    p. 4f.
Trewin, J. C. <u>Illustrated London News</u>, August 10,
    1968, p. 30.
Wardle, Irving. <u>The Times</u>, July 30, 1968, p. 11c.
Young, B. A. <u>Financial Times</u>, July 31, 1968, p. 22h.

HIRSON, Roger O.
    <u>Pippin</u>. See: Schwartz, Stephen

    <u>World War 2 1/2</u>.
    New: April 13, 1967-June 3, 1967 (60)

Barker, Felix. <u>Evening News</u>, April 14, 1967, p. 3a.
Bryden, Ronald. <u>Observer</u>, April 16, 1967, p. 24f.

Darlington, W. A. Daily Telegraph, April 14, 1967,
    p. 19c.
Hobson, Harold. Sunday Times, April 16, 1967, p.
    49e.
Hope-Wallace, Philip. Manchester Guardian, April
    14, 1967, p. 9c.
Kingston, Jeremy. Punch, April 10, 1967, pp. 577-
    578.
Kretzmer, Herbert. Daily Express, April 14, 1967,
    p. 7b.
Nathan, David. Sun, April 14, 1967, p. 7c.
Shulman, Milton. Evening Standard, April 14, 1967,
    p. 4e.
Trewin, J. C. Illustrated London News, April 22,
    1967, p. 33.
Wardle, Irving. The Times, April 14, 1967, p. 8c.
Young, B. A. Financial Times, April 15, 1967, p.
    7c.

HOWE, Bill
    The Wayward Way. See: Huycke, Lorne

HOWITT, Arnold
    Plain and Fancy. See: Hague, Albert

HUGHES, Langston
    Black Nativity.
    Criterion: August 14, 1962-September 8, 1962, trans-
    ferred to Phoenix: September 10, 1962-October 13, 1962
    (80)

Barker, Felix. Evening News, August 15, 1962, p. 5a.
Gellert, Roger. New Statesman, August 24, 1962, p.
    237.
Higgins, John. Financial Times, August 16, 1962,
    p. 16a.
Hobson, Harold. Sunday Times, August 19, 1962, p.
    25c.
Hope-Wallace, Philip. Manchester Guardian, August
    15, 1962, p. 7a.
Keown, Eric. Punch, August 22, 1962, p. 281.
Kretzmer, Herbert. Daily Express, August 15, 1962,
    p. 4b.
Lewis, Peter. Daily Mail, August 15, 1962, p. 3b.
Nathan, David. Daily Herald, August 15, 1962, p. 4g.
Rutherford, Malcolm. Spectator, August 24, 1962,
    pp. 272-273.
Shulman, Milton. Evening Standard, August 15, 1962,
    p. 14c.
The Times, August 15, 1962, p. 13a.
Tynan, Kenneth. Observer, August 19, 1962, p. 18d.

HUGHES, Langston
    Black Nativity (Return Engagement).
    Vaudeville: October 2, 1964-October 31, 1964 (39)

Green, Benny. Observer, October 11, 1964, p. 24d.
The Times, October 3, 1964, p. 12a.

Simply Heavenly.
Adelphi: May 20, 1958-June 14, 1958 (16)

Barber, John. Daily Express, May 21, 1958, p. 7g.
Barker, Felix. Evening News, May 21, 1958, p. 7a.
Fay, Gerald. Manchester Guardian, May 22, 1958, p.
   7c.
Gibbs, Patrick. Daily Telegraph, May 21, 1958, p.
   10f.
Shulman, Milton. Evening Standard, May 21, 1958,
   p. 6a.
The Times, May 21, 1958, p. 3c.
Tynan, Kenneth. Observer, May 25, 1958, p. 15c.
W., D. Financial Times, May 21, 1958, p. 15h.
Wilson, Cecil. Daily Mail, May 21, 1958, p. 3b.

HUNTER, Evan
The Easter Man.
Globe: June 30, 1964-July 18, 1964 (24)

Barker, Felix. Evening News, July 1, 1964, p. 6a.
Bryden, Ronald. New Statesman, July 10, 1964, p.
   64.
Hope-Wallace, Philip. Manchester Guardian, July 1,
   1964, p. 7c.
Kingston, Jeremy. Punch, July 8, 1964, p. 65.
Kretzmer, Herbert. Daily Express, July 1, 1964, p.
   5e.
Lambert, J. W. Sunday Times, July 5, 1964, p. 33a.
Levin, Bernard. Daily Mail, July 2, 1964, p. 10b.
Nathan, David. Daily Herald, July 1, 1964, p. 3b.
Rutherford, Malcolm. Spectator, July 10, 1964, p.
   47.
Shulman, Milton. Evening Standard, July 1, 1964,
   p. 14e.
The Times, July 1, 1964, p. 15g.
Trewin, J. C. Illustrated London News, July 11,
   1964, p. 68.
Young, B. A. Financial Times, July 2, 1964, p. 27c.

HUSSON, Albert
Cuisine des Anges. See: Spewack, Sam and Bella, My
Three Angels

HUYCKE, Lorne
The Wayward Way. Musical version of The Drunkard by
William Henry Smith. Music by Lorne Huycke; lyrics by
Bill Howe.
New Lyric, Hammersmith: November 16, 1964-December 28,
1964* (49)

Barker, Felix. Evening News, November 17, 1964, p.
   9e.

Higgins, John. Financial Times, November 17, 1964,
    p. 24a.
Hobson, Harold. Sunday Times, November 22, 1964, p.
    43e.
Kingston, Jeremy. Punch, December 2, 1964, pp. 851-
    852.
Nathan, David. Sun, November 17, 1964, p. 9a.
Shorter, Eric. Daily Telegraph, November 17, 1964,
    p. 18d.
Shulman, Milton. Evening Standard, November 17,
    1964, p. 4c.
The Times, November 17, 1964, p. 5c.
Trewin, J. C. Illustrated London News, November 28,
    1964, p. 852.
Walsh, Michael. Daily Express, November 17, 1964,
    p. 8b.

The Wayward Way.
Vaudeville: January 27, 1965-February 27, 1965 (36)

Barker, Felix. Evening News, January 28, 1965, p.
    5h.
Bryden, Ronald. New Statesman, February 5, 1965,
    pp. 211-212.
Darlington, W. A. Daily Telegraph, January 28, 1965,
    p. 18f.
Kingston, Jeremy. Punch, February 3, 1965, pp. 178-
    179.
Rutherford, Malcolm. Spectator, February 5, 1965,
    p. 170.
The Times, January 28, 1965, p. 18e.

HYMAN, Mac
No Time for Sargeants. See: Levin, Ira

INGE, William
Dark at the Top of the Stairs.
Pembroke, Croydon: February 14, 1961-February 26, 1961
(14)

Holland, Julian. Evening News, February 15, 1961,
    p. 7e.
Lewis, Peter. Daily Mail, February 15, 1961, p. 7b.
Shorter, Eric. Daily Telegraph, February 15, 1961,
    p. 14e.
Slater, Dan. Daily Herald, February 15, 1961, p. 3f.
The Times, February 15, 1961, p. 4g.
Wardle, Irving. Observer, February 19, 1961, p. 30f.

A Loss of Roses.
Pembroke, Croydon: January 22, 1962-February 3, 1962
(14)

Barker, Felix. Evening News, January 23, 1962, p.
    7g.
Lambert, J. W. Sunday Times, January 28, 1962, p.
    39d.

Muller, Robert. Daily Mail, January 23, 1962, p. 3g.
Nathan, David. Daily Herald, January 23, 1962, p.
    3d.
Shorter, Eric. Daily Telegraph, January 23, 1962,
    p. 14e.
The Times, January 23, 1962, p. 13a.
Trewin, J. C. Illustrated London News, February 3,
    1962, p. 192.
Wardle, Irving. Observer, January 28, 1962, p. 27c.
Worsley, T. C. Financial Times, January 23, 1962,
    p. 28a.

ISHERWOOD, Christopher
    I Am a Camera. See: Kander, John, Cabaret.

JACOBS, Jim
    Grease. Book, lyrics, and music by Jim Jacobs and
    Warren Casey.
    New London: June 26, 1973-February 16, 1974 (258)

    Barker, Felix. Evening News, June 27, 1973, p. 2d.
    Billington, Michael. Manchester Guardian, June 27,
        1973, p. 10b.
    Cushman, Robert. Observer, July 1, 1973, p. 30d.
    Hurren, Kenneth. Spectator, July 7, 1973, p. 22.
    Kingston, Jeremy. Punch, July 4, 1973, p. 26.
    Kretzmer, Herbert. Daily Express, June 27, 1973,
        p. 6d.
    Nightingale, Benedict. New Statesman, July 6, 1973,
        p. 27.
    Shulman, Milton. Evening Standard, June 27, 1973,
        p. 27c.
    Tinker, Jack. Daily Mail, June 28, 1973, p. 21e.
    Trewin, J. C. Illustrated London News, September
        1973, p. 96.
    Wardle, Irving. The Times, June 27, 1973, p. 11c.
    Young, B. A. Financial Times, June 27, 1973, p. 3a.

JAMES, Henry
    The Ambassadors. See: Gohman, Don

JONES, LeRoi
    Dutchman. Performed with Neighbors by James Saunders.
    Opened at Hampstead Theatre Club: May 8, 1967
    Mayfair: June 27, 1967-July 8, 1967 (18)

    Bryden, Ronald. Observer, May 14, 1967, p. 25b.
    Hobson, Harold. Sunday Times, May 14, 1967, p. 47c.
    Jones, D. A. N. New Statesman, May 12, 1967, p. 667.
    Kingston, Jeremy. Punch, May 17, 1967, p. 730.
    Lewis, Peter. Daily Mail, May 11, 1967, p. 12c.
    Malcolm, Derek. Manchester Guardian, May 9, 1967,
        p. 7e.
    Meyer, Caren. Evening News, June 28, 1967, p. 11c.
    Shorter, Eric. Daily Telegraph, May 9, 1967, p. 19a.
    Shulman, Milton. Evening Standard, May 10, 1967,
        p. 4a.

Shulman, Milton. The Times, May 10, 1967, p. 8g.
Trewin, J. C. Illustrated London News, May 20, 1967,
     p. 35.
Young, B. A. Financial Times, May 11, 1967, p. 30a.

JONES, Tom
     The Fantasticks. See: Schmidt, Harvey
     I Do! I Do! See: Schmidt, Harvey
     110 in the Shade. See: Schmidt, Harvey

KANDER, John
     Cabaret. Based on I Am a Camera by John Van Druten from
     stories by Christopher Isherwood. Music by John Kander;
     book by Joe Masteroff; lyrics by Fredd Ebb.
     Palace: February 28, 1968-November 30, 1968 (316)

          Barker, Felix. Evening News, February 29, 1968, p.
               3b.
          Bryden, Ronald. Observer, March 3, 1968, p. 31b.
          French, Philip. New Statesman, March 15, 1968, p.
               355.
          Hobson, Harold. Sunday Times, March 3, 1968, p. 26d.
          Hope-Wallace, Philip. Manchester Guardian, February
               29, 1968, p. 6e.
          Kingston, Jeremy. Punch, March 6, 1968, p. 355.
          Kretzmer, Herbert. Daily Express, February 29, 1968,
               p. 4f.
          Lewis, Peter. Daily Mail, March 1, 1968, p. 10c.
          Nathan, David. Sun, February 29, 1968, p. 7b.
          Shorter, Eric. Daily Telegraph, February 29, 1968,
               p. 19a.
          Shulman, Milton. Evening Standard, February 29,
               1968, p. 4a.
          Spurling, Hilary. Spectator, March 8, 1968, p. 303.
          Trewin, J. C. Illustrated London News, March 9,
               1968, p. 32.
          Wardle, Irving. The Times, February 29, 1968, p.
               15a.

     Zorba. Book by Joseph Stein. Based on the novel Zorba,
     The Greek by Nikos Kazantzakis. Lyrics by Fredd Ebb;
     music by John Kander.
     Company Theatre, Greenwich: November 27, 1973-December
     21, 1973 (30)

          Cushman, Robert. Observer, December 2, 1973, p. 33c.
          Frame, Colin. Evening News, November 28, 1973, p.
               4f.
          Hurren, Kenneth. Spectator, December 8, 1973, p.
               757.
          Kingston, Jeremy. Punch, December 12, 1973, p. 959.
          Nightingale, Benedict. New Statesman, December 7,
               1973, p. 879.
          Wardle, Irving. The Times, November 28, 1973, p.
               13b.
          Young, B. A. Financial Times, November 28, 1973,
               p. 3a.

KANIN, Garson
   Born Yesterday (Revival).
   Greenwich: April 19, 1973-May 12, 1973 (25)

       Barker, Felix. Evening News, April 21, 1973, p. 4e.
       Coveney, Michael. Financial Times, April 24, 1973,
          p. 3a.
       Hobson, Harold. Sunday Times, April 22, 1973, p.
          33b.
       Hurren, Kenneth. Spectator, April 28, 1973, p. 528.
       Lewsen, Charles. The Times, April 21, 1973, p. 9e.
       Nightingale, Benedict. New Statesman, May 4, 1973,
          p. 667.
       Trewen, J. C. Illustrated London News, June 1973,
          p. 109.

   Do Re Mi. See: Styne, Jule

KAUFMAN, George S.
   Solid Gold Cadillac. See: Teichmann, Howard

KAZANTZAKIS, Nikos
   Zorba the Greek. See: Kander, John

KELLY, George
   The Show-Off.
   Hampstead Theatre Club: March 12, 1974-April 6, 1974
   (26)

       Billington, Michael. Manchester Guardian, March 13,
          1974, p. 10d.
       Hobson, Harold. Sunday Times, March 17, 1974, p.
          37d.
       Hurren, Kenneth. Spectator, March 23, 1974, p. 369.
       Kretzmer, Herbert. Daily Express, March 13, 1974,
          p. 10e.
       Shorter, Eric. Daily Telegraph, March 13, 1974, p.
          13g.
       Shulman, Milton. Evening News, March 13, 1974, p.
          23c.
       Wardle, Irving. The Times, March 13, 1974, p. 19g.
       Young, B. A. Financial Times, March 13, 1974, p. 3a.

KERN, Jerome
   Show Boat (Revival). Book and lyrics by Oscar Hammer-
   stein, II. Based on the novel by Edna Ferber.
   Adelphi: July 29, 1971-September 29, 1973 (910)

       Barber, John. Daily Telegraph, July 30, 1971, p.
          11g.
       Barker, Felix. Evening News, July 30, 1971, p. 30.
       Brahms, Caryl. Manchester Guardian, July 30, 1971,
          p. 8a.
       Bryden, Ronald. Observer, August 1, 1971, p. 24a.
       Caslin, Fergus. Sun, July 30, 1971, p. 5c.
       Hobson, Harold. Sunday Times, August 1, 1971, p.
          23f.

Hurren, Kenneth. Spectator, August 7, 1971, p. 219.
Kretzmer, Herbert. Daily Express, July 30, 1971, p.
    10a.
Lewis, Peter. Daily Mail, July 30, 1971, p. 17a.
Shulman, Milton. Evening Standard, July 30, 1971,
    p. 19d.
Young, B. A. Financial Times, July 30, 1971, p. 3g.

KERR, Jean
    Finishing Touches.
    Apollo: September 4, 1973-October 13, 1973 (47)

    Billington, Michael. Manchester Guardian, September
        5, 1973, p. 8c.
    Cushman, Robert. Observer, September 9, 1973, p.
        35h.
    Humphries, Barry. Punch, September 12, 1973, p. 356.
    Nightingale, Benedict. Spectator, September 15,
        1973, pp. 349-350.
    Shulman, Milton. Evening Standard, September 5,
        1973, p. 24c.
    Trewin, J. C. Illustrated London News, November
        1973, p. 100.
    Wardle, Irving. The Times, September 5, 1973, p.
        16g.
    Young, B. A. Financial Times, September 5, 1973,
        p. 3a.

    Mary, Mary.
    Queens: February 27, 1963-August 31, 1963, transferred
    to Globe: September 2, 1963-February 8, 1964 (396)

    Barker, Felix. Evening News, February 28, 1963, p.
        7g.
    Darlington, W. A. Daily Telegraph, February 28,
        1963, p. 14c.
    Gascoigne, Bamber. Spectator, March 8, 1963, p.
        296.
    Gellert, Roger. New Statesman, March 8, 1963, p.
        352.
    Hope-Wallace, Philip. Manchester Guardian, February
        28, 1963, p. 7a.
    Kretzmer, Herbert. Daily Express, February 28,
        1963, p. 4a.
    Lambert, J. W. Sunday Times, March 3, 1963, p. 41a.
    Levin, Bernard. Daily Mail, February 28, 1963, p.
        3a.
    Nathan, David. Daily Herald, February 28, 1963, p.
        4a.
    Shulman, Milton. Evening Standard, February 28,
        1963, p. 4d.
    The Times, February 28, 1963, p. 16d.
    Trewin, J. C. Illustrated London News, March 16,
        1963, p. 398.
    Tynan, Kenneth. Observer, March 3, 1963, p. 26g.
    Worsley, T. C. Financial Times, March 1, 1963, p.
        24a.
    Young, B. A. Punch, March 6, 1963, p. 351.

KERR, Walter
    Touch and Go. See: Gorney, Jay

KESSELRING, Joseph
    Arsenic and Old Lace (Revival).
    Vaudeville: February 23, 1966-November 12, 1966 (300)

        Barker, Felix. Evening News, February 24, 1966, p.
            9a.
        Bryden, Ronald. New Statesman, March 4, 1966, p.
            308.
        Darlington, W. A. Daily Telegraph, February 24,
            1966, p. 21a.
        Gilliatt, Penelope. Observer, February 27, 1966,
            p. 24e.
        Hobson, Harold. Sunday Times, February 27, 1966,
            p. 29b.
        Hope-Wallace, Philip. Manchester Guardian, February
            24, 1966, p. 7a.
        Kingston, Jeremy. Punch, March 2, 1966, p. 321.
        Kretzmer, Herbert. Daily Express, February 24, 1966,
            p. 4g.
        Levin, Bernard. Daily Mail, February 25, 1966, p.
            16d.
        Nathan, David. Sun, February 24, 1966, p. 5a.
        Shulman, Milton. Evening Standard, February 24,
            1966, p. 4a.
        Spurling, Hilary. Spectator, March 4, 1966, p. 260.
        The Times, February 24, 1966, p. 16e.
        Trewin, J. C. Illustrated London News, March 5,
            1966, p. 34.
        Young, B. A. Financial Times, February 25, 1966,
            p. 28c.

KILTY, Jerome
    Dear Love.
    Comedy: May 16, 1973-June 16, 1973 (27)

        Barker, Felix. Evening News, May 17, 1973, p. 2e.
        Gebler Davies, Stan. Evening Standard, May 17, 1973,
            p. 26e.
        Hurren, Kenneth. Spectator, May 26, 1973, p. 656.
        Kretzmer, Herbert. Daily Express, May 17, 1973, p.
            8f.
        Nightingale, Benedict. New Statesman, May 25, 1973,
            p. 785.
        Tinker, Jack. Daily Mail, May 18, 1973, p. 25d.
        Wardle, Irving. The Times, May 17, 1973, p. 13h.
        Young, B. A. Financial Times, May 17, 1973, p. 3f.

    The Ides of March. Based on the novel by Thornton
    Wilder.
    Haymarket: August 8, 1963-September 28, 1963 (60)

        Barker, Felix. Evening News, August 9, 1963, p. 3a.
        Barry, Gerald. Punch, August 21, 1963, p. 283.

Darlington, W. A.   Daily Telegraph, August 9, 1963,
    p. 14d.
Driver, Christopher.   Manchester Guardian, August 9,
    1963, p. 7a.
Gellert, Roger.   New Statesman, August 16, 1963, p.
    204.
Hobson, Harold.   Sunday Times, August 11, 1963, p.
    29a.
Kretzmer, Herbert.   Daily Express, August 9, 1963,
    p. 6e.
Nathan, David.   Daily Herald, August 9, 1963, p. 5a.
Pryce-Jones, David.   Spectator, August 16, 1963, p.
    205.
Shulman, Milton.   Evening Standard, August 9, 1963,
    p. 4a.
The Times, August 9, 1963, p. 11c.
Trewin, J. C.   Illustrated London News, August 24,
    1963, p. 286.
Tynan, Kenneth.   Observer, August 11, 1963, p. 19e.
Worsley, T. C.   Financial Times, August 10, 1963,
    p. 9f.

KINGSLEY, Sidney
    Detective Story.
    Princess: March 25, 1950-April 29, 1950   (41)

Barber, John.   Daily Express, March 27, 1950, p. 3e.
Brown, Ivor.   Observer, March 26, 1950, p. 10a.
Conway, Harold.   Evening Standard, March 27, 1950,
    p. 6c.
Darlington, W. A.   Daily Telegraph, March 27, 1950,
    p. 7e.
Fleming, Peter.   Spectator, March 31, 1950, p. 425.
Hayes, Walter.   Daily Sketch, March 27, 1950, p. 7a.
Hope-Wallace, Philip.   Manchester Guardian, March
    27, 1950, p. 5f.
Keown, Eric.   Punch, April 5, 1950, p. 384.
Mannock, P. L.   Daily Herald, March 27, 1950, p. 3g.
The Times, March 27, 1950, p. 8c.
Trewin, J. C.   Illustrated London News, April 8,
    1950, p. 552.
V., A.   New Statesman, April 1, 1950, p. 371.
Wilson, Cecil.   Daily Mail, March 27, 1950, p. 3b.

KNOBLOCK, Edward
    Kismet.   See: Wright, Robert

KOBER, Arthur and LOGAN, Joshua
    Wish You Were Here.   See: Rome, Harold

KOPIT, Arthur
    Indians (World Premier).
    Aldwych: July 4, 1968   (34 performances in repertory)

Barker, Felix.   Evening News, July 5, 1968, p. 3a.
Bryden, Ronald.   Observer, July 7, 1968, p. 24f.

Darlington, W. A. Daily Telegraph, July 5, 1968,
    p. 19a.
Hobson, Harold. Sunday Times, July 7, 1968, p. 49f.
Hope-Wallace, Philip. Manchester Guardian, July 5,
    1968, p. 8e.
Kingston, Jeremy. Punch, July 17, 1968, p. 88.
Kretzmer, Herbert. Daily Express, July 5, 1968, p.
    10a.
Nathan, David. Sun, July 5, 1968, p. 3h.
Spurling, Hilary. Spectator, July 12, 1968, p. 61.
Trewin, J. C. Illustrated London News, July 13,
    1968, p. 30.
Wardle, Irving. The Times, July 5, 1968, p. 7a.

Oh Dad, Poor Dad, Mamma's Hung You in the Closet and
I'm Feeling So Sad.
Lyric, Hammersmith: July 5, 1961-July 15, 1961 (13)

Darlington, W. A. Daily Telegraph, July 6, 1961,
    p. 16d.
Gascoigne, Bamber. Spectator, July 14, 1961, p. 60.
Gellert, Roger. New Statesman, July 14, 1961, p.
    64.
Hobson, Harold. Sunday Times, July 9, 1961, p. 35c.
Hope-Wallace, Philip. Manchester Guardian, July 6,
    1961, p. 9a.
Keown, Eric. Punch, July 19, 1961, p. 112.
Meyer, Caren. Evening News, July 6, 1961, p. 6e.
Muller, Robert. Daily Mail, July 6, 1961, p. 3d.
Nathan, David. Daily Herald, July 6, 1961, p. 5a.
Shulman, Milton. Evening Standard, July 6, 1961,
    p. 20b.
The Times, July 6, 1961, p. 19a.
Trewin, J. C. Illustrated London News, July 22,
    1961, p. 144.
Tynan, Kenneth. Observer, July 9, 1961, p. 22a.

Oh Dad, Poor Dad . . . (Revival).
Piccadilly: October 6, 1965-November 20, 1965 (53)

Boothroyd, Basil. Punch, October 13, 1965, pp. 546-
    547.
Bryden, Ronald. New Statesman, October 15, 1965,
    p. 576.
Darlington, W. A. Daily Telegraph, October 7, 1965,
    p. 18d.
Gilliatt, Penelope. Observer, October 10, 1965, p.
    24e.
Hobson, Harold. Sunday Times, October 10, 1965, p.
    49f.
Hope-Wallace, Philip. Manchester Guardian, October
    7, 1965, p. 9c.
Kretzmer, Herbert. Daily Express, October 7, 1965,
    p. 4f.
Nathan, David. Sun, October 7, 1965, p. 5a.
Shulman, Milton. Evening Standard, October 7, 1965,
    p. 4d.

Spurling, Hilary. Spectator, October 15, 1965, p.
    484.
The Times, October 7, 1965, p. 16b.
Trewin, J. C. Illustrated London News, October 16,
    1965, p. 49.

KORNGOLD, Eric
    The Great Waltz. Music by Eric Korngold; lyrics by
    George Forrest and Robert Wright; book by Jerome
    Chodorov.
    Drury Lane: July 9, 1970-February 18, 1972 (706)

    Barber, John. Daily Telegraph, July 11, 1970, p.
        8b.
    Bryden, Ronald. Observer, July 12, 1970, p. 23b.
    Cushman, Robert. Spectator, July 25, 1970, p. 80.
    Frame, Colin. Evening News, July 10, 1970, p. 3e.
    Hobson, Harold. Sunday Times, July 12, 1970, p. 25a.
    Hope-Wallace, Philip. Manchester Guardian, July 10,
        1970, p. 8f.
    Kingston, Jeremy. Punch, July 22, 1970, p. 149.
    Kretzmer, Herbert. Daily Express, July 10, 1970,
        p. 10c.
    Shulman, Milton. Evening Standard, July 10, 1970,
        p. 17e.
    Trewin, J. C. Illustrated London News, July 25,
        1970, p. 39.
    Wardle, Irving. The Times, July 10, 1970, p. 13a.
    Young, B. A. Financial Times, July 10, 1970, p. 3a.

KRAMM, Joseph
    The Shrike.
    Princess: February 13, 1953-March 21, 1953 (43)

    Barber, John. Daily Express, February 14, 1953, p.
        3c.
    Brown, Ivor. Observer, February 15, 1953, p. 11b.
    Conway, Harold. Evening Standard, February 14, 1953,
        p. 5c.
    Darlington, W. A. Daily Telegraph, February 14,
        1953, p. 9g.
    Fleming, Peter. Spectator, February 20, 1953, p.
        212.
    Hayes, Walter. Daily Sketch, February 14, 1953, p.
        6d.
    Hobson, Harold. Sunday Times, February 15, 1953,
        p. 9b.
    Holt, Paul. Daily Herald, February 14, 1953, p. 2b.
    Keown, Eric. Punch, February 25, 1953, p. 274.
    The Times, February 14, 1953, p. 8c.
    Trewin, J. C. Illustrated London News, February 28,
        1953, p. 326.
    Williams, Stephen. Evening News, February 14, 1953,
        p. 3c.
    Wilson, Cecil. Daily Mail, February 14, 1953, p.
        5d.

KRASNA, Norman
   Bunny.
   Criterion: December 18, 1972-February 3, 1973   (56)

      Barber, John. Daily Telegraph, December 19, 1972,
        p. 13a.
      Billington, Michael. Manchester Guardian, December
        19, 1972, p. 10e.
      Hobson, Harold. Sunday Times, December 24, 1972,
        p. 31b.
      Hurren, Kenneth. Spectator, December 30, 1972, p.
        1052.
      Kingston, Jeremy. Punch, January 3, 1973, p. 28.
      Kretzmer, Herbert. Daily Express, December 19,
        1972, p. 10c.
      Lewsen, Charles. The Times, December 19, 1972, p.
        10f.
      Nightingale, Benedict. New Statesman, December 29,
        1972, p. 986.
      Shulman, Milton. Evening Standard, December 19,
        1972, p. 29a.
      Trewin, J. C. Illustrated London News, February
        1973, p. 56.
      Young, B. A. Financial Times, December 19, 1972,
        p. 3a.

KURNITZ, Harry
   Once More With Feeling.
   New: July 9, 1959-August 22, 1959   (52)

      Brien, Alan. Spectator, July 24, 1959, pp. 99-100.
      Darlington, W. A. Daily Telegraph, July 10, 1959,
        p. 8d.
      Hobson, Harold. Sunday Times, July 12, 1959, p.
        12g.
      Keown, Eric. Punch, August 12, 1959, p. 27.
      Levin, Bernard. Daily Express, July 10, 1959, p.
        3h.
      Nathan, David. Daily Herald, July 12, 1959, p. 3d.
      Pryce-Jones, Alan. Observer, July 12, 1959, p. 10c.
      Shulman, Milton. Evening Standard, July 12, 1959,
        p. 10e.
      The Times, July 10, 1959, p. 9a.
      W., M. W. Manchester Guardian, July 11, 1959, p. 5d.
      Wainwright, David. Evening News, July 10, 1959, p.
        5c.
      Wilson, Cecil. Daily Mail, July 10, 1959, p. 3h.
      Worsley, T. C. Financial Times, July 10, 1959, p.
        11g.

LAURENTS, Arthur
   Gypsy. See: Styne, Jule
   West Side Story. See: Bernstein, Leonard

LAWRENCE, Jerome
   Auntie Mame. By Jerome Lawrence and Robert E. Lee.
   Adelphi: September 10, 1958-May 30, 1959   (301)

Barber, John. Daily Express, September 11, 1958,
     p. 9d.
Brien, Alan. Spectator, September 19, 1958, p. 369.
Darlington, W. A. Daily Telegraph, September 11,
     1958, p. 10f.
Hobson, Harold. Sunday Times, September 14, 1958,
     p. 11a.
Hope-Wallace, Philip. Manchester Guardian, September
     12, 1958, p. 5f.
Keown, Eric. Punch, September 24, 1958, p. 416.
Nevard, Mike. Daily Herald, September 11, 1958, p.
     2e.
Shulman, Milton. Evening Standard, September 11,
     1958, p. 13a.
The Times, September 11, 1958, p. 4e.
Trewin, J. C. Illustrated London News, September
     27, 1958, p. 534.
Tynan, Kenneth. Observer, September 14, 1958, p.
     15b.
W., T. C. New Statesman, September 30, 1958, p. 380.
Wainwright, David. Evening News, September 11, 1958,
     p. 5d.
Wilson, Cecil. Daily Mail, September 11, 1958, p.
     3g.
Worsley, T. C. Financial Times, September 11, 1958,
     p. 15f.

Inherit the Wind.
Pembroke, Croydon: February 16, 1960, reopened in the
West End at St. Martin's: March 16, 1960-May 14, 1960
(68)

Alvarez, A. New Statesman, February 27, 1960, p.
     286.
Brien, Alan. Spectator, March 25, 1960, pp. 429-
     430.
Findlater, Richard. Financial Times, February 17,
     1960, p. 15g.
Hobson, Harold. Sunday Times, February 21, 1960,
     p. 23d.
Hope-Wallace, Philip. Manchester Guardian, February
     18, 1960, p. 9c.
Keown, Eric. Punch, March 23, 1960, p. 432.
Levin, Bernard. Daily Express, February 17, 1960,
     p. 4f.
Shulman, Milton. Evening Standard, February 17,
     1960, p. 16e.
The Times, February 17, 1960, p. 13c.
Wainwright, David. Evening News, February 17, 1960,
     p. 11a.
Wilson, Cecil. Daily Mail, February 17, 1960, p. 3b.

St. Martin's: March 16, 1960-May 14, 1960 (68)

Darlington, W. A. Daily Telegraph, March 17, 1960,
     p. 15c.

Shulman, Milton. The Times, March 17, 1960, p. 16f.
Trewin, J. C. Illustrated London News, April 2,
1960, p. 566.

Mame. See: Herman, Jerry

LEDERER, Charles
Kismet. See: Wright, Robert

LEE, Gypsy Rose
Gypsy. See: Styne, Jule

LEE, Robert E.
Auntie Mame. See: Lawrence, Jerome
Inherit the Wind. See: Lawrence, Jerome
Mame. See: Herman, Jerry

LEIGH, Carolyn
Little Me. See: Coleman, Cy

LEIGH, Mitch
Man of La Mancha. Music by Mitch Leigh; play by Dale
Wasserman.
Piccadilly: April 24, 1968-November 30, 1968 (253)

Barker, Felix. Evening News, April 25, 1968, p. 3d.
Billington, Michael. The Times, April 25, 1968, p.
15a.
Bryden, Ronald. Observer, April 28, 1968, p. 30g.
Christie, Ian. Daily Express, April 25, 1968, p. 4b.
French, Philip. New Statesman, May 3, 1968, p. 591.
Hobson, Harold. Sunday Times, April 28, 1968, p.
53a.
Kingston, Jeremy. Punch, May 1, 1968, p. 648.
Nathan, David. Sun, April 25, 1968, p. 7g.
Pritchett, Oliver. Manchester Guardian, April 25,
1968, p. 8e.
Shorter, Eric. Daily Telegraph, April 25, 1968, p.
21e.
Shulman, Milton. Evening Standard, April 26, 1968,
p. 4e.
Trewin, J. C. Illustrated London News, May 4, 1968,
p. 29.

LENNART, Isabel
Funny Girl. See: Styne, Jule

LERNER, Alan J.
Camelot. See: Loewe, Frederick
My Fair Lady. See: Loewe, Frederick
Paint Your Wagon. See: Loewe, Frederick

LETTON, Francis
The Young Elizabeth. See: Dowling, Jennette

LEVIN, Ira
Critic's Choice.
Vaudeville: December 6, 1961-May 26, 1962 (190)

Barker, Felix. Evening News, December 7, 1961, p.
    11c.
Darlington, W. A. Daily Telegraph, December 7, 1961,
    p. 16d.
Gascoigne, Bamber. Spectator, December 15, 1961, p.
    902.
Hobson, Harold. Sunday Times, December 10, 1961, p.
    39a.
Hope-Wallace, Philip. Manchester Guardian, December
    7, 1961, p. 9c.
Levin, Bernard. Daily Express, December 7, 1961, p.
    16g.
Mallory, Leslie. Daily Herald, December 7, 1961, p.
    6c.
Muller, Robert. Daily Mail, December 7, 1961, p. 3e.
Shulman, Milton. Evening Standard, December 7, 1961,
    p. 4c.
The Times, December 7, 1961, p. 17c.
Trewin, J. C. Illustrated London News, December 23,
    1961, p. 1118.
Wardle, Irving. Observer, December 19, 1961, p. 25a.
Worsley, T. C. Financial Times, December 7, 1961,
    p. 22a.
Young, B. A. Punch, December 13, 1961, p. 878.

No Time for Sergeants. From the novel by Mac Hyman.
Her Majesty's: August 23, 1956-November 30, 1957 (411)

Barber, John. Daily Express, August 24, 1956, p. 3h.
Barker, Felix. Evening News, August 24, 1956, p. 5d.
Carthew, Anthony. Daily Herald, August 24, 1956, p.
    5h.
Gibbs, Patrick. Daily Telegraph, August 24, 1956,
    p. 9e.
Granger, Derek. Financial Times, August 24, 1956,
    p. 2g.
Keown, Eric. Punch, September 5, 1956, p. 288.
Lambert, J. W. Sunday Times, August 26, 1956, p. 4h.
Shulman, Milton. Evening Standard, August 24, 1956,
    p. 6c.
The Times, August 24, 1956, p. 5c.
Trewin, J. C. Illustrated London News, September 8,
    1956, p. 400.
Tynan, Kenneth. Observer, August 26, 1956, p. 10c.
Wilson, Cecil. Daily Mail, August 24, 1956, p. 3b.

LEVITT, Saul
    The Andersonville Trial.
    Mermaid: June 6, 1961-July 15, 1961 (67)

Gascoigne, Bamber. Spectator, June 16, 1961, p.
    882.
Gellert, Roger. New Statesman, June 23, 1961, p.
    1018.
Hart, Denis. Manchester Guardian, June 8, 1961,
    p. 9a.

Hastings, Ronald. Daily Telegraph, June 7, 1961, p.
    16e.
Higgins, John. Financial Times, June 7, 1961, p.
    22d.
Hobson, Harold. Sunday Times, June 11, 1961, p. 41a.
Keown, Eric. Punch, June 14, 1961, p. 914.
Levin, Bernard. Daily Express, June 7, 1961, p. 10f.
Muller, Robert. Daily Mail, June 7, 1961, p. 3e.
Piler, Jack. Daily Herald, June 7, 1961, p. 7a.
Thompson, J. W. M. Evening Standard, June 7, 1961,
    p. 12d.
The Times, June 7, 1961, p. 17a.
Trewin, J. C. Illustrated London News, June 17,
    1961, p. 1044.
Tynan, Kenneth. Observer, June 11, 1961, p. 28a.

LINDSAY, Howard
    Anything Goes. See: Porter, Cole

    Remains to Be Seen. By Howard Lindsay and Russel
    Crouse.
    Her Majesty's: December 16, 1952-December 20, 1952   (7)

        Barber, John. Daily Express, December 17, 1952, p.
            3h.
        Conway, Harold. Evening Standard, December 17,
            1952, p. 5d.
        Darlington, W. A. Daily Telegraph, December 17,
            1952, p. 8e.
        Hayes, Walter. Daily Sketch, December 17, 1952, p.
            5e.
        Hobson, Harold. Sunday Times, December 21, 1952,
            p. 4b.
        Hope-Wallace, Philip. Manchester Guardian, December
            18, 1952, p. 3g.
        Mannock, P. L. Daily Herald, December 17, 1952, p.
            3g.
        The Times, December 17, 1952, p. 3e.
        Trewin, J. C. Observer, December 21, 1952, p. 6b.
        Williams, Stephen. Evening News, December 17, 1952,
            p. 3b.
        Wilson, Cecil. Daily Mail, December 17, 1952, p. 6d.
        Worsley, T. C. New Statesman, December 27, 1952, p.
            778.

    The Sound of Music. See: Rodgers, Richard

LOESSER, Frank
    Guys and Dolls. Music and lyrics by Frank Loesser; play
    by Cy Feuer and Ernest Martin; book by Jo Swerling and
    Abe Burrows.
    Coliseum: May 28, 1953-September 25, 1954   (545)

        Barber, John. Daily Express, May 29, 1953, p. 6a.
        Brown, Ivor. Observer, May 31, 1953, p. 14b.
        Darlington, W. A. Daily Telegraph, May 29, 1953,
            p. 10e.

Hamilton, Iain. Spectator, June 5, 1953, p. 727.
Hayes, Walter. Daily Sketch, May 29, 1953, p. 5c.
Hobson, Harold. Sunday Times, May 31, 1953, p. 9b.
Holt, Paul. Daily Herald, May 29, 1953, p. 5a.
Hope-Wallace, Philip. Manchester Guardian, May 30,
      1953, p. 3g.
Keown, Eric. Punch, June 10, 1953, p. 698.
The Times, May 29, 1953, p. 6d.
Trewin, J. C. Illustrated London News, June 20,
      1953, p. 1036.
Tynan, Kenneth. Evening Standard, May 29, 1953, p.
      10a.
Williams, Stephen. Evening News, May 29, 1953, p.
      4d.
Wilson, Cecil. Daily Mail, May 29, 1953, p. 8a.
Worsley, T. C. New Statesman, June 6, 1953, pp.
      671-672.

Hans Anderson. Book by Beverly Cross. Based on motion
picture production by Samuel Goldwyn. Music and lyrics
by Frank Loesser.
London Palladium: December 18, 1974-November 1, 1975
(383)

Barker, Felix. Evening News, December 24, 1974, p.
      10c.
Cushman, Robert. Observer, December 22, 1974, p.
      21e.
Davis, Clifford. Daily Mirror, December 18, 1974,
      p. 16c.
Hobson, Harold. Sunday Times, December 29, 1974,
      p. 25b.
Hurren, Kenneth. Spectator, December 28, 1974, p.
      832.
Kretzmer, Herbert. Daily Express, December 19, 1974,
      p. 10e.
Tinker, Jack. Daily Mail, December 18, 1974, p. 22d.
Young, B. A. Financial Times, December 19, 1974, p.
      3g.

How to Succeed in Business Without Really Trying. Music
and lyrics by Frank Loesser; book by Abe Burrows, Jack
Weinstock, and Willie Gilbert. Based on the book by
Shepherd Mead.
Shaftesbury: March 28, 1963-June 27, 1964 (520)

Barker, Felix. Evening News, March 29, 1963, p. 7d.
Gascoigne, Bamber. Spectator, April 5, 1963, p. 434.
Gellert, Roger. New Statesman, April 5, 1963, pp.
      499-500.
Hobson, Harold. Sunday Times, March 31, 1963, p.
      41d.
Hope-Wallace, Philip. Manchester Guardian, March
      29, 1963, p. 9a.
Kretzmer, Herbert. Daily Express, March 29, 1963,
      p. 4e.

Levin, Bernard. Daily Mail, March 29, 1963, p. 3d.
Nathan, David. Daily Herald, March 29, 1963, p. 7e.
Shorter, Eric. Daily Telegraph, March 29, 1963, p.
    16d.
Shulman, Milton. Evening Standard, March 29, 1963,
    p. 4d.
The Times, March 29, 1963, p. 15a.
Worsley, T. C. Financial Times, March 29, 1963, p.
    9f.
Young, B. A. Punch, April 3, 1963, p. 495.

The Most Happy Fella. Based on They Knew What They
Wanted by Sidney Howard.
Coliseum: April 21, 1960-January 21, 1961 (290)

Alvarez, A. New Statesman, April 30, 1960, p. 622.
Barker, Felix. Evening News, April 22, 1960, p. 9e.
Brien, Alan. Spectator, April 29, 1960, p. 612.
Hall, Angus. Daily Sketch, April 22, 1960, p. 5a.
Hobson, Harold. Sunday Times, April 24, 1960, p.
    25a.
Keown, Eric. Punch, April 27, 1960, p. 597.
Levin, Bernard. Daily Express, April 22, 1960, p.
    15d.
Muller, Robert. Daily Mail, April 22, 1960, p. 3b.
Nathan, David. Daily Herald, April 22, 1960, p. 3a.
Pryce-Jones, Alan. Observer, April 24, 1960, p. 21a
Russell, John. Manchester Guardian, April 23, 1960,
    p. 5e.
Shulman, Milton. Evening Standard, April 22, 1960,
    p. 17c.
The Times, April 22, 1960, p. 18a.
Trewin, J. C. Illustrated London News, May 7, 1960,
    p. 788.
Worsley, T. C. Financial Times, April 22, 1960, p.
    19e.

Where's Charley? (a musical). Book by George Abbott.
Based on Charley's Aunt by Brandon Thomas.
Palace: February 20, 1958-February 26, 1959 (404)

Barber, John. Daily Express, February 26, 1958, p.
    7c.
Barker, Felix. Evening News, February 21, 1958, p.
    5a.
Darlington, W. A. Daily Telegraph, February 21,
    1958, p. 10d.
Granger, Derek. Financial Times, February 21, 1958,
    p. 13f.
Hobson, Harold. Sunday Times, February 23, 1958,
    p. 23b.
Keown, Eric. Punch, February 29, 1958, p. 304.
Shulman, Milton. Evening Standard, February 21,
    1958, p. 10d.
The Times, February 21, 1958, p. 3a.
Trewin, J. C. Illustrated London News, March 8,
    1958, p. 400.

Tynan, Kenneth. Observer, February 23, 1958, p. 15b.
Weaver, Harry. Daily Herald, February 21, 1958, p.
    2g.
Wilson, Cecil. Daily Mail, February 21, 1958, p. 3a.
Worsley, T. C. New Statesman, March 1, 1958, p. 271.

LOEWE, Frederick
    Camelot. Based on The Once and Future King by T. H.
    White. Book and lyrics by Alan Jay Lerner.
    Drury Lane: August 19, 1964-November 13, 1965 (518)

    Barker, Felix. Evening News, August 20, 1964, p. 4e.
    Bryden, Ronald. New Statesman, August 28, 1964, pp.
        291-292.
    Fay, Gerard. Manchester Guardian, August 20, 1964,
        p. 9a.
    Frost, David. Punch, August 26, 1964, p. 315.
    Gascoigne, Bamber. Observer, August 23, 1964, p.
        23h.
    Hobson, Harold. Sunday Times, August 23, 1964, p.
        25a.
    Kretzmer, Herbert. Daily Express, August 20, 1964,
        p. 3g.
    Levin, Bernard. Daily Mail, August 21, 1964, p. 14b.
    Nathan, David. Daily Herald, August 20, 1964, p. 3c.
    Rutherford, Malcolm. Spectator, August 28, 1964, p.
        276.
    Shulman, Milton. Evening Standard, August 20, 1964,
        p. 4c.
    The Times, August 20, 1964, p. 12a.
    Trewin, J. C. Illustrated London News, September
        5, 1964, p. 348.

    My Fair Lady. Based on Pygmalion by George Bernard
    Shaw.
    Drury Lane: April 30, 1958-October 26, 1963 (2,281)

    Barber, John. Daily Express, May 1, 1958, p. 5a.
    Barker, Felix. Evening News, May 1, 1958, p. 5c.
    Brien, Alan. Spectator, May 9, 1958, pp. 586-587.
    Darlington, W. A. Daily Telegraph, May 1, 1958, p.
        10f.
    Fay, Gerard. Manchester Guardian, May 2, 1958, p.
        5e.
    Granger, Derek. Financial Times, May 1, 1958, p.
        15f.
    Hobson, Harold. Sunday Times, May 4, 1958, p. 11a.
    Keown, Eric. Punch, May 7, 1958, p. 622.
    Robertson, Ker. Daily Sketch, May 1, 1958, p. 9e.
    Shulman, Milton. Evening Standard, May 1, 1958, p.
        6a.
    The Times, May 1, 1958, p. 3a.
    Trewin, J. C. Illustrated London News, May 17, 1958,
        p. 827.
    Tynan, Kenneth. Observer, May 4, 1958, p. 15b.
    Weaver, Harry. Daily Herald, May 1, 1958, p. 3a.

Wilson, Cecil. Daily Mail, May 1, 1958, p. 3c.
Worsley, T. C. New Statesman, May 10, 1958, p. 598.

Paint Your Wagon.
Her Majesty's: February 11, 1953-April 3, 1954 (478)

Barber, John. Daily Express, February 12, 1953, p.
   3c.
Brown, Ivor. Observer, February 15, 1953, p. 11b.
Conway, Harold. Evening Standard, February 12, 1953
   p. 5c.
Daily Sketch, February 12, 1953, p. 8d.
Darlington, W. A. Daily Telegraph, February 12,
   1953, p. 8e.
Hamilton, Iain. Spectator, February 20, 1953, p.
   212.
Hobson, Harold. Sunday Times, February 15, 1953,
   p. 9a.
Holt, Paul. Daily Herald, February 12, 1953, p. 3a.
Hope-Wallace, Philip. Manchester Guardian, February
   13, 1953, p. 5f.
Keown, Eric. Punch, March 4, 1953, p. 305.
The Times, February 12, 1953, p. 11a.
Trewin, J. C. Illustrated London News, February 28,
   1953, p. 326.
Williams, Stephen. Evening News, February 12, 1953,
   p. 2c.
Wilson, Cecil. Daily Mail, February 12, 1953, p.
   6d.

LOGAN, Joshua
   Fanny. See: Rome, Harold
   Mister Roberts. See: Heggen, Thomas
   Wish You Were Here. See: Rome, Harold

LONG, Arthur Sumner
   Never Too Late.
   Prince of Wales: September 24, 1963-March 7, 1964 (189

Barker, Felix. Evening News, September 25, 1963,
   p. 4e.
Bryden, Ronald. New Statesman, October 4, 1963, p.
   460.
Darlington, W. A. Daily Telegraph, September 25,
   1963, p. 14d.
Gascoigne, Bamber. Observer, September 29, 1963,
   p. 26h.
Kretzmer, Herbert. Daily Express, September 25,
   1963, p. 8e.
Nathan, David. Daily Herald, September 25, 1963,
   p. 5a.
Shulman, Milton. Evening Standard, September 25,
   1963, p. 4d.
The Times, September 25, 1963, p. 13a.
Worsley, T. C. Financial Times, September 26, 1963,
   p. 26d.
Young, B. A. Punch, October 2, 1963, p. 503.

Looking for Action.
(A revue by Second City group from Chicago.)
Prince Charles: April 23, 1963-June 1, 1963   (50)

Clurman, Harold. Observer, April 28, 1963, p. 28d.
Darlington, W. A. Daily Telegraph, April 24, 1963,
p. 17a.
Dent, Alan. Punch, May 1, 1963, pp. 642-643.
Gellert, Roger. New Statesman, May 3, 1963, p. 689.
Hobson, Harold. Sunday Times, April 28, 1963, p.
41d.
Hope-Wallace, Philip. Manchester Guardian, April
24, 1963, p. 7a.
Levin, Bernard. Daily Mail, April 24, 1963, p. 3f.
Trewin, J. C. Illustrated London News, May 11, 1963,
p. 740.
Worsley, T. C. Financial Times, April 24, 1963, p.
22a.

LOOS, Anita
Gentlemen Prefer Blondes. See: Styne, Jule

Gigi. Based on a work by Colette.
New: May 23, 1956-September 1, 1956   (117)*

Barber, John. Daily Express, May 24, 1956, p. 3c.
Darlington, W. A. Daily Telegraph, May 24, 1956,
p. 8d.
Granger, Derek. Financial Times, May 24, 1956, p.
2g.
Hartley, Anthony. Spectator, June 1, 1956, p. 761.
Hobson, Harold. Sunday Times, May 27, 1956, p. 13a.
Hope-Wallace, Philip. Manchester Guardian, May 25,
1956, p. 5c.
Keown, Eric. Punch, May 29, 1956, p. 663.
Raymond, John. New Statesman, June 2, 1956, p. 627.
Shulman, Milton. Evening Standard, May 24, 1956,
p. 8c.
The Times, May 24, 1956, p. 3a.
Trewin, J. C. Illustrated London News, June 9, 1956,
p. 704.
Tynan, Kenneth. Observer, May 27, 1956, p. 11b.
Williams, Stephen. Evening News, May 24, 1956, p.
5a.
Wilson, Cecil. Daily Mail, May 24, 1956, p. 3g.

LOWE, Frank
The Thirteen Clocks. By James Thurber, adapted for the
stage by Frank Lowe.
Arts: December 22, 1966-January 7, 1967   (16)

Darlington, W. A. Daily Telegraph, December 23,
1966, p. 11g.
Gray, David. Manchester Guardian, December 23, 1966,
p. 5e.
Hobson, Harold. Sunday Times, January 1, 1967, p.
37h.

Kingston, Jeremy. Punch, January 4, 1967, pp. 26-27.
Kretzmer, Herbert. Daily Express, December 23, 1966,
    p. 4e.
Shulman, Milton. Evening Standard, December 23, 1966,
    p. 4a.
The Times, December 23, 1966, p. 4e.
Trewin, J. C. Illustrated London News, January 7,
    1967, p. 30.
Wells, Alexandra. Sun, December 23, 1966, p. 5f.
Young, B. A. Financial Times, December 23, 1966,
    p. 16a.

LOWELL, Robert
    Benito Cereno.
    Mermaid: March 8, 1967-April 1, 1967 (37)

        Barker, Felix. Evening News, March 9, 1967, p. 9e.
        Bryden, Ronald. Observer, March 12, 1967, p. 25a.
        Darlington, W. A. Daily Telegraph, March 9, 1967,
            p. 21c.
        Hobson, Harold. Sunday Times, March 12, 1967, p.
            49a.
        Hope-Wallace, Philip. Manchester Guardian, March
            9, 1967, p. 6d.
        Jones, D. A. N. New Statesman, March 17, 1967, p.
            382.
        Kingston, Jeremy. Punch, March 15, 1967, p. 389.
        Kretzmer, Herbert. Daily Express, March 9, 1967,
            p. 4f.
        Lewis, Peter. Daily Mail, March 10, 1967, p. 18b.
        Nathan, David. Sun, March 9, 1967, p. 7d.
        Shulman, Milton. Evening Standard, March 9, 1967,
            p. 8e.
        Spurling, Hilary. Spectator, March 17, 1967, p.
            314.
        Trewin, J. C. Illustrated London News, March 18,
            1967, p. 30.
        Wardle, Irving. The Times, March 9, 1967, p. 10c.
        Young, B. A. Financial Times, March 10, 1967, p.
            30c.

    Prometheus Bound.
    Mermaid: June 24, 1971-July 24, 1971 (31)

        Barker, Felix. Evening News, June 25, 1971, p. 3a.
        Bryden, Ronald. Observer, June 27, 1971, p. 26a.
        Hobson, Harold. Sunday Times, June 27, 1971, p. 27e.
        Hope-Wallace, Philip. Manchester Guardian, June 25,
            1971, p. 8a.
        Hurren, Kenneth. Spectator, July 3, 1971, p. 26.
        Kretzmer, Herbert. Daily Express, June 25, 1971,
            p. 14f.
        Pryce Jones, David. Financial Times, June 25, 1971,
            p. 3a.
        Shorter, Eric. Daily Telegraph, June 25, 1971, p.
            14a.

Shulman, Milton. <u>Evening Standard</u>, June 25, 1971,
    p. 21f.
Trewin, J. C. <u>Illustrated London News</u>, September
    1971, p. 55.
Wardle, Irving. <u>The Times</u>, June 25, 1971, p. 18a.

MacARTHUR, Charles
    <u>The Front Page</u>. See: Hecht, Ben

McCLURE, Michael
    <u>The Beard</u>.
    Royal Court: November 4, 1968-January 4, 1969 (50)

    Barker, Felix. <u>Evening News</u>, November 5, 1968, p.
        7c.
    Bryden, Ronald. <u>Observer</u>, November 10, 1968, p. 22e.
    Hobson, Harold. <u>Sunday Times</u>, November 10, 1968, p.
        59c.
    Jongh, Nicholas De. <u>Manchester Guardian</u>, November
        6, 1968, p. 6a.
    Kingston, Jeremy. <u>Punch</u>, November 13, 1968, p. 703.
    Lewis, Peter. <u>Daily Mail</u>, November 6, 1968, p. 12b.
    Nightingale, Benedict. <u>New Statesman</u>, November 15,
        1968, p. 682.
    Shulman, Milton. <u>Evening Standard</u>, November 5, 1968,
        p. 21a.
    Spurling, Hilary. <u>Spectator</u>, November 15, 1968, p.
        709.
    Wardle, Irving. <u>The Times</u>, November 6, 1968, p. 14a.

McCULLERS, Carson
    <u>The Member of the Wedding</u>.
    Royal Court: February 5, 1957-March 9, 1957 (36)

    Ayre, Leslie. <u>Evening News</u>, February 6, 1957, p. 3d.
    Barber, John. <u>Daily Express</u>, February 6, 1957, p.
        3e.
    Gibbs, Patrick. <u>Daily Telegraph</u>, February 6, 1957,
        p. 8d.
    Granger, Derek. <u>Financial Times</u>, February 6, 1957,
        p. 2g.
    Hobson, Harold. <u>Sunday Times</u>, February 10, 1957,
        p. 5a.
    Hope-Wallace, Philip. <u>Manchester Guardian</u>, February
        7, 1957, p. 7c.
    Keown, Eric. <u>Punch</u>, February 13, 1957, p. 258.
    Shulman, Milton. <u>Evening Standard</u>, February 6, 1957,
        p. 10a.
    <u>The Times</u>, February 6, 1957, p. 3e.
    Trewin, J. C. <u>Illustrated London News</u>, February 16,
        1957, p. 276.
    Tynan, Kenneth. <u>Observer</u>, February 10, 1957, p. 11a.
    Watt, David. <u>Spectator</u>, February 15, 1957, p. 212.
    Wilson, Cecil. <u>Daily Mail</u>, February 6, 1957, p. 7e.
    Worsley, T. C. <u>New Statesman</u>, February 16, 1957,
        pp. 201-202.

The Square Root of Wonderful.
Hampstead Theatre Club: March 9, 1970-March 28, 1970
(23)

  Barber, John. Daily Telegraph, March 10, 1970, p.
   14a.
  Bryden, Ronald. Observer, March 15, 1970, p. 35d.
  Hobson, Harold. Sunday Times, March 15, 1970, p.
   53b.
  Kretzmer, Herbert. Daily Express, March 10, 1970,
   p. 16h.
  Nightingale, Benedict. New Statesman, March 20,
   1970, p. 422.
  Trewin, J. C. Illustrated London News, March 21,
   1970, p. 33.
  Wardle, Irving. The Times, March 10, 1970, p. 16d.
  Young, B. A. Financial Times, March 10, 1970, p. 3c.

MacDERMOT, Galt
 Hair. By Gerome Ragni and James Rado. Music by Galt
 MacDermot.
 Shaftesbury: September 27, 1968-July 19, 1973   (1,998)

  Barker, Felix. Evening News, September 28, 1968,
   p. 7c.
  Bryden, Ronald. Observer, September 29, 1968, p.
   25a.
  De'ath, Wilfred. Illustrated London News, October
   12, 1968, p. 43.
  Hobson, Harold. Sunday Times, September 29, 1968,
   p. 59a.
  Hope-Wallace, Philip. Manchester Guardian, September
   28, 1968, p. 6e.
  Kingston, Jeremy. Punch, October 9, 1968, p. 517.
  Kretzmer, Herbert. Daily Express, September 28,
   1968, p. 12a.
  Nathan, David. Sun, September 28, 1968, p. 3b.
  Nightingale, Benedict. New Statesman, October 4,
   1968, p. 437.
  Shulman, Milton. Evening Standard, September 30,
   1968, p. 4a.
  Spurling, Hilary. Spectator, October 4, 1968, pp.
   481-482.
  Wardle, Irving. The Times, September 28, 1968, p.
   18g.

 Hair (Revival).
 Queen's Theatre: June 25, 1974-September 28, 1974   (111)

  Barber, John. Daily Telegraph, June 26, 1974, p.
   15c.
  Coveney, Michael. Financial Times, June 26, 1974,
   p. 3g.
  Hobson, Harold. Sunday Times, June 30, 1974, p.
   37a.
  Hurren, Kenneth. Spectator, July 6, 1974, p. 25.

Kretzmer, Herbert. Daily Express, June 26, 1974,
     p. 10d.
Meyer, Caren. Evening News, June 26, 1974, p. 6d.
Nightingale, Benedict. New Statesman, July 12, 1974,
     p. 61.
Radin, Victoria. Observer, June 30, 1974, p. 31c.
Tinker, Jack. Daily Mail, June 26, 1974, p. 14c.

Hair (Revival).
Her Majesty's: June 7, 1975-September 27, 1975 (128)

     Atkins, Harold. Daily Telegraph, June 9, 1975, p.
          6c.
     Young, B. A. Financial Times, June 9, 1975, p. 3d.

Isabel's a Jezebel. Book by William Dumares; music by
Galt MacDermot.
Duchess: December 19, 1970-February 6, 1971 (61)

     Barber, John. Daily Telegraph, December 19, 1970,
          p. 5a.
     Barker, Felix. Evening News, December 19, 1970, p.
          3d.
     Hobson, Harold. Sunday Times, December 20, 1970,
          p. 23b.
     Hope-Wallace, Philip. Manchester Guardian, December
          19, 1970, p. 6e.
     Kingston, Jeremy. Punch, December 30, 1970, p. 944.
     Kretzmer, Herbert. Daily Express, December 19, 1970,
          p. 6b.
     Shulman, Milton. Evening Standard, December 21,
          1970, p. 15f.
     Thirkell, Arthur. Daily Mirror, December 21, 1970,
          p. 14e.
     Trewin, J. C. Illustrated London News, January 2,
          1971, p. 33.
     Young, B. A. Financial Times, December 21, 1970,
          p. 3c.

Two Gentlemen of Verona. Book by John Guare and Mel
Shapiro adapted from the play by William Shakespeare.
Lyrics by John Guare; music by Galt MacDermot.
Phoenix: April 26, 1973-November 10, 1973 (237)

     Billington, Michael. Manchester Guardian, April 27,
          1973, p. 14d.
     Frame, Colin. Evening News, April 27, 1973, p. 2d.
     Hobson, Harold. Sunday Times, April 29, 1973, p.
          35d.
     Hurren, Kenneth. Spectator, May 5, 1973, p. 562.
     Kingston, Jeremy. Punch, May 9, 1973, p. 663.
     Kretzmer, Herbert. Daily Express, April 27, 1973,
          p. 8d.
     Nightingale, Benedict. New Statesman, May 4, 1973,
          p. 667.
     Shulman, Milton. Evening News, April 27, 1973, p.
          24e.

Trewin, J. C. Illustrated London News, June 1973,
     p. 109.
Wardle, Irving. The Times, April 27, 1973, p. 9g.
Young, B. A. Financial Times, April 27, 1973, p. 3a.

MACLEISH, Archibald
   J. B.
   Phoenix: March 23, 1961-April 8, 1961 (19)

Barker, Felix. Evening News, March 24, 1961, p. 5a.
Boothroyd, J. B. Punch, April 5, 1961, p. 550.
Craig, H. A. L. New Statesman, March 31, 1961, p.
     524.
Darlington, W. A. Daily Telegraph, March 24, 1961,
     p. 16d.
Gascoigne, Bamber. Spectator, March 31, 1961, p.
     444.
Hobson, Harold. Sunday Times, March 26, 1961, p.
     35b.
Hope-Wallace, Philip. Manchester Guardian, March
     25, 1961, p. 5b.
Levin, Bernard. Daily Express, March 24, 1961, p.
     9a.
Muller, Robert. Daily Mail, March 24, 1961, p. 3c.
Nathan, David. Daily Herald, March 24, 1961, p. 3a.
Shulman, Milton. Evening Standard, March 24, 1961,
     p. 19a.
The Times, March 24, 1961, p. 18a.
Trewin, J. C. Illustrated London News, April 8,
     1961, p. 600.
Wardle, Irving. Observer, March 26, 1961, p. 30a.
Worsley, T. C. Financial Times, March 24, 1961, p.
     22d.

McNALLY, Terence
   Next and Sweet Eros (a double bill).
   Open Space: July 13, 1971-August 7, 1971 (20)

Hobson, Harold. Sunday Times, July 18, 1971, p. 25f.
O'Connor, Garry. Financial Times, July 14, 1971, p.
     3g.
Shulman, Milton. Evening Standard, July 14, 1971,
     p. 9a.
Wardle, Irving. The Times, July 14, 1971, p. 9g.

MAGDALAMY, Peter
   Section Nine. Produced by the Royal Shakespeare Company.
   The Place: October 11, 1973-December 6, 1973 (64)*;
   reopened at the Aldwych January 23, 1974 and ran in
   repertory for 47 performances. Last performance: April
   23, 1974

Billington, Michael. Manchester Guardian, October
     12, 1973, p. 12c.
Cushman, Robert. Observer, October 14, 1973, p. 36b.
Hurren, Kenneth. Spectator, October 20, 1973, pp.
     519-520.

Lewsen, Charles. The Times, October 12, 1973, p.
   15c.
Nightingale, Benedict. New Statesman, October 19,
   1973, pp. 572-573.
Trewin, J. C. Illustrated London News, April 1974,
   p. 73.

MANDEL, Frank
   Desert Song. See: Romberg, Sigmund

MANHOFF, Bill
   The Owl and the Pussycat.
   Criterion: March 2, 1966-August 20, 1966   (196)

   Barker, Felix. Evening News, March 3, 1966, p. 7a.
   Darlington, W. A. Daily Telegraph, March 3, 1966,
      p. 21c.
   Gilliatt, Penelope. Observer, March 6, 1966, p. 24e.
   Higgins, John. Financial Times, March 4, 1966, p.
      24c.
   Hobson, Harold. Sunday Times, March 6, 1966, p. 29b.
   Kingston, Jeremy. Punch, March 9, 1966, p. 357.
   Kretzmer, Herbert. Daily Express, March 3, 1966,
      p. 4e.
   Levin, Bernard. Daily Mail, March 4, 1966, p. 16b.
   Nathan, David. Sun, March 3, 1966, p. 8f.
   Shulman, Milton. Evening Standard, March 3, 1966,
      p. 4e.
   The Times, March 3, 1966, p. 18f.
   Trewin, J. C. Illustrated London News, March 12,
      1966, p. 48.

MARASCO, Robert
   Child's Play.
   Queen's: March 16, 1971-June 12, 1971   (106)

   Barker, Felix. Evening News, March 17, 1971, p. 3b.
   Bryden, Ronald. Observer, March 21, 1971, p. 34e.
   Hobson, Harold. Sunday Times, March 21, 1971, p.
      37d.
   Hurren, Kenneth. Spectator, March 27, 1971, p. 429.
   Jongh, Nicholas De. Manchester Guardian, March 17,
      1971, p. 10b.
   Kingston, Jeremy. Punch, March 24, 1971, p. 423.
   Kretzmer, Herbert. Daily Express, March 17, 1971,
      p. 16e.
   Shorter, Eric. Daily Telegraph, March 17, 1971, p.
      16c.
   Shulman, Milton. Evening Standard, March 17, 1971,
      p. 22d.
   Trewin, J. C. Illustrated London News, March 27,
      1971, p. 23.
   Young, B. A. Financial Times, March 17, 1971, p. 3g.

MARCH, William
   The Bad Seed. See: Anderson, Maxwell

MARTIN, Ernest
    Guys and Dolls. See: Loesser, Frank

MARX, Arthur
    The Impossible Years. See: Fisher, Bob

MASON, Richard L.
    The World of Suzie Wong. See: Osborn, Paul

MASTEROFF, Joe
    Cabaret. See: Kander, John
    She Loves Me. See: Bock, Jerry

MASTERS, Edgar Lee
    Spoon River. See: Aidman, Charles

MEAD, Shepherd
    How to Succeed in Business Without Really Trying. See:
    Loesser, Frank

MELFI, Leonard
    Birdbath and Lunchtime.
    Basement: January 4, 1971-January 14, 1971* (9)

        B., J. Daily Telegraph, January 6, 1971, p. 10d.
        Wardle, Irving. The Times, January 5, 1971, p. 9f.
        Young, B. A. Financial Times, January 5, 1971, p.
            3h.

MELVILLE, Herman
    Moby Dick. See: Welles, Orson

MERRILL, Bob
    Carnival. Music and lyrics by Bob Merrill; book by
    Michael Stewart. Based on material by Helen Deutsch.
    Lyric: February 8, 1963-March 9, 1963 (36)

        Barker, Felix. Evening News, February 9, 1963, p.
            3b.
        Darlington, W. A. Daily Telegraph, February 9,
            1963, p. 10c.
        Gellert, Roger. New Statesman, February 15, 1963,
            p. 247.
        Hobson, Harold. Sunday Times, February 10, 1963,
            p. 33c.
        Hope-Wallace, Philip. Manchester Guardian, February
            9, 1963, p. 4f.
        Kretzmer, Herbert. Daily Express, February 9, 1963,
            p. 9g.
        Levin, Bernard. Daily Mail, February 9, 1963, p.
            3c.
        Nathan, David. Daily Herald, February 9, 1963, p.
            3g.
        The Times, February 9, 1963, p. 4a.
        Trewin, J. C. Illustrated London News, February 23,
            1963, p. 278.

Tynan, Kenneth. Observer, February 17, 1963, p. 26d.
Young, B. A. Punch, February 20, 1963, p. 278.

Funny Girl. See: Styne, Jule

MILLER, Arthur
   All My Sons (Revival).
   Sadler's Wells: April 10, 1972-April 29, 1972 (22)

      Christie, Ian. Daily Express, April 11, 1972, p.
        14h.
      Hobson, Harold. Sunday Times, April 16, 1972, p.
        37f.
      Lewis, Peter. Daily Mail, April 12, 1972, p. 31c.
      Lewsen, Charles. The Times, April 12, 1972, p. 14g.
      O'Connor, Garry. Financial Times, April 11, 1972,
        p. 3c.
      Shorter, Eric. Daily Telegraph, April 11, 1972, p.
        12b.

   The Crucible.
   Royal Court: April 9, 1956-June 23, 1956 (36)

      Barber, John. Daily Express, April 10, 1956, p. 3g.
      Gibbs, Patrick. Daily Telegraph, April 10, 1956, p.
        8d.
      Granger, Derek. Financial Times, April 10, 1956, p.
        2g.
      Hartley, Anthony. Spectator, April 20, 1956, p. 547.
      Hobson, Harold. Sunday Times, April 15, 1956, p.
        15b.
      Hope-Wallace, Philip. Manchester Guardian, April
        11, 1956, p. 5f.
      Keown, Eric. Punch, April 25, 1956, p. 504.
      Shulman, Milton. Evening Standard, April 10, 1956,
        p. 5c.
      The Times, April 10, 1956, p. 3c.
      Trewin, J. C. Illustrated London News, April 21,
        1956, p. 370.
      Tynan, Kenneth. Observer, April 15, 1956, p. 15b.
      Williams, Stephen. Evening News, April 10, 1956,
        p. 5a.
      Wilson, Cecil. Daily Mail, April 10, 1956, p. 3h.
      Worsley, T. C. New Statesman, April 14, 1956, pp.
        370-371.

   The Crucible (Revival).
   Old Vic: January 19, 1965 (part 1964/65 season, repertory) (36)

      Barker, Felix. Evening News, January 20, 1965, p.
        7b.
      Bryden, Ronald. New Statesman, January 29, 1965,
        p. 174.
      Darlington, W. A. Daily Telegraph, January 20,
        1965, p. 18d.

Gilliatt, Penelope. Observer, January 24, 1965, p.
    24c.
Hobson, Harold. Sunday Times, January 24, 1965, p.
    41g.
Hope-Wallace, Philip. Manchester Guardian, January
    20, 1965, p. 11a.
Kingston, Jeremy. Punch, January 27, 1965, p. 142.
Kretzmer, Herbert. Daily Express, January 20, 1965,
    p. 6f.
Nathan, David. Sun, January 20, 1965, p. 9e.
Rutherford, Malcolm. Spectator, January 29, 1965,
    p. 137.
Shulman, Milton. Evening Standard, January 20,
    1965, p. 4d.
The Times, January 20, 1965, p. 13a.

Incident at Vichy.
Phoenix: January 26, 1966-April 16, 1966   (91)

Barker, Felix. Evening News, January 27, 1966, p.
    11e.
Bryden, Ronald. New Statesman, February 4, 1966,
    p. 170.
Darlington, W. A. Daily Telegraph, January 27, 1966,
    p. 19a.
Gilliatt, Penelope. Observer, January 30, 1966, p.
    25a.
Hobson, Harold. Sunday Times, January 30, 1966, p.
    45f.
Hope-Wallace, Philip. Manchester Guardian, January
    27, 1966, p. 9e.
Kingston, Jeremy. Punch, February 2, 1966, p. 173.
Kretzmer, Herbert. Daily Express, January 27, 1966,
    p. 4e.
Levin, Bernard. Daily Mail, January 28, 1966, p.
    12b.
Shulman, Milton. Evening Standard, January 27, 1966,
    p. 4a.
Spurling, Hilary. Spectator, February 4, 1966, p.
    137.
The Times, January 27, 1966, p. 9b.
Trewin, J. C. Illustrated London News, February 5,
    1966, p. 42.
Young, B. A. Financial Times, January 28, 1966, p.
    26a.

The Price.
Duke of York's: March 4, 1969-February 14, 1970   (404)

Barber, John. Daily Telegraph, March 5, 1969, p.
    19a.
Barker, Felix. Evening News, March 5, 1969, p. 11e.
Bryden, Ronald. Observer, March 9, 1969, p. 26c.
Hobson, Harold. Sunday Times, March 9, 1969, p. 55a.
Hope-Wallace, Philip. Manchester Guardian, March 5,
    1969, p. 6f.

Kingston, Jeremy. <u>Punch</u>, March 12, 1969, p. 394.
Nathan, David. <u>Sun</u>, March 5, 1969, p. 11c.
Nightingale, Benedict. <u>New Statesman</u>, March 5,
    1969, p. 384.
Shulman, Milton. <u>Evening Standard</u>, March 5, 1969,
    p. 9a.
Spurling, Hilary. <u>Spectator</u>, March 14, 1969, p. 344.
Trewin, J. C. <u>Illustrated London News</u>, March 15,
    1969, p. 29.
Wardle, Irving. <u>The Times</u>, March 5, 1969, p. 14f.
Young, B. A. <u>Financial Times</u>, March 5, 1969, p. 3g.

A View from the Bridge.
Comedy: October 11, 1956-April 20, 1957 (220)

Barber, John. <u>Daily Express</u>, October 12, 1956, p.
    5c.
Darlington, W. A. <u>Daily Telegraph</u>, October 12, 1956,
    p. 9c.
Granger, Derek. <u>Financial Times</u>, October 12, 1956,
    p. 2g.
Hartley, Anthony. <u>Spectator</u>, October 19, 1956, pp.
    539-540.
Hobson, Harold. <u>Sunday Times</u>, October 14, 1956, p.
    15a.
Hope-Wallace, Philip. <u>Manchester Guardian</u>, October
    13, 1956, p. 5c.
Keown, Eric. <u>Punch</u>, October 17, 1956, pp. 481-482.
Shulman, Milton. <u>Evening Standard</u>, October 12, 1956,
    p. 14c.
<u>The Times</u>, October 12, 1956, p. 3d.
Trewin, J. C. <u>Illustrated London News</u>, October 27,
    1956, p. 720.
Tynan, Kenneth. <u>Observer</u>, October 14, 1956, p. 15a.
Williams, Stephen. <u>Evening News</u>, October 12, 1956,
    p. 5a.
Wilson, Cecil. <u>Daily Mail</u>, October 12, 1956, p. 13f.
Worsley, T. C. <u>New Statesman</u>, October 20, 1956, p.
    482.

MILLER, Jason
    That Championship Season.
    Garrick: May 6, 1974-May 25, 1974 (24)

Barker, Felix. <u>Evening News</u>, May 7, 1974, p. 4a.
Billington, Michael. <u>Manchester Guardian</u>, May 7,
    1974, p. 12a.
Cushman, Robert. <u>Observer</u>, May 12, 1974, p. 35c.
Hobson, Harold. <u>Sunday Times</u>, May 12, 1974, p. 38g.
Hurren, Kenneth. <u>Spectator</u>, May 18, 1974, p. 616.
Kingston, Jeremy. <u>Punch</u>, May 15, 1974, p. 830.
Kretzmer, Herbert. <u>Daily Express</u>, May 7, 1974, p.
    10d.
Nightingale, Benedict. <u>New Statesman</u>, May 17, 1974,
    p. 704.
Shorter, Eric. <u>Daily Telegraph</u>, May 7, 1974, p. 13c.

Thirkell, Arthur. Daily Mirror, May 7, 1974, p. 22c.
Tinker, Jack. Daily Mail, May 7, 1974, p. 3f.
Wardle, Irving. The Times, May 7, 1974, p. 13f.
Young, B. A. Financial Times, May 7, 1974, p. 3a.

MILLIS, Robin
   Dames at Sea. See: Wise, Jim

MITCHELL, Margaret
   Gone With the Wind. See: Rome, Harold

MORRIS, Edmund
   Wooden Dish.
   Phoenix: July 27, 1954-September 11, 1954 (54)

      Barber, John. Daily Express, July 28, 1954, p. 3e.
      Brown, Ivor. Observer, August 1, 1954, p. 6b.
      Darlington, W. A. Daily Telegraph, July 28, 1954,
         p. 8f.
      Granger, Derek. Financial Times, July 28, 1954, p.
         5d.
      Hartley, Anthony. Spectator, August 6, 1954, p. 165.
      Hobson, Harold. Sunday Times, August 1, 1954, p. 9a.
      Hope-Wallace, Philip. Manchester Guardian, July 29,
         1954, p. 3c.
      Keown, Eric. Punch, August 11, 1954, p. 214.
      Shulman, Milton. Evening Standard, July 28, 1954,
         p. 6b.
      The Times, July 28, 1954, p. 7e.
      Trewin, J. C. Illustrated London News, August 14,
         1954, p. 270.
      Williams, Stephen. Evening News, July 28, 1954, p.
         5g.
      Wilson, Cecil. Daily Mail, July 28, 1954, p. 6f.
      Worsley, T. C. New Statesman, August 7, 1954, p.
         156.

MYERS, Robert Manson
   The Spoils of Poynton. Based on the novel by Henry
   James.
   Mayfair: September 2, 1969-September 13, 1969 (12)

      Barber, John. Daily Telegraph, September 3, 1969,
         p. 17b.
      Bryden, Ronald. Observer, September 7, 1969, p. 27e.
      Frame, Colin. Evening News, September 9, 1969, p.
         2g.
      Jongh, Nicholas De. Manchester Guardian, September
         3, 1969, p. 8a.
      Kretzmer, Herbert. Daily Express, September 3,
         1969, p. 10h.
      Lewis, Peter. Daily Mail, September 4, 1969, p. 14b.
      Nathan, David. Sun, September 3, 1969, p. 5a.
      Raynor, Henry. The Times, September 3, 1969, p. 7d.
      Shulman, Milton. Evening Standard, September 3,
         1969, p. 44e.

NASH, Richard
       110 in the Shade. See: Schmidt, Harvey

       The Rainmaker.
       St. Martin's: May 31, 1956-December 15, 1956 (228)

              Barber, John. Daily Express, June 1, 1956, p. 3h.
              Carthew, Anthony. Daily Herald, June 1, 1956, p.
                  5c.
              Darlington, W. A. Daily Telegraph, June 1, 1956,
                  p. 11c.
              Granger, Derek. Financial Times, June 1, 1956, p.
                  2g.
              Hartley, Anthony. Spectator, June 8, 1956, pp. 794-
                  795.
              Hobson, Harold. Sunday Times, June 3, 1956, p. 13b.
              Keown, Eric. Punch, June 6, 1956, p. 692.
              Shulman, Milton. Evening Standard, June 1, 1956,
                  p. 6a.
              The Times, June 1, 1956, p. 3e.
              Trewin, J. C. Illustrated London News, June 16,
                  1956, p. 746.
              Tynan, Kenneth. Observer, June 3, 1956, p. 9a.
              Williams, Stephen. Evening News, June 1, 1956, p.
                  5a.
              Wilson, Cecil. Daily Mail, June 1, 1956, p. 3g.
              Worsley, T. C. New Statesman, June 9, 1956, p. 651.

       The Rainmaker (Revival).
       Greenwood: October 20, 1975-October 25, 1975 (8)*

              Chaillet, Ned. The Times, October 21, 1975, p. 10g.
              Coveney, Michael. Financial Times, October 21,
                  1975, p. 3e.
              Shorter, Eric. Daily Telegraph, October 21, 1975,
                  p. 13e.

O'BRIEN, Liam
       The Remarkable Mr. Pennypacker.
       New: May 18, 1955-May 19, 1956 (421)

              Barber, John. Daily Express, May 19, 1955, p. 5e.
              Gibbs, Patrick. Daily Telegraph, May 19, 1955, p.
                  8e.
              Granger, Derek. Financial Times, May 19, 1955, p.
                  7e.
              Hartley, Anthony. Spectator, May 27, 1955, p. 682.
              Hobson, Harold. Sunday Times, May 22, 1955, p. 7a.
              Hope-Wallace, Philip. Manchester Guardian, May 29,
                  1955, p. 7f.
              Keown, Eric. Punch, June 1, 1955, p. 690.
              Shulman, Milton. Evening Standard, May 19, 1955,
                  p. 9e.
              The Times, May 19, 1955, p. 3a.
              Trewin, J. C. Illustrated London News, June 4,
                  1955, p. 1026.

Tynan, Kenneth. Observer, May 22, 1955, p. 15a.
Williams, Stephen. Evening News, May 19, 1955, p.
     9a.
Wilson, Cecil. Daily Mail, May 19, 1955, p. 12d.
Worsley, T. C. New Statesman, June 4, 1955, pp.
     781-782.

O'DAY, Nell
     Bride of Denmark Hill. See: Williams, Lawrence

ODETS, Clifford
     Awake and Sing (Revival).
     Saville: October 24, 1950-November 11, 1950 (20)

          Daily Mail, October 25, 1950, p. 5f.
          G., R. P. M. Daily Telegraph, October 25, 1950, p.
               6f.
          Hayes, Walter. Daily Sketch, October 25, 1950, p.
               4b.
          Observer, October 29, 1950, p. 6c.
          Trewin, J. C. Illustrated London News, November 11,
               1950, p. 780.
          Worsley, T. C. New Statesman, November 4, 1950, p.
               411.

     Awake and Sing (Revival).
     Hampstead Theatre Club: September 27, 1971-October 20,
     1971* (27)

          Barber, John. Daily Telegraph, September 28, 1971,
               p. 13f.
          Hurren, Kenneth. Spectator, October 2, 1971, p. 483.
          Peter, John. Sunday Times, October 3, 1971, p. 38c.
          Wardle, Irving. The Times, September 28, 1971, p.
               10c.
          Young, B. A. Financial Times, September 28, 1971,
               p. 3a.

     The Big Knife.
     Duke of York's: January 1, 1954, transferred to
     Westminster: March 29, 1954-May 1, 1954 (138)

          Barber, John. Daily Express, January 22, 1954, p.
               3c.
          Brown, Ivor. Observer, January 3, 1954, p. 6a.
          Darlington, W. A. Daily Telegraph, January 2, 1954,
               p. 7f.
          Foster, Paul. Daily Herald, January 2, 1954, p. 2h.
          Granger, Derek. Financial Times, January 2, 1954,
               p. 5e.
          Hartley, Anthony. Spectator, January 8, 1954, p. 37.
          Hobson, Harold. Sunday Times, January 3, 1954, p.
               4a.
          Hope-Wallace, Philip. Manchester Guardian, January
               4, 1954, p. 10d.
          Keown, Eric. Punch, January 13, 1954, p. 104.

Shulman, Milton. Evening Standard, January 2, 1954,
    p. 10e.
The Times, January 2, 1954, p. 8d.
Trewin, J. C. Illustrated London News, January 16,
    1954, p. 90.
Tynan, Kenneth. Daily Sketch, January 2, 1954, p.
    6c.
Williams, Stephen. Evening News, January 2, 1954,
    p. 3g.
Wilson, Cecil. Daily Mail, January 2, 1954, p. 3f.
Worsley, T. C. New Statesman, January 9, 1954, p.
    40.

Golden Boy. See: Strouse, Charles

Winter Journey (American title: The Country Girl).
St. James': April 3, 1952-November 1, 1952 (243)

Barber, John. Daily Express, April 4, 1952, p. 3h.
Baxter, Becerly. Evening Standard, April 4, 1952,
    p. 11d.
Brown, Ivor. Observer, April 6, 1952, p. 6a.
Darlington, W. A. Daily Telegraph, April 4, 1952,
    p. 5f.
Hayes, Walter. Daily Sketch, April 4, 1952, p. 3c.
Hobson, Harold. Sunday Times, April 6, 1952, p. 2f.
Hope-Wallace, Philip. Manchester Guardian, April
    5, 1952, p. 3a.
Keown, Eric. Punch, April 16, 1952, p. 492.
Mannock, P. L. Daily Herald, April 4, 1952, p. 3g.
The Times, April 4, 1952, p. 6d.
Trewin, J. C. Illustrated London News, April 26,
    1952, p. 722.
Tynan, Kenneth. Spectator, April 11, 1952, p. 481.
Williams, Stephen. Evening News, April 4, 1952, p.
    4f.
Wiltshire, Maurice. Daily Mail, April 4, 1952, p.
    6f.
Worsley, T. C. New Statesman, April 12, 1952, p.
    433.

O'HARA, John
    Pal Joey. See: Rodgers, Richard

O'NEILL, Eugene
    Hughie. Includes: "In the Zone," "Before Breakfast,"
    and "Hughie."
    Duchess: June 18, 1963-June 29, 1963 (14) (Opened
    in Bath on June 10, 1963 at the Theatre Royal--reviewed
    by The Times. See below.)

Barry, Gerald. Punch, June 26, 1963, pp. 934-935.
Darlington, W. A. Daily Telegraph, June 19, 1963,
    p. 16e.
Frame, Colin. Evening News, June 19, 1963, p. 5e.
Gellert, Roger. New Statesman, June 28, 1963, p.
    984.

Kretzmer, Herbert. Daily Express, June 19, 1963,
    p. 4c.
Lambert, J. W. Sunday Times, June 23, 1963, p. 37b.
Nathan, David. Daily Herald, June 19, 1963, p. 6f.
Pryce-Jones, David. Spectator, June 28, 1963, p.
    838.
Shrapnel, Norman. Manchester Guardian, June 19,
    1963, p. 7a.
Shulman, Milton. Evening Standard, June 19, 1963,
    p. 4a.
The Times, June 11, 1963, p. 15a. (Opening at
    Theatre Royal, Bath.)
The Times, June 19, 1963, p. 5c.
Trewin, J. C. Illustrated London News, June 29,
    1963, p. 1024.
Tynan, Kenneth. Observer, June 23, 1963, p. 27a.

The Iceman Cometh.
Arts: January 29, 1958, transferred to Winter Gardens:
March 29, 1958-May 10, 1958 (31)

Barber, John. Daily Express, January 30, 1958, p.
    7d.
Barker, Felix. Evening News, January 29, 1958, p.
    3d.
Darlington, W. A. Daily Telegraph, January 30, 1958,
    p. 10f.
Fay, Gerard. Spectator, February 7, 1958, p. 174.
Granger, Derek. Financial Times, January 30, 1958,
    p. 11g.
Hobson, Harold. Sunday Times, February 2, 1958, p.
    21c.
Hope-Wallace, Philip. Manchester Guardian, January
    30, 1958, p. 7a.
Keown, Eric. Punch, February 5, 1958, p. 218.
Shulman, Milton. Evening Standard, January 31, 1958,
    p. 6e.
Smith, Andrew. Daily Herald, January 30, 1958, p.
    2g.
The Times, January 30, 1958, p. 3a.
Trewin, J. C. Illustrated London News, February 15,
    1958, p. 276.
Tynan, Kenneth. Observer, February 2, 1958, p. 13b.
Wilson, Cecil. Daily Mail, January 30, 1958, p. 3c.
Worsley, T. C. New Statesman, February 8, 1958, pp.
    165-166.

Long Day's Journey Into Night.
Globe: September 24, 1958-January 3, 1959 (108)

Barber, John. Daily Express, September 25, 1958,
    p. 7c.
Barker, Felix. Evening News, September 25, 1958,
    p. 3a.
Brien, Alan. Spectator, September 29, 1958, p. 369.
Darlington, W. A. Daily Telegraph, September 25,
    1958, p. 10e.

Hobson, Harold. Sunday Times, September 28, 1958,
    p. 19a.
Keown, Eric. Punch, September 17, 1958, p. 380.
Nevard, Mike. Daily Herald, September 25, 1958, p.
    3d.
New Statesman, October 4, 1958, pp. 444-445.
Shrapnel, Norman. Manchester Guardian, September
    26, 1958, p. 5b.
Shulman, Milton. Evening Standard, September 25,
    1958, p. 13a.
The Times, September 25, 1958, p. 14c.
Trewin, J. C. Illustrated London News, September
    29, 1958, p. 486.
Tynan, Kenneth. Observer, September 28, 1958, p.
    19a.
Wilson, Cecil. Daily Mail, September 25, 1958, p.
    3f.
Worsley, T. C. Financial Times, September 25, 1958,
    p. 15f.

Long Day's Journey Into Night (Revival). Produced by
the National Theatre Company for the 1971/72 season.
New: December 21, 1971-January 8, 1973 (122 in repertory)

Barber, John. Daily Telegraph, December 22, 1971,
    p. 7a.
Barker, Felix. Evening News, December 22, 1971, p.
    3a.
Billington, Michael. Manchester Guardian, December
    22, 1971, p. 8c.
Dawson, Helen. Observer, January 2, 1972, p. 24a.
Hobson, Harold. Sunday Times, January 2, 1972, p.
    14a.
Hurren, Kenneth. Spectator, January 1, 1972, p. 17.
Kretzmer, Herbert. Daily Express, December 22, 1971,
    p. 13a.
Shulman, Milton. Evening News, December 22, 1971,
    p. 7d.
Young, B. A. Financial Times, December 22, 1971,
    p. 3a.

Moon for the Misbegotten.
Arts: January 20, 1960-February 26, 1960* (44)*
(Closing date estimated on basis of next production,
which opened March 1, 1960.)

Alvarez, A. New Statesman, January 30, 1960, pp.
    149-150.
Barker, Felix. Evening News, January 21, 1960, p.
    7d.
Brien, Alan. Spectator, January 29, 1960, pp. 137-
    138.
Darlington, W. A. Daily Telegraph, January 21, 1960,
    p. 12f.
Hobson, Harold. Sunday Times, January 24, 1960, p.
    23c.

Hope-Wallace, Philip. _Manchester Guardian_, January
    22, 1960, p. 9a.
Keown, Eric. _Punch_, January 27, 1960, p. 174.
Levin, Bernard. _Daily Express_, January 21, 1960,
    p. 4d.
Pryce-Jones, David. _Observer_, January 24, 1960, p.
    21a.
Shulman, Milton. _Evening Standard_, January 21, 1960,
    p. 12e.
The Times, January 21, 1960, p. 3d.
Trewin, J. C. _Illustrated London News_, February 6,
    1960, p. 226.
Wilson, Cecil. _Daily Mail_, January 21, 1960, p. 5a.
Worsley, T. C. _Financial Times_, January 21, 1960,
    p. 17g.

More Stately Mansions.
Greenwich: September 19, 1974-October 12, 1974 (25)

Billington, Michael. _Manchester Guardian_, September
    20, 1974, p. 10c.
Hobson, Harold. _Sunday Times_, September 22, 1974,
    p. 3e.
Kingston, Jeremy. _Punch_, October 2, 1974, p. 543.
Spurling, Hilary. _Observer_, September 22, 1974,
    p. 26a.
Wardle, Irving. _The Times_, September 20, 1974, p.
    8f.
Young, B. A. _Financial Times_, September 21, 1974,
    p. 10e.

Mourning Becomes Electra (Revival).
Arts: June 9, 1955-August 2, 1955 (62)*

Barber, John. _Daily Express_, June 10, 1955, p. 3e.
Forster, Peter. _Financial Times_, June 11, 1955, p.
    7g.
Gibbs, Patrick. _Daily Telegraph_, June 10, 1955,
    p. 8d.
Hartley, Anthony. _Spectator_, June 17, 1955, p. 772.
Hobson, Harold. _Sunday Times_, June 12, 1955, p. 4b.
Hope-Wallace, Philip. _Manchester Guardian_, June 11,
    1955, p. 5f.
Shulman, Milton. _Evening Standard_, June 10, 1955,
    p. 20b.
The Times, June 10, 1955, p. 10a.
Trewin, J. C. _Illustrated London News_, June 25,
    1955, p. 1160.
Tynan, Kenneth. _Observer_, June 12, 1955, p. 6b.
Williams, Stephen. _Evening News_, June 10, 1955, p.
    5d.
Wilson, Cecil. _Daily Mail_, June 10, 1955, p. 8e.
Worsley, T. C. _New Statesman_, June 25, 1955, p. 886.

Mourning Becomes Electra (Revival).
Old Vic: November 21, 1961-December 13, 1961 (24)

Barker, Felix. Evening News, November 22, 1961, p.
     9h.
Darlington, W. A. Daily Telegraph, November 22,
     1961, p. 14d.
Gascoigne, Bamber. Spectator, December 1, 1961, p.
     820.
Gellert, Roger. New Statesman, December 1, 1961,
     p. 856.
Hobson, Harold. Sunday Times, November 26, 1961,
     p. 41f.
Hope-Wallace, Philip. Manchester Guardian, November
     21, 1961, p. 7g.
Levin, Bernard. Daily Express, November 22, 1961,
     p. 15h.
Muller, Robert. Daily Mail, November 22, 1961, p.
     3e.
Nathan, David. Daily Herald, November 22, 1961,
     p. 5a.
Shulman, Milton. Evening Standard, November 22,
     1961, p. 21a.
The Times, November 22, 1961, p. 15b.
Trewin, J. C. Illustrated London News, December 2,
     1961, p. 984.
Wardle, Irving. Observer, November 26, 1961, p. 26c.
Worsley, T. C. Financial Times, November 22, 1961,
     p. 18a.
Young, B. A. Punch, November 29, 1961, p. 801.

Mourning Becomes Electra (Revival). The Traverse Theatre
of Edinbourgh designed this production to be played in
the Temple of Bacchus at the Baalbeck Festival.
Arts: June 27, 1967-July 2, 1967 (5)*

Hastings, Ronald. Daily Telegraph, June 28, 1967,
     p. 17e.
Hobson, Harold. Sunday Times, July 2, 1967, p. 25e.
Malcolm, Derek. Manchester Guardian, June 29, 1967,
     p. 6f.
Raynor, Henry. The Times, June 28, 1967, p. 8d.

A Touch of the Poet.
Ashcroft, Croydon: September 16, 1963-September 28,
1963 (14)

Barker, Felix. Evening News, September 17, 1963,
     p. 4d.
Bryden, Ronald. New Statesman, September 27, 1963,
     p. 420.
Hobson, Harold. Sunday Times, September 22, 1963,
     p. 33d.
Hope-Wallace, Philip. Manchester Guardian, September
     17, 1963, p. 7a.
Pacey, Ann. Daily Herald, September 17, 1963, p. 7c.
Shorter, Eric. Daily Telegraph, September 17, 1963,
     p. 14d.
Shulman, Milton. Evening Standard, September 17,
     1963, p. 4a.

The Times, September 17, 1963, p. 16g.
Worsley, T. C. Financial Times, September 18, 1963,
      p. 22a.

OSBORN, Paul
   Morning's at Seven. (First London production. Opened,
   New York, 1938.)
   Comedy: December 14, 1955-January 21, 1956 (46)

      Barber, John. Daily Express, December 15, 1955, p.
         3e.
      Carthew, Anthony. Daily Herald, December 15, 1955,
         p. 3c.
      Darlington, W. A. Daily Telegraph, December 15,
         1955, p. 9e.
      Granger, Derek. Financial Times, December 15, 1955,
         p. 2g.
      Hartley, Anthony. Spectator, December 23, 1955, p.
         869.
      Hobson, Harold. Sunday Times, December 18, 1955,
         p. 11a.
      Hope-Wallace, Philip. Manchester Guardian, December
         15, 1955, p. 7c.
      Keown, Eric. Punch, December 21, 1955, pp. 743-744.
      Shulman, Milton. Evening Standard, December 15,
         1955, p. 18b.
      The Times, December 15, 1955, p. 5a.
      Trewin, J. C. Illustrated London News, December 31,
         1955, p. 1146.
      Tynan, Kenneth. Observer, December 18, 1955, p. 9a.
      Williams, Stephen. Evening News, December 15, 1955,
         p. 5b.
      Wilson, Cecil. Daily Mail, December 15, 1955, p.
         10d.
      Worsley, T. C. New Statesman, December 24, 1955,
         p. 854.

   The World of Suzie Wong. (Based on the novel by Richard
   L. Mason.)
   Prince of Wales: November 17, 1959-August 5, 1961
   (823)

      Alvarez, A. New Statesman, November 28, 1959, p.
         746.
      Barker, Felix. Evening News, November 18, 1959, p.
         8h.
      Brien, Alan. Spectator, December 4, 1959, p. 829.
      Carthew, Anthony. Daily Herald, November 18, 1959,
         p. 4g.
      Darlington, W. A. Daily Telegraph, November 18,
         1959, p. 14d.
      Hobson, Harold. Sunday Times, November 22, 1959,
         p. 25c.
      Hope-Wallace, Philip. Manchester Guardian, November
         19, 1959, p. 9a.
      Keown, Eric. Punch, November 25, 1959, p. 509.

Levin, Bernard. <u>Daily Express</u>, November 18, 1959,
    p. 4c.
Pryce-Jones, Alan. <u>Observer</u>, November 22, 1959, p.
    25b.
Shulman, Milton. <u>Evening Standard</u>, November 18,
    1959, p. 15d.
<u>The Times</u>, November 18, 1959, p. 4a.
Trewin, J. C. <u>Illustrated London News</u>, December 5,
    1959, p. 818.
Wilson, Cecil. <u>Daily Mail</u>, November 18, 1959, p.
    3b.
Worsley, T. C. <u>Financial Times</u>, November 18, 1959,
    p. 19f.

PAGNOL, Marcel
    <u>Fanny</u>. See: Rome, Harold

PATINKIN, Sheldon
    <u>The Star Spangled Jack Show</u>. By Sheldon Patinkin and
    Bernard Sahlins. Revue developed at Second City,
    Chicago. (Called by <u>The Times</u> "an Anglo-American revue"
    with three Americans and three Britons. Since it is
    half American, I have included it.)
    Comedy: August 17, 1965-September 4, 1965 (22)

    Barker, Felix. <u>Evening News</u>, August 18, 1965, p.
        7a.
    Darlington, W. A. <u>Daily Telegraph</u>, August 18, 1965,
        p. 14c.
    Gilliatt, Penelope. <u>Observer</u>, August 22, 1965, p.
        19d.
    Holland, Julian. <u>Daily Mail</u>, August 18, 1965, p.
        12b.
    Hope-Wallace, Philip. <u>Manchester Guardian</u>, August
        18, 1965, p. 7a.
    Kretzmer, Herbert. <u>Daily Express</u>, August 18, 1965,
        p. 4f.
    Lambert, J. W. <u>Sunday Times</u>, August 22, 1965, p.
        31b.
    Lewis, Jenny. <u>Financial Times</u>, August 19, 1965,
        p. 20c.
    Nathan, David. <u>Sun</u>, August 18, 1965, p. 6f.
    <u>The Times</u>, August 18, 1965, p. 11a.
    Trewin, J. C. <u>Illustrated London News</u>, September
        4, 1965, p. 41.

PATRICK, John
    <u>Everybody Loves Opal</u>.
    Vaudeville: April 1, 1964-April 4, 1964 (5)

    Barker, Felix. <u>Evening News</u>, April 2, 1964, p. 6b.
    Boothroyd, Basil. <u>Punch</u>, April 8, 1964, p. 538.
    Cashin, Fergus. <u>Daily Sketch</u>, April 2, 1964, p. 9a.
    Fay, Gerard. <u>Manchester Guardian</u>, April 2, 1964,
        p. 7c.
    Gascoigne, Bamber. <u>Observer</u>, April 5, 1964, p. 24e.
    Higgins, John. <u>Financial Times</u>, April 2, 1964, p.
        24d.

Hobson, Harold. Sunday Times, April 5, 1964, p. 33c.
Kretzmer, Herbert. Daily Express, April 2, 1964, p. 4h.
Levin, Bernard. Daily Mail, April 3, 1964, p. 14f.
Nathan, David. Daily Herald, April 2, 1964, p. 7a.
Shulman, Milton. Evening Standard, April 2, 1964, p. 4b.
The Times, April 2, 1964, p. 16a.

The Teahouse of the August Moon.
Her Majesty's: April 22, 1954-August 11, 1956 (964)

Barber, John. Daily Express, April 23, 1954, p. 3h.
Brown, Ivor. Observer, April 25, 1954, p. 11a.
Gibbs, Patrick. Daily Telegraph, April 23, 1954, p. 9d.
Granger, Derek. Financial Times, April 23, 1954, p. 7d.
Hartley, Anthony. Spectator, April 30, 1954, p. 512.
Holt, Paul. Daily Herald, April 23, 1954, p. 3d.
Hope-Wallace, Philip. Manchester Guardian, April 24, 1954, p. 3d.
Keown, Eric. Punch, April 28, 1954, p. 535.
Lambert, J. W. Sunday Times, April 25, 1954, p. 11a.
Shulman, Milton. Evening Standard, April 23, 1954, p. 17c.
The Times, April 23, 1954, p. 10a.
Trewin, J. C. Illustrated London News, May 8, 1954, p. 762.
Williams, Stephen. Evening News, April 23, 1954, p. 5f.
Wiltshire, Maurice. Daily Mail, April 23, 1954, p. 6a.
Worsley, T. C. New Statesman, May 1, 1954, p. 560.

PATRICK, Robert
Kennedy's Children.
King's Head Theatre Club: October 30, 1974-March 29, 1975 (137); reopened at the Arts Theatre Club: April 17, 1975-December 21, 1975 (216)

Cushman, Robert. Observer, November 3, 1974, p. 30c.
Hobson, Harold. Sunday Times, November 10, 1974, p. 35b.
Hurren, Kenneth. Spectator, December 7, 1974, p. 742.
Nightingale, Benedict. New Statesman, November 15, 1974, p. 712.
Shorter, Eric. Daily Telegraph, April 18, 1975, p. 13d.
Wardle, Irving. The Times, October 31, 1974, p. 9f.

Play by Play.
King's Head: October 20, 1975-December 6, 1975 (56)*

B., J. [John Barber]. Daily Telegraph, October 21, 1975, p. 13b.

Billington, Michael. <u>Manchester Guardian</u>, October
  21, 1975, p. 10a.
Hurren, Kenneth. <u>Spectator</u>, November 1, 1975, pp.
  578-579.
Lewsen, Charles. <u>The Times</u>, October 21, 1975, p.
  10c.
Shulman, Milton. <u>Evening Standard</u>, October 21,
  1975, p. 15e.
Spurling, Hilary. <u>Observer</u>, October 26, 1975, p.
  30d.
Young, B. A. <u>Financial Times</u>, October 21, 1975, p.
  3e.

PLAUTUS
  Plays. See: Sondheim, Stephen, <u>A Funny Thing Happened
  on the Way to the Forum</u>

POHLMAN, Ray
  <u>Catch My Soul</u>. See: Good, Jack

PONTAC, Perry
  <u>The Old Man's Comforts</u>.
  Open Space: December 21, 1972-January 6, 1973 (32)

  B., J. <u>Daily Telegraph</u>, December 22, 1972, p. 7e.
  Billington, Michael. <u>Manchester Guardian</u>, December
    22, 1972, p. 8d.
  Brustein, Robert. <u>Observer</u>, December 24, 1972, p.
    21f.
  Kingston, Jeremy. <u>Punch</u>, January 3, 1973, p. 28.
  Kretzmer, Herbert. <u>Daily Express</u>, December 22, 1972,
    p. 10d.
  Nightingale, Benedict. <u>New Statesman</u>, December 29,
    1972, p. 986.
  Wardle, Irving. <u>The Times</u>, December 22, 1972, p.
    10g.
  Young, B. A. <u>Financial Times</u>, December 22, 1972,
    p. 3a.

PORTER, Cole
  <u>Anything Goes</u> (Revival). Book by Howard Lindsay and
  Russel Crouse.
  Saville: November 18, 1969-November 29, 1969 (15)

  Barber, John. <u>Daily Telegraph</u>, November 19, 1969,
    p. 13a.
  Barker, Felix. <u>Evening News</u>, November 19, 1969, p.
    2d.
  Bryden, Ronald. <u>Observer</u>, November 23, 1969, p. 29e.
  Cashin, Fergus. <u>Sun</u>, November 19, 1969, p. 28c.
  Hobson, Harold. <u>Sunday Times</u>, November 23, 1969, p.
    53d.
  Hope-Wallace, Philip. <u>Manchester Guardian</u>, November
    19, 1969, p. 8c.
  Kingston, Jeremy. <u>Punch</u>, November 26, 1969, p. 883.
  Raynor, Henry. <u>The Times</u>, November 19, 1969, p. 8c.

Shulman, Milton. Evening Standard, November 19,
    1969, p. 19a.
Trewin, J. C. Illustrated London News, November 29,
    1969, p. 31.
Young, B. A. Financial Times, November 19, 1969,
    p. 3a.

Can-Can. Book by Abe Burrows.
Coliseum: October 14, 1954-September 24, 1955 (375)

Barber, John. Daily Express, October 15, 1954, p.
    3e.
Darlington, W. A. Daily Telegraph, October 15, 1954,
    p. 9c.
Granger, Derek. Financial Times, October 15, 1954,
    p. 7d.
Hartley, Anthony. Spectator, October 22, 1954, p.
    489.
Hobson, Harold. Sunday Times, October 17, 1954, p.
    11a.
Holt, Paul. Daily Sketch, October 15, 1954, p. 3a.
Hope-Wallace, Philip. Manchester Guardian, October
    15, 1954, p. 5d.
Keown, Eric. Punch, October 29, 1954, pp. 517-518.
Shulman, Milton. Evening Standard, October 15,
    1954, p. 6d.
The Times, October 15, 1954, p. 5d.
Trewin, J. C. Illustrated London News, October 30,
    1954, p. 760.
Tynan, Kenneth. Observer, October 17, 1954, p. 11a.
Williams, Stephen. Evening News, October 15, 1954,
    p. 5g.
Wiltshire, Maurice. Daily Mail, October 15, 1954,
    p. 6d.

Kiss Me Kate. Book by Sam and Bella Spewack.
Coliseum: March 8, 1951-February 23, 1952 (501)

Barber, John. Daily Express, March 9, 1951, p. 3b.
Baxter, Beverly. Evening Standard, March 9, 1951,
    p. 9d.
Brown, Ivor. Observer, March 11, 1951, p. 6a.
C., H. E. Daily Sketch, March 9, 1951, p. 12a.
Darlington, W. A. Daily Telegraph, March 9, 1951,
    p. 5d.
Hobson, Harold. Sunday Times, March 11, 1951, p.
    2d.
Hope-Wallace, Philip. Manchester Guardian, March
    10, 1951, p. 3d.
Hopkins, Kenneth. Spectator, March 16, 1951, p.
    341.
Keown, Eric. Punch, March 21, 1951, p. 374.
Mannock, P. L. Daily Herald, March 9, 1951, p. 3d.
The Times, March 9, 1951, p. 8d.
Trewin, J. C. Illustrated London News, March 17,
    1951, p. 417.

Williams, Stephen. <u>Evening News</u>, March 9, 1951, p.
    5.
Wilson, Cecil. <u>Daily Mail</u>, March 9, 1951, p. 3d.
Worsley, T. C. <u>New Statesman</u>, March 17, 1951, p.
    302.

<u>Kiss Me Kate</u> (Revival).
Coliseum: December 24, 1970-January 23, 1971 (22)

Aprahamian, Felix. <u>Sunday Times</u>, January 3, 1971,
    p. 40c.
Ayre, Leslie. <u>Evening News</u>, December 28, 1970, p.
    7f.
Barber, John. <u>Daily Telegraph</u>, December 28, 1970,
    p. 8a.
Edwards, Sydney. <u>Evening Standard</u>, December 28,
    1970, p. 27f.
Goodwin, Noel. <u>Daily Express</u>, December 28, 1970,
    p. 6b.
Hope-Wallace, Philip. <u>Manchester Guardian</u>, December
    28, 1970, p. 6f.
Mann, William. <u>The Times</u>, December 28, 1970, p. 5c.
Mason, Eric. <u>Daily Mail</u>, December 28, 1970, p. 2g.
Nightingale, Benedict. <u>New Statesman</u>, January 15,
    1971, p. 90.
Young, B. A. <u>Financial Times</u>, December 28, 1970,
    p. 3a.

<u>Kiss Me Kate</u> (Reopened). Ran in repertory for 1971
season.
Coliseum: July 19, 1971

Edwards, Sydney. <u>Evening Standard</u>, July 20, 1971,
    p. 15c.
Greenfield, Edward. <u>Manchester Guardian</u>, July 20,
    1971, p. 8b.
Milnes, Rodney. <u>Spectator</u>, July 24, 1971, p. 146.
P., A. E. <u>Daily Telegraph</u>, July 16, 1971, p. 8f.
Pankhurst, H. J. <u>Evening News</u>, July 20, 1971, p.
    3b.
Widdicombe, Gillian. <u>Financial Times</u>, July 20, 1971,
    p. 3g.

RADO, James
    <u>Hair</u>. See: MacDermot, Galt

RAGNI, Gerome
    <u>Hair</u>. See: MacDermot, Galt

REGAN, Sylvia
    <u>The Fifth Season</u>.
    Cambridge: February 24, 1954-May 22, 1954 (101)

Barber, John. <u>Daily Express</u>, February 25, 1954,
    p. 3b.
Brown, Ivor. <u>Observer</u>, February 28, 1954, p. 11b.

Darlington, W. A. Daily Telegraph, February 25,
    1954, p. 8f.
Granger, Derek. Financial Times, February 25, 1954,
    p. 7e.
Hobson, Harold. Sunday Times, February 28, 1954,
    p. 11b.
Hope-Wallace, Philip. Manchester Guardian, February
    26, 1954, p. 5f.
Keown, Eric. Punch, March 3, 1954, p. 304.
The Times, February 25, 1954, p. 10b.
Trewin, J. C. Illustrated London News, March 13,
    1954, p. 416.
Tynan, Kenneth. Daily Sketch, February 26, 1954,
    p. 13b.
Williams, Stephen. Evening News, February 25, 1954,
    p. 5b.
Wilson, Cecil. Daily Mail, February 25, 1954, p. 6f.

RESNICK, Muriel
    Any Wednesday.
    Apollo: August 4, 1965-January 1, 1966, transferred to
    Wyndham's: January 3, 1966-January 29, 1966 (205)

    Barker, Felix. Evening News, August 5, 1965, p. 7f.
    Benedictus, David. Spectator, August 13, 1965, p.
        209.
    Bryden, Ronald. New Statesman, August 13, 1965, p.
        229.
    Darlington, W. A. Daily Telegraph, August 5, 1965,
        p. 14d.
    Gilliatt, Penelope. Observer, August 8, 1965, p.
        19d.
    Hobson, Harold. Sunday Times, August 8, 1965, p.
        33b.
    Holland, Julian. Daily Mail, August 6, 1965, p. 10b.
    Hope-Wallace, Philip. Manchester Guardian, August
        5, 1965, p. 7c.
    Kingston, Jeremy. Punch, August 11, 1965, p. 213.
    Kretzmer, Herbert. Daily Express, August 5, 1965,
        p. 4h.
    Nathan, David. Sun, August 5, 1965, p. 3b.
    The Times, August 5, 1965, p. 5a.
    Trewin, J. C. Illustrated London News, August 14,
        1965, p. 36.
    Young, B. A. Financial Times, August 6, 1965, p.
        20a.

RICE, Elmer
    The Winner.
    Pembroke, Croydon: October 2, 1961-October 16, 1961
    (17)

    Gellert, Roger. New Statesman, October 13, 1961,
        p. 530.
    Last, Richard. Daily Herald, October 3, 1961, p. 9d.
    The Times, October 3, 1961, p. 16c.

Trewin, J. C. Illustrated London News, October 14,
    1961, p. 636.

RINTELS, David
    Clarence Darrow.
    Piccadilly: July 16, 1975-September 20, 1975 (47)

        Barker, Felix. Evening News, July 17, 1975, p. 10e.
        Curtis, Anthony. Financial Times, July 17, 1975,
            p. 3a.
        Davie, Michael. Observer, July 20, 1975, p. 22e.
        Hurren, Kenneth. Spectator, July 26, 1975, pp. 129-
            130.
        Kretzmer, Herbert. Daily Express, July 17, 1975,
            p. 10d.
        Lewsen, Charles. The Times, July 17, 1975, p. 11g.
        Nightingale, Benedict. New Statesman, July 25, 1975,
            p. 121.
        Shorter, Eric. Daily Telegraph, July 17, 1975, p.
            13c.
        Shulman, Milton. Evening Standard, July 17, 1975,
            p. 16d.
        Tinker, Jack. Daily Mail, July 18, 1975, p. 22d.
        Walker, Martin. Manchester Guardian, July 17, 1975,
            p. 10b.
        Wardle, Irving. The Times, July 17, 1975, p. 11g.

ROBIN, Leo
    Gentlemen Prefer Blondes. See: Styne, Jule

RODGERS, Mary
    Once Upon a Mattress. Music by Mary Rodgers; book by
    Jay Thompson, Marshall Baker, and Dean Fuller; lyrics
    by Marshall Baker.
    Adelphi: September 20, 1960-October 22, 1960 (38)

        Barker, Felix. Evening News, September 21, 1960,
            p. 11b.
        Boothroyd, J. B. Punch, September 28, 1960, p. 465.
        Brien, Alan. Spectator, September 30, 1960, p. 490.
        Brooks, Jeremy. New Statesman, October 1, 1960, p.
            470.
        Darlington, W. A. Daily Telegraph, September 21,
            1960, p. 16e.
        Hobson, Harold. Sunday Times, September 25, 1960,
            p. 35b.
        Hope-Wallace, Philip. Manchester Guardian, September
            22, 1960, p. 9a.
        Levin, Bernard. Daily Express, September 21, 1960,
            p. 12c.
        Muller, Robert. Daily Mail, September 21, 1960, p.
            3b.
        Nathan, David. Daily Herald, September 21, 1960,
            p. 7a.
        Shulman, Milton. Evening Standard, September 21,
            1960, p. 20c.

The Times, September 21, 1960, p. 16d.
Trewin, J. C. Illustrated London News, October 1,
     1960, p. 578.
Tynan, Kenneth. Observer, September 25, 1960, p.
     24b.
Worsley, T. C. Financial Times, September 21, 1960,
     p. 19e.

RODGERS, Richard
     The Boys from Syracuse. Lyrics by Lorenz Hart; book by
     George Abbott.
     Drury Lane: November 7, 1963-February 1, 1964 (100)
     (First London production.)

          Barker, Felix. Evening News, November 8, 1963, p.
               17b.
          Darlington, W. A. Daily Telegraph, November 8, 1963,
               p. 18d.
          Gascoigne, Bamber. Observer, November 10, 1963, p.
               26c.
          Gellert, Roger. New Statesman, November 15, 1963,
               p. 715.
          Hobson, Harold. Sunday Times, November 10, 1963,
               p. 33a.
          Hope-Wallace, Philip. Manchester Guardian, November
               8, 1963, p. 11e.
          Kretzmer, Herbert. Daily Express, November 8, 1963,
               p. 4d.
          Levin, Bernard. Daily Mail, November 9, 1963, p.
               3c.
          Nathan, David. Daily Herald, November 8, 1963, p.
               3e.
          Pryce-Jones, David. Spectator, November 15, 1963,
               p. 629.
          Shulman, Milton. Evening Standard, November 8, 1963,
               p. 5a.
          The Times, November 8, 1963, p. 16b.
          Trewin, J. C. Illustrated London News, November 23,
               1963, p. 872.
          Young, B. A. Punch, November 13, 1963, p. 720.

     Carousel. Book and lyrics by Oscar Hammerstein, II.
     Based on Liliom by Ferenc Molnar.
     Drury Lane: June 7, 1950-October 13, 1951 (567)

          Barber, John. Daily Express, June 8, 1950, p. 5g.
          Bishop, George. Daily Telegraph, June 8, 1950, p.
               6f.
          Evening Standard, June 8, 1950, p. 6e.
          Hayes, Walter. Daily Sketch, June 8, 1950, p. 3b.
          Hobson, Harold. Sunday Times, June 11, 1950, p. 4d.
          Hope-Wallace, Philip. Manchester Guardian, June 9,
               1950, p. 5f.
          Keown, Eric. Punch, June 21, 1950, p. 692.
          Mannock, P. L. Daily Herald, June 8, 1950, p. 3d.
          The Times, June 8, 1950, p. 8e.

Trewin, J. C. <u>Illustrated London News</u>, July 1, 1950,
    p. 22.
Trewin, J. C. <u>Observer</u>, June 11, 1950, p. 6a.
Williams, Stephen. <u>Evening News</u>, June 9, 1950, p.
    4f.
Wilson, Cecil. <u>Daily Mail</u>, June 8, 1950, p. 3f.
Worsley, T. C. <u>New Statesman</u>, June 24, 1950, p.
    712.

<u>Cinderella</u>. Book and lyrics by Oscar Hammerstein, II.
<u>Coliseum:</u> December 18, 1958-April 11, 1959 (168)

Barker, Felix. <u>Evening News</u>, December 19, 1958, p.
    3e.
Darlington, W. A. <u>Daily Telegraph</u>, December 19,
    1958, p. 10f.
Keown, Eric. <u>Punch</u>, December 31, 1958, p. 878.
Shulman, Milton. <u>Evening Standard</u>, December 19,
    1958, p. 11e.
Thompson, John. <u>Daily Express</u>, December 19, 1958,
    p. 7d.
<u>The Times</u>, December 19, 1958, p. 7b.
Wilson, Angus. <u>Observer</u>, December 21, 1958, p. 11a.
Wilson, Cecil. <u>Daily Mail</u>, December 19, 1958, p.
    17g.
Worsley, T. C. <u>Financial Times</u>, December 19, 1958,
    p. 17g.

<u>Flower Drum Song</u>. Lyrics by Oscar Hammerstein, II; book
by Joseph Fields and Oscar Hammerstein, II.
Palace: March 24, 1960-April 29, 1961 (464)

Atkinson, Alex. <u>Punch</u>, March 30, 1960, p. 464.
Barker, Felix. <u>Evening News</u>, March 25, 1960, p. 8h.
Brien, Alan. <u>Spectator</u>, April 8, 1960, p. 507.
Carthew, Anthony. <u>Daily Herald</u>, March 25, 1960, p.
    3a.
Darlington, W. A. <u>Daily Telegraph</u>, March 25, 1960,
    p. 16f.
Hall, Unity. <u>Daily Sketch</u>, March 25, 1960, p. 12b.
Hobson, Harold. <u>Sunday Times</u>, March 27, 1960, p.
    25b.
Hope-Wallace, Philip. <u>Manchester Guardian</u>, March
    26, 1960, p. 5a.
Levin, Bernard. <u>Daily Express</u>, March 25, 1960, p.
    4b.
Muller, Robert. <u>Daily Mail</u>, March 25, 1960, p. 4c.
Pryce-Jones, Alan. <u>Observer</u>, March 27, 1960, p. 24g.
Shulman, Milton. <u>Evening Standard</u>, March 25, 1960,
    p. 11a.
<u>The Times</u>, March 25, 1960, p. 16c.
Trewin, J. C. <u>Illustrated London News</u>, April 9,
    1960, p. 612.
Worsley, T. C. <u>Financial Times</u>, March 25, 1960, p.
    19f.

The King and I. Book and lyrics by Oscar Hammerstein,
II.
Drury Lane: October 8, 1953-January 14, 1956 (926)

    Barber, John. Daily Express, October 9, 1953, p. 3a.
    Brown, Ivor. Observer, October 11, 1953, p. 13a.
    Darlington, W. A. Daily Telegraph, October 9, 1953,
       p. 9e.
    Granger, Derek. Financial Times, October 9, 1953,
       p. 7g.
    Hobson, Harold. Sunday Times, October 11, 1953, p.
       9a.
    Holt, Paul. Daily Herald, October 9, 1953, p. 3a.
    Hope-Wallace, Philip. Manchester Guardian, October
       10, 1953, p. 3c.
    Keown, Eric. Punch, October 14, 1953, p. 471.
    Monsey, Derek. Spectator, October 16, 1953, p. 421.
    Shulman, Milton. Evening Standard, October 9, 1953,
       p. 11c.
    The Times, October 9, 1953, p. 13a.
    Trewin, J. C. Illustrated London News, October 24,
       1953, p. 664.
    Tynan, Kenneth. Daily Sketch, October 9, 1953, p.
       4a.
    Williams, Stephen. Evening News, October 9, 1953,
       p. 5e.
    Wilson, Cecil. Daily Mail, October 9, 1953, p. 6a.
    Worsley, T. C. New Statesman, October 17, 1953, pp.
       446-447.

The King and I (Revival).
Adelphi: October 10, 1973-May 25, 1974 (260)

    Billington, Michael. Manchester Guardian, October
       11, 1973, p. 14c.
    Cushman, Robert. Observer, October 14, 1973, p. 36c.
    Frame, Colin. Evening News, October 11, 1973, p. 4b.
    Hurren, Kenneth. Spectator, October 20, 1973, p.
       521.
    Kingston, Jeremy. Punch, October 17, 1973, p. 559.
    Lewsen, Charles. The Times, October 11, 1973, p.
       12f.
    Nightingale, Benedict. New Statesman, October 19,
       1973, p. 573.
    Shulman, Milton. Evening Standard, October 11,
       1973, p. 31c.
    Tinker, Jack. Daily Mail, October 12, 1973, p. 23d.
    Young, B. A. Financial Times, October 11, 1973, p.
       3c.

No Strings. Music and lyrics by Richard Rodgers; book
by Samuel Taylor.
Her Majesty's: December 30, 1963-May 9, 1964 (151)

    Barker, Felix. Evening News, December 31, 1963, p.
       7b.

Darlington, W. A. Daily Telegraph, December 31, 1963,
    p. 10d.
Gascoigne, Bamber. Observer, January 5, 1964, p.
    23d.
Gellert, Roger. New Statesman, January 10, 1964, p.
    56.
Kretzmer, Herbert. Daily Express, December 31, 1963,
    p. 3f.
Lambert, J. W. Sunday Times, January 5, 1964, p.
    25b.
Nathan, David. Daily Herald, December 31, 1963, p.
    7a.
Pryce-Jones, David. Spectator, January 10, 1964,
    p. 47.
Shulman, Milton. Evening Standard, December 31, 1963,
    p. 4a.
The Times, December 31, 1963, p. 7a.
Trewin, J. C. Illustrated London News, January 11,
    1964, p. 68.
Young, B. A. Punch, January 8, 1964, p. 66.

Pal Joey. Book by John O'Hara; lyrics by Lorenz Hart.
Princess: March 31, 1954-October 30, 1954 (245)

Balfour, John. Daily Sketch, April 1, 1954, p. 10a.
Barber, John. Daily Express, April 1, 1954, p. 3h.
Brown, Ivor. Observer, April 4, 1954, p. 11a.
Darlington, W. A. Daily Telegraph, April 1, 1954,
    p. 8f.
Granger, Derek. Financial Times, April 1, 1954, p.
    9d.
Hartley, Anthony. Spectator, April 9, 1954, p. 430.
Hobson, Harold. Sunday Times, April 4, 1954, p. 11a.
Holt, Paul. Daily Herald, April 1, 1954, p. 3a.
Hope-Wallace, Philip. Manchester Guardian, April 2,
    1954, p. 5c.
Keown, Eric. Punch, April 7, 1954, pp. 451-452.
Shulman, Milton. Evening Standard, April 2, 1954,
    p. 17d.
The Times, April 1, 1954, p. 8d.
Trewin, J. C. Illustrated London News, April 17,
    1954, p. 630.
Williams, Stephen. Evening News, April 1, 1954, p.
    5e.
Wilson, Cecil. Daily Mail, April 1, 1954, p. 6c.

The Sound of Music. Music by Richard Rodgers; lyrics
by Oscar Hammerstein, II; book by Howard Lindsay and
Russel Crouse.
Palace: May 18, 1961-January 14, 1967 (2,385)

Barker, Felix. Evening News, May 19, 1961, p. 12d.
Darlington, W. A. Daily Telegraph, May 19, 1961, p.
    16f.
Dickinson, Peter. Punch, May 31, 1961, p. 842.
Gellert, Roger. New Statesman, May 26, 1961, p.
    847.

Hobson, Harold. Sunday Times, May 21, 1961, p. 35b.
Hope-Wallace, Philip. Manchester Guardian, May 20,
     1961, p. 3f.
Levin, Bernard. Daily Express, May 19, 1961, p. 9e.
Muller, Robert. Daily Mail, May 19, 1961, p. 3a.
Nathan, David. Daily Herald, May 19, 1961, p. 5b.
Shulman, Milton. Evening Standard, May 19, 1961,
     p. 4a.
The Times, May 19, 1961, p. 19a.
Trewin, J. C. Illustrated London News, June 3, 1961,
     p. 944.
Wardle, Irving. Observer, May 21, 1961, p. 22g.
Worsley, T. C. Financial Times, May 19, 1961, p.
     20c.

South Pacific. Lyrics by Oscar Hammerstein, II; book
by Joshua Logan and Oscar Hammerstein, II.
Drury Lane: November 1, 1951-September 26, 1953 (792)

Barber, John. Daily Express, November 2, 1951, p.
     3b.
Baxter, Beverly. Evening Standard, November 2,
     1951, p. 11c.
Brown, Ivor. Observer, November 4, 1951, p. 6a.
Darlington, W. A. Daily Telegraph, November 2, 1951,
     p. 7e.
Hayes, Walter. Daily Sketch, November 2, 1951, p.
     6c.
Hobson, Harold. Sunday Times, November 4, 1951, p.
     2f.
Hope-Wallace, Philip. Manchester Guardian, November
     3, 1951, p. 3f.
Keown, Eric. Punch, November 14, 1951, p. 556.
Mannock, P. L. Daily Herald, November 2, 1951, p.
     3e.
The Times, November 2, 1951, p. 7a.
Trewin, J. C. Illustrated London News, November 24,
     1951, p. 868.
Tynan, Kenneth. Spectator, November 9, 1951, p. 600.
Williams, Stephen. Evening News, November 2, 1951,
     p. 2g.
Wilson, Cecil. Daily Mail, November 2, 1951, p. 6f.
Worsley, T. C. New Statesman, November 10, 1951,
     p. 531.

ROMBERG, Sigmund
     The Desert Song (Revival). Music by Sigmund Romberg;
     book by Otto Harbach, Oscar Hammerstein, II, and Frank
     Mandel; lyrics by Otto Harbach and Oscar Hammerstein, II.
     Palace: May 13, 1967-February 10, 1968, transferred to
     Cambridge: February 13, 1968-May 25, 1968 (433)

     Barker, Felix. Evening News, May 14, 1967, p. 3c.
     Billington, Michael. The Times, May 15, 1967, p.
          8h.
     Bryden, Ronald. Observer, May 21, 1967, p. 24h.

Christie, Ian. Daily Mail, May 15, 1967, p. 10b.
Hope-Wallace, Philip. Manchester Guardian, May 16,
    1967, p. 7f.
Kingston, Jeremy. Punch, May 24, 1967, p. 768.
Lambert, J. W. Sunday Times, May 21, 1967, p. 48h.
Nathan, David. Sun, May 15, 1967, p. 6f.
Shorter, Eric. Daily Telegraph, May 15, 1967, p.
    15a.
Shulman, Milton. Evening Standard, May 15, 1967,
    p. 4f.
Spurling, Hilary. Spectator, May 26, 1967, p. 624.
Trewin, J. C. Illustrated London News, May 27, 1967,
    p. 3g.

ROME, Harold
    Fanny. Music and lyrics by Harold Rome; book and play
    by S. N. Behrman and Joshua Logan. Based on a trilogy
    by Marcel Pagnol.
    Drury Lane: November 15, 1956-September 14, 1957 (347)

    Barber, John. Daily Express, November 16, 1956, p.
        3b.
    Daily Herald, November 16, 1956, p. 3b.
    Gibbs, Patrick. Daily Telegraph, November 16, 1956,
        p. 12d.
    Granger, Derek. Financial Times, November 16, 1956,
        p. 2g.
    Hobson, Harold. Sunday Times, November 18, 1956, p.
        15f.
    Hope-Wallace, Philip. Manchester Guardian, November
        17, 1956, p. 5c.
    Keown, Eric. Punch, November 28, 1956, p. 662.
    Shulman, Milton. Evening Standard, November 16,
        1956, p. 6a.
    The Times, November 16, 1956, p. 3c.
    Trewin, J. C. Illustrated London News, December 1,
        1956, p. 942.
    Tynan, Kenneth. Observer, November 18, 1956, p. 13b.
    W., D. Spectator, November 23, 1956, p. 718.
    Williams, Stephen. Evening News, November 15, 1956,
        p. 5c.
    Wilson, Cecil. Daily Mail, November 16, 1956, p. 3f.

Gone With the Wind. Book by Horton Foote, based on the
novel by Margaret Mitchell. Music and lyrics by Harold
Rome.
Drury Lane: May 3, 1972-April 7, 1973 (387)

    Barber, John. Daily Telegraph, May 4, 1972, p. 14b.
    Barker, Felix. Evening News, May 4, 1972, p. 3a.
    Billington, Michael. Manchester Guardian, May 4,
        1972, p. 12b.
    Hurren, Kenneth. Spectator, May 13, 1972, p. 744.
    Kingston, Jeremy. Punch, May 10, 1972, pp. 662-663.
    Kretzmer, Herbert. Daily Express, May 4, 1972, p.
        16d.

Lambert, J. W. Sunday Times, May 7, 1972, p. 35a.
Mortimer, John. Observer, May 7, 1972, p. 36a.
Nightingale, Benedict. New Statesman, May 12, 1972,
    p. 651.
Shulman, Milton. Evening Standard, May 4, 1972, p.
    15e.
Tinker, Jack. Daily Mail, May 5, 1972, p. 19a.
Trewin, J. C. Illustrated London News, July 1972,
    p. 50.
Wardle, Irving. The Times, May 4, 1972, p. 9d.
Young, B. A. Financial Times, May 4, 1972, p. 3a.

Wish You Were Here. Book by Arthur Kober and Joshua
Logan; music and lyrics by Harold Rome. Based on Having
Wonderful Time by Arthur Kober.
Casino: October 10, 1953-June 12, 1954 (282)

Barber, John. Daily Express, October 12, 1953, p.
    5g.
Brown, Ivor. Observer, October 18, 1953, p. 13b.
Darlington, W. A. Daily Telegraph, October 12, 1953,
    p. 9e.
Hope-Wallace, Philip. Manchester Guardian, October
    12, 1953, p. 3e.
Monsey, Derek. Spectator, October 23, 1953, p. 451.
The Times, October 12, 1953, p. 12c.
Trewin, J. C. Illustrated London News, October 24,
    1953, p. 664.
Tynan, Kenneth. Daily Sketch, October 12, 1953, p.
    4c.
Williams, Stephen. Evening News, October 12, 1953,
    p. 5h.
Wiltshire, Maurice. Daily Mail, October 12, 1953,
    p. 5c.
Worsley, T. C. New Statesman, October 17, 1953, p.
    447.

ROSE, Reginald
    Twelve Angry Men.
    Queen's: July 9, 1964-August 15, 1964, transferred to
    Lyric: August 24, 1964-October 10, 1964 (99)

Barker, Felix. Evening News, July 10, 1964, p. 7a.
Bryden, Ronald. New Statesman, July 17, 1964, p.
    96.
Gascoigne, Bamber. Observer, July 12, 1964, p. 24g.
Higgins, John. Financial Times, July 10, 1964, p.
    28a.
Hope-Wallace, Philip. Manchester Guardian, July 10,
    1964, p. 11e.
Kingston, Jeremy. Punch, July 15, 1964, p. 99.
Lambert, J. W. Sunday Times, July 12, 1964, p. 25b.
Nathan, David. Daily Herald, July 10, 1964, p. 7c.
Shulman, Milton. Evening Standard, July 10, 1964,
    p. 4a.
The Times, July 10, 1964, p. 7a.

Trewin, J. C. Illustrated London News, July 25,
    1964, p. 13b.
Walsh, Michael. Daily Express, July 10, 1964, p. 7b.

ROSEN, Al
    Mary Had a Little. See: Hertzog, Arthur

ROSENTHAL, Andrew
    Horses in Midstream.
    Vaudeville: September 22, 1960-October 1, 1960   (12)

        Boothroyd, J. B. Punch, September 28, 1960, p. 465.
        Brooks, Jeremy. New Statesman, October 1, 1960, p.
            470.
        Darlington, W. A. Daily Telegraph, September 23,
            1960, p. 16d.
        Hobson, Harold. Sunday Times, September 25, 1960,
            p. 35a.
        Hope-Wallace, Philip. Manchester Guardian, September
            24, 1960, p. 5a.
        Levin, Bernard. Daily Express, September 23, 1960,
            p. 17f.
        Muller, Robert. Daily Mail, September 23, 1960, p.
            3b.
        Shulman, Milton. Evening Standard, September 23,
            1960, p. 10d.
        Smith, Andrew. Daily Herald, September 23, 1960,
            p. 3c.
        The Times, September 23, 1960, p. 18f.
        Trewin, J. C. Illustrated London News, October 8,
            1960, p. 620.
        Worsley, T. C. Financial Times, September 23, 1960,
            p. 19e.

    Innocent as Hell (musical).
    Lyric, Hammersmith: June 29, 1960-July 9, 1960   (13)

        Barker, Felix. Evening News, June 30, 1960, p. 7d.
        Barnes, Clive. Daily Express, June 30, 1960, p.
            11d.
        Darlington, W. A. Daily Telegraph, June 30, 1960,
            p. 14e.
        Higgins, John. Financial Times, June 30, 1960, p.
            17c.
        Muller, Robert. Daily Mail, June 30, 1960, p. 3a.
        Nathan, David. Daily Herald, June 30, 1960, p. 3c.
        The Times, June 30, 1960, p. 6d.
        Wardle, Irving. Observer, July 3, 1960, p. 25d.

    Red Letter Day.
    Garrick: February 21, 1952-May 24, 1952   (107)

        Barber, John. Daily Express, February 22, 1952, p.
            3h.
        Brown, Ivor. Observer, February 24, 1952, p. 6b.
        Darlington, W. A. Daily Telegraph, February 22,
            1952, p. 7d.

Hayes, Walter. Daily Sketch, February 23, 1952, p.
     3c.
Hobson, Harold. Sunday Times, February 24, 1952, p.
     2e.
Hope-Wallace, Philip. Manchester Guardian, February
     23, 1952, p. 3c.
Keown, Eric. Punch, March 12, 1952, p. 352.
Mannock, P. L. Daily Herald, February 22, 1952, p.
     3g.
The Times, February 22, 1952, p. 4e.
Trewin, J. C. Illustrated London News, March 15,
     1952, p. 466.
Tynan, Kenneth. Spectator, February 29, 1952, p.
     260.
Williams, Stephen. Evening News, February 22, 1952,
     p. 2g.
Wilson, Cecil. Daily Mail, February 22, 1952, p. 4d.
Worsley, T. C. New Statesman, March 1, 1952, p. 243.

Third Person.
Arts: October 30, 1951-November 28, 1951   (35)*
Criterion: January 3, 1952-April 5, 1952   (107)

Conway, Harold. Evening Standard, October 31, 1951,
     p. 5b.
Darlington, W. A. Daily Telegraph, October 31, 1951,
     p. 6f.
Hope-Wallace, Philip. Manchester Guardian, November
     1, 1951, p. 5c.
The Times, October 31, 1951, p. 4e.
Wiltshire, Maurice. Daily Mail, October 31, 1951,
     p. 4f.
Worsley, T. C. New Statesman, November 17, 1951,
     p. 562.

Duncan, Ronald. Evening Standard, January 4, 1952,
     p. 9e.
Hamilton, Iain. Spectator, January 11, 1952, p. 44.
Hayes, Walter. Daily Sketch, January 4, 1952, p.
     3e.
Hobson, Harold. Sunday Times, January 6, 1952, p.
     2f.
Hope-Wallace, Philip. Manchester Guardian, November
     1, 1952, p. 5c.
Keown, Eric. Punch, January 16, 1952, p. 124.
Levin, Bernard. Daily Express, January 4, 1952, p.
     3b.
Mannock, P. L. Daily Herald, January 4, 1952, p.
     3d.
The Times, January 4, 1952, p. 7c.
Wilson, Cecil. Daily Mail, January 4, 1952, p. 7c.
Worsley, T. C. New Statesman, November 17, 1952, p.
     562.

ROSS, Jerry
    Damn Yankees. Music by Jerry Ross; lyrics by Richard
    Adler; book by George Abbott and Douglas Wallop. (Based
    on the novel, The Year the Yankees Lost the Pennant, by
    Douglas Wallop.)
    Coliseum: March 28, 1957-November 9, 1957 (258)

        Barber, John. Daily Express, March 29, 1957, p. 3c.
        Conway, Harold. Daily Sketch, March 29, 1957, p.
            6e.
        Darlington, W. A. Daily Telegraph, March 29, 1957,
            p. 10f.
        Granger, Derek. Financial Times, March 29, 1957, p.
            2g.
        Hobson, Harold. Sunday Times, March 31, 1957, p.
            19c.
        Hope-Wallace, Philip. Manchester Guardian, March
            30, 1957, p. 5b.
        Keown, Eric. Punch, April 3, 1957, p. 453.
        L., J. A. New Statesman, April 6, 1957, p. 441.
        Shulman, Milton. Evening Standard, March 29, 1957,
            p. 6c.
        The Times, March 29, 1957, p. 3g.
        Trewin, J. C. Illustrated London News, April 13,
            1957, p. 600.
        Tynan, Kenneth. Observer, March 31, 1957, p. 13b.
        Watt, David. Spectator, April 12, 1957, p. 488.
        Williams, Stephen. Evening News, March 29, 1957,
            p. 5e.
        Wilson, Cecil. Daily Mail, March 29, 1957, p. 3a.

    The Pajama Game. Music and lyrics by Jerry Ross and
    Richard Adler; musical play and book by George Abbott
    and Richard Bissell. (Based on 7-1/2 Cents by Richard
    Bissell.)
    Coliseum: October 13, 1955-March 9, 1957 (588)

        Barber, John. Daily Express, October 13, 1955, p.
            3a.
        Carthew, Anthony. Daily Herald, October 14, 1955,
            p. 3c.
        Conway, Harold. Daily Sketch, October 14, 1955,
            p. 7a.
        Darlington, W. A. Daily Telegraph, October 14,
            1955, p. 9e.
        Granger, Derek. Financial Times, October 14, 1955,
            p. 2g.
        Hartley, Anthony. Spectator, October 21, 1955, p.
            531.
        Hobson, Harold. Sunday Times, October 16, 1955, p.
            7a.
        Hope-Wallace, Philip. Manchester Guardian, October
            15, 1955, p. 5a.
        Keown, Eric. Punch, October 19, 1955, p. 470.
        Shulman, Milton. Evening Standard, October 14,
            1955, p. 5c.

The Times, October 14, 1955, p. 3b.
Trewin, J. C. Illustrated London News, October 29,
     1955, p. 742.
Tynan, Kenneth. Observer, October 16, 1955, p. 11a.
Williams, Stephen. Evening News, October 14, 1955,
     p. 2h.
Wilson, Cecil. Daily Mail, October 14, 1955, p. 3g.

ROSSETT, Alan
     High Time.
     Hampstead Theatre Club: April 10, 1972-May 6, 1972 (28)

          Barber, John. Daily Telegraph, April 11, 1972, p.
               12d.
          Hurren, Kenneth. Spectator, April 22, 1972, p. 630.
          Kretzmer, Herbert. Daily Express, April 11, 1972,
               p. 14g.
          Mortimer, John. Observer, April 16, 1972, p. 30b.
          Shulman, Milton. Evening Standard, April 11, 1972,
               p. 21e.
          Tinker, Jack. Daily Mail, April 12, 1972, p. 31b.
          Wardle, Irving. The Times, April 11, 1972, p. 8c.
          Young, B. A. Financial Times, April 11, 1972, p.
               3c.

RUSSEL, Gordon
     Masterpiece. See: Ward, Larry

SACKLER, Howard
     The Pastime of Monsieur Robert.
     Hampstead Theatre Club: February 7, 1966-February 25,
     1966 (21)

          Bryden, Ronald. New Statesman, February 18, 1966,
               p. 234.
          Gilliatt, Penelope. Observer, February 13, 1966,
               p. 25c.
          Hobson, Harold. Sunday Times, February 13, 1966,
               p. 31h.
          Kingston, Jeremy. Punch, February 16, 1966, p. 245.
          The Times, February 8, 1966, p. 15a.
          Trewin, J. C. Illustrated London News, February 19,
               1966, p. 38.

SAHLINS, Bernard
     The Star Spangled Jack Show. See: Patinkin, Sheldon

SAROYAN, William
     Sam the Highest Jumper of Them All.
     Theatre Royal, Stratford: April 6, 1960-April 30, 1960
     (26)

          Alvarez, A. New Statesman, April 16, 1960, pp. 554-
               555.
          Brien, Alan. Spectator, April 22, 1960, pp. 573-
               574.

Darlington, W. A. Daily Telegraph, April 7, 1960,
    p. 14f.
Hope-Wallace, Philip. Manchester Guardian, April 8,
    1960, p. 11a.
Lambert, J. W. Sunday Times, April 10, 1960, p. 25c.
Levin, Bernard. Daily Express, April 7, 1960, p.
    14f.
Muller, Robert. Daily Mail, April 7, 1960, p. 3b.
Nathan, David. Daily Herald, April 7, 1960, p. 3h.
The Times, April 7, 1960, p. 3d.
Trewin, J. C. Illustrated London News, April 23,
    1960, p. 704.
Worsley, T. C. Financial Times, April 7, 1960, p.
    23e.

Settled Out of Court. By William Saroyan and Henry
Cecil.
Strand: October 19, 1960-April 29, 1961 (222)

Barker, Felix. Evening News, October 20, 1960, p.
    9d.
Brien, Alan. Spectator, October 28, 1960, p. 655.
Brooks, Jeremy. New Statesman, October 29, 1960,
    p. 648.
Gibbs, Patrick. Daily Telegraph, October 20, 1960,
    p. 16d.
Hobson, Harold. Sunday Times, October 23, 1960, p.
    35b.
Keown, Eric. Punch, October 26, 1960, pp. 608-609.
Levin, Bernard. Daily Express, October 20, 1960,
    p. 7c.
Muller, Robert. Daily Mail, October 20, 1960, p. 3c.
Shrapnel, Norman. Manchester Guardian, October 21,
    1960, p. 11h.
Shulman, Milton. Evening Standard, October 20, 1960,
    p. 21a.
Smith, Andrew. Daily Herald, October 20, 1960, p.
    3e.
The Times, October 20, 1960, p. 8a.
Trewin, J. C. Illustrated London News, November 5,
    1960, p. 818.
Tynan, Kenneth. Observer, October 23, 1960, p. 26d.
Worsley, T. C. Financial Times, October 20, 1960,
    p. 21g.

Two Plays: Talking to You and Across the Board on
Tomorrow Morning.
Duke of York's: October 4, 1962-October 13, 1962 (12)

Barker, Felix. Evening News, October 5, 1962, p. 7c.
Gellert, Roger. New Statesman, October 19, 1962, p.
    543.
Hobson, Harold. Sunday Times, October 7, 1962, p.
    41c.
Keown, Eric. Punch, October 10, 1962, p. 537.
Kretzmer, Herbert. Daily Express, October 5, 1962,
    p. 4c.

Levin, Bernard. Daily Mail, October 5, 1962, p. 3e.
Nathan, David. Daily Herald, October 5, 1962, p.
    3f.
Shulman, Milton. Evening Standard, October 5, 1962,
    p. 4a.
The Times, October 5, 1962, p. 18g.
Trewin, J. C. Illustrated London News, October 20,
    1962, p. 622.
Tynan, Kenneth. Observer, October 7, 1962, p. 26c.

SAUNDERS, James
    Neighbors. See: Jones, LeRoi, The Dutchman

SCHAFER, Jerry
    Belle Starr. See: Allen, Steve

SCHISGAL, Murray
    Ducks and Lovers.
    Arts: October 19, 1961-November 14, 1961 (30)*

Barker, Felix. Evening News, October 20, 1961, p.
    3a.
Gascoigne, Bamber. Spectator, October 27, 1961, p.
    577.
Gellert, Roger. New Statesman, October 27, 1961,
    p. 624.
Hobson, Harold. Sunday Times, October 22, 1961, p.
    41g.
Jenkins, Peter. Manchester Guardian, October 20,
    1961, p. 9f.
Keown, Eric. Punch, October 25, 1961, pp. 620-621.
Levin, Bernard. Daily Express, October 20, 1961,
    p. 8f.
Muller, Robert. Daily Mail, October 20, 1961, p.
    3f.
Nathan, David. Daily Herald, October 20, 1961, p.
    7f.
Shorter, Eric. Daily Telegraph, October 20, 1961,
    p. 16e.
Shulman, Milton. Evening Standard, October 20, 1961,
    p. 22b.
The Times, October 20, 1961, p. 16c.
Trewin, J. C. Illustrated London News, November 4,
    1961, p. 788.
Tynan, Kenneth. Observer, October 22, 1961, p. 27h.
Worsley, T. C. Financial Times, October 20, 1961,
    p. 20a.

    Luv.
    Arts: April 24, 1963-May 18, 1963 (31)

Barker, Felix. Evening News, April 25, 1963, p.
    13c.
Clurman, Harold. Observer, April 28, 1963, p. 28d.
Darlington, W. A. Daily Telegraph, April 25, 1963,
    p. 18e.

Dent, Alan. <u>Punch</u>, May 1, 1963, p. 643.
Fay, Gerard. <u>Manchester Guardian</u>, April 25, 1963,
    p. 9c.
Gascoigne, Bamber. <u>Spectator</u>, May 3, 1963, p. 569.
Gellert, Roger. <u>New Statesman</u>, May 3, 1963, p. 689.
Hobson, Harold. <u>Sunday Times</u>, April 28, 1963, p.
    41d.
Kretzmer, Herbert. <u>Daily Express</u>, April 25, 1963,
    p. 19b.
Levin, Bernard. <u>Daily Mail</u>, April 25, 1963, p. 3a.
Nathan, David. <u>Daily Herald</u>, April 25, 1963, p. 9b.
Shulman, Milton. <u>Evening Standard</u>, April 25, 1963,
    p. 4b.
<u>The Times</u>, April 25, 1963, p. 16g.
Trewin, J. C. <u>Illustrated London News</u>, May 11,
    1963, p. 740.
Worsley, T. C. <u>Financial Times</u>, April 25, 1963, p.
    24d.

<u>The Tiger and the Typists</u>.
Globe: May 25, 1964-June 27, 1964   (40)

Barker, Felix. <u>Evening News</u>, May 26, 1964, p. 4e.
Bryden, Ronald. <u>New Statesman</u>, June 5, 1964, p. 888.
Gascoigne, Bamber. <u>Observer</u>, May 31, 1964, p. 24e.
Hobson, Harold. <u>Sunday Times</u>, May 31, 1964, p. 34e.
Kingston, Jeremy. <u>Punch</u>, June 3, 1964, p. 835.
Levin, Bernard. <u>Daily Mail</u>, May 27, 1964, p. 16b.
Nathan, David. <u>Daily Herald</u>, May 26, 1964, p. 7f.
Pryce-Jones, David. <u>Spectator</u>, June 5, 1964, p.
    757.
Shrapnel, Norman. <u>Manchester Guardian</u>, May 26,
    1964, p. 9d.
Shulman, Milton. <u>Evening Standard</u>, May 26, 1964,
    p. 4a.
<u>The Times</u>, May 26, 1964, p. 14a.
Trewin, J. C. <u>Illustrated London News</u>, June 6,
    1964, p. 912.
Young, B. A. <u>Financial Times</u>, May 26, 1964, p. 24c.

SCHMIDT, Harvey
    <u>The Fantasticks</u>. Book and lyrics by Tom Jones.
    Apollo: September 7, 1961-October 14, 1961   (44)

Darlington, W. A. <u>Daily Telegraph</u>, September 8,
    1961, p. 14d.
Gascoigne, Bamber. <u>Spectator</u>, September 22, 1961,
    pp. 353-354.
Gellert, Roger. <u>New Statesman</u>, September 22, 1961,
    p. 400.
Holland, Julian. <u>Evening News</u>, September 8, 1961,
    p. 6h.
Hope-Wallace, Philip. <u>Manchester Guardian</u>, September
    8, 1961, p. 9a.
Keown, Eric. <u>Punch</u>, October 4, 1961, p. 512.
Lambert, J. W. <u>Sunday Times</u>, September 10, 1961,
    p. 35a.

Levin, Bernard. Daily Express, September 8, 1961,
     p. 11d.
Nathan, David. Daily Herald, September 8, 1961, p.
     7b.
Shulman, Milton. Evening Standard, September 8,
     1961, p. 21e.
The Times, September 8, 1961, p. 16a.
Tynan, Kenneth. Observer, September 19, 1961, p.
     23c.

I Do! I Do! Music by Harvey Schmidt; lyrics by Tom
Jones. Musical based on The Fourposter by Jan de Hartog.
Lyric: May 16, 1968-August 24, 1968 (116)

Barker, Felix. Evening News, May 17, 1968, p. 3a.
Bryden, Ronald. Observer, May 19, 1968, p. 31b.
Hobson, Harold. Sunday Times, May 19, 1968, p. 55f.
Hope-Wallace, Philip. Manchester Guardian, May 17,
     1968, p. 10e.
Kingston, Jeremy. Punch, May 29, 1968, p. 788.
Kretzmer, Herbert. Daily Express, May 17, 1968,
     p. 9g.
Lewis, Peter. Daily Mail, May 18, 1968, p. 4f.
Nathan, David. Sun, May 17, 1968, p. 4a.
Shorter, Eric. Daily Telegraph, May 17, 1968, p.
     21a.
Shulman, Milton. Evening Standard, May 17, 1968,
     p. 21a.
Trewin, J. C. Illustrated London News, May 25,
     1968, p. 54.
Wardle, Irving. The Times, May 17, 1968, p. 19c.

110 in the Shade. Music by Harvey Schmidt; lyrics by
Tom Jones; book by Richard Nash.
Palace: February 8, 1967-May 8, 1967 (101)

Barker, Felix. Evening News, February 9, 1967, p.
     4g.
Bryden, Ronald. Observer, February 12, 1967, p. 25a.
Darlington, W. A. Daily Telegraph, February 9, 1967,
     p. 17a.
Hobson, Harold. Sunday Times, February 12, 1967, p.
     49a.
Hope-Wallace, Philip. Manchester Guardian, February
     9, 1967, p. 10e.
Jones, D. A. N. New Statesman, February 24, 1967,
     p. 270.
Kingston, Jeremy. Punch, February 15, 1967, p. 242.
Kretzmer, Herbert. Daily Express, February 9, 1967,
     p. 6a.
Lewis, Peter. Daily Mail, February 10, 1967, p. 10b.
Nathan, David. Sun, February 9, 1967, p. 3e.
Shulman, Milton. Evening Standard, February 9, 1967,
     p. 4f.
Trewin, J. C. Illustrated London News, February 18,
     1967, p. 29.

Wardle, Irving. The Times, February 9, 1967, p. 4f.
Young, B. A. Financial Times, February 10, 1967, p.
      26a.

SCHWARTZ, Stephen
    Godspell, a rock musical. Book by John-Michael Tehelak;
    music by Stephen Schwartz.
    Round House, transferred to Wyndham's: November 17,
    1971-October 12, 1974 (1,128)

        Barber, John. Daily Telegraph, November 18, 1971,
            p. 14c.
        Billington, Michael. Manchester Guardian, November
            18, 1971, p. 12a.
        Dawson, Helen. Observer, November 21, 1971, p. 31e.
        Frame, Colin. Evening News, November 18, 1971, p.
            3d.
        Hobson, Harold. Sunday Times, November 21, 1971, p.
            37a.
        Hurren, Kenneth. Spectator, November 27, 1971, p.
            777.
        Kretzmer, Herbert. Daily Express, November 18, 1971,
            p. 20f.
        Shulman, Milton. Evening Standard, November 18,
            1971, p. 18d.
        Wardle, Irving. The Times, November 18, 1971, p.
            11c.
        Young, B. A. Financial Times, November 18, 1971,
            p. 3a.

    Godspell (Revival).
    Phoenix: June 10, 1975-September 20, 1975 (119)

        Barber, John. Daily Telegraph, June 11, 1975, p.
            11a.
        Young, B. A. Financial Times, June 11, 1975, p. 3a.

    Pippin. Book by Roger O. Hirson; music and lyrics by
    Stephen Schwartz.
    Her Majesty's: October 30, 1973-January 12, 1974 (85)

        Barker, Felix. Evening News, October 31, 1973, p.
            4g.
        Billington, Michael. Manchester Guardian, October
            31, 1973, p. 10e.
        Cushman, Robert. Observer, November 4, 1973, p. 37g.
        Hurren, Kenneth. Spectator, November 10, 1973, p.
            615.
        Nightingale, Benedict. New Statesman, November 16,
            1973, p. 749.
        Shulman, Milton. Evening Standard, October 31,
            1973, p. 24c.
        Trewin, J. C. Illustrated London News, January
            1974, p. 69.
        Wardle, Irving. The Times, October 31, 1973, p. 15c.
        Young, B. A. Financial Times, October 31, 1973, p.
            3a.

SHAPIRO, Mel
    Two Gentlemen of Verona. See: MacDermot, Galt

SHEARER, Toni
    Mother Earth. Book and lyrics by Ron Thronson; music
    by Toni Shearer.
    Roundhouse: September 19, 1972-September 30, 1972
    (16)

        Barber, John. Daily Telegraph, September 21, 1972,
            p. 13f.
        Barker, Felix. Evening News, September 21, 1972,
            p. 11c.
        Kretzmer, Herbert. Daily Express, September 21,
            1972, p. 20a.
        O'Connor, Garry. Financial Times, September 21,
            1972, p. 3a.
        Peter, John. Sunday Times, September 24, 1972, p.
            37d.
        Shulman, Milton. Evening Standard, September 21,
            1972, p. 30a.
        Wardle, Irving. The Times, September 21, 1972, p.
            10d.

SHEPARD, Sam
    Tooth of Crime.
    Royal Court: June 5, 1974-July 6, 1974 (30)

        Barber, John. Daily Telegraph, June 6, 1974, p. 14a.
        Barker, Felix. Evening News, June 6, 1974, p. 6h.
        Billington, Michael. Manchester Guardian, June 6,
            1974, p. 12b.
        Coveney, Michael. Financial Times, June 6, 1974, p.
            3a.
        Hurren, Kenneth. Spectator, June 15, 1974, p. 744.
        Lambert, J. W. Sunday Times, June 9, 1974, p. 35d.
        Nightingale, Benedict. New Statesman, June 21, 1974,
            p. 895.
        Radin, Victoria. Observer, June 9, 1974, p. 31c.
        Thirkell, Arthur. Daily Mirror, June 6, 1974, p.
            18a.
        Tinker, Jack. Daily Mail, June 6, 1974, p. 3f.
        Wardle, Irving. The Times, June 6, 1974, p. 9c.

    The Unseen Hand.
    Theatre Upstairs, Royal Court: March 12, 1973-March
    31, 1973 (24)*

        Brustein, Robert. Observer, March 18, 1973, p. 34a.
        Hurren, Kenneth. Spectator, March 17, 1973, p. 338.
        Kingston, Jeremy. Punch, March 21, 1973, p. 402.
        Nightingale, Benedict. New Statesman, March 23,
            1973, p. 435.
        Shulman, Milton. Evening Standard, March 13, 1973,
            p. 24c.
        Tinker, Jack. Daily Mail, March 16, 1973, p. 21d.

Wardle, Irving. The Times, March 13, 1973, p. 12d.
Young, B. A. Financial Times, March 13, 1973, p.
    3a.

SHERWOOD, Robert
    Reunion in Vienna (Revival).
    Piccadilly: February 17, 1972-March 25, 1972   (44)

    Barber, John. Daily Telegraph, February 18, 1972,
        p. 11e.
    Barker, Felix. Evening News, February 18, 1972, p.
        3a.
    Billington, Michael. Manchester Guardian, February
        18, 1972, p. 10d.
    Dawson, Helen. Observer, February 20, 1972, p. 27e.
    Kretzmer, Herbert. Daily Express, February 18, 1972,
        p. 17a.
    Lambert, J. W. Sunday Times, February 20, 1972, p.
        29g.
    O'Connor, Garry. Financial Times, February 18, 1972,
        p. 3a.
    Shulman, Milton. Evening Standard, February 18,
        1972, p. 15d.
    Trewin, J. C. Illustrated London News, April 1972,
        p. 57.
    Wardle, Irving. The Times, February 18, 1972, p.
        10a.

SHEVELOVE, Burt
    A Funny Thing Happened on the Way to the Forum. See:
    Sondheim, Stephen

SHULMAN, Max
    The Tender Trap. By Max Shulman and Robert Paul Smith.
    Saville: May 3, 1955-May 29, 1955 (22)

    Barber, John. Daily Express, May 4, 1955, p. 3b.
    Carson, Peter. Evening Standard, May 4, 1955, p.
        20c.
    Darlington, W. A. Daily Telegraph, May 4, 1955,
        p. 8f.
    Granger, Derek. Financial Times, May 4, 1955, p.
        9c.
    Hartley, Anthony. Spectator, May 13, 1955, p. 618.
    Hobson, Harold. Sunday Times, May 8, 1955, p. 7b.
    Holt, Paul. Daily Herald, May 4, 1955, p. 3d.
    Hope-Wallace, Philip. Manchester Guardian, May 5,
        1955, p. 5g.
    Keown, Eric. Punch, May 11, 1955, p. 594.
    The Times, May 4, 1955, p. 16b.
    Trewin, J. C. Illustrated London News, May 21,
        1955, p. 936.
    Tynan, Kenneth. Observer, May 8, 1955, p. 15a.
    Williams, Stephen. Evening News, May 4, 1955, p. 5c.
    Wilson, Cecil. Daily Mail, May 4, 1955, p. 12b.

SIMON, Neil
  Barefoot in the Park.
  Piccadilly: November 24, 1965-June 25, 1966   (243)

        Barker, Felix. Evening News, November 25, 1965, p.
            7d.
        Benedictus, David. Observer, November 28, 1965, p.
            24f.
        Darlington, W. A. Daily Telegraph, November 25,
            1965, p. 18f.
        Hobson, Harold. Sunday Times, November 28, 1965,
            p. 27b.
        Hope-Wallace, Philip. Manchester Guardian, November
            25, 1965, p. 7e.
        Kingston, Jeremy. Punch, December 1, 1965, p. 810.
        Kretzmer, Herbert. Daily Express, November 25, 1965,
            p. 4h.
        Lewis, Peter. Daily Mail, November 26, 1965, p. 20b.
        Nathan, David. Sun, November 25, 1965, p. 7a.
        Shulman, Milton. Evening Standard, November 25,
            1965, p. 11a.
        The Times, November 25, 1965, p. 5d.
        Trewin, J. C. Illustrated London News, December 4,
            1965, p. 44.
        Young, B. A. Financial Times, November 26, 1965,
            p. 26a.

  Come Blow Your Horn.
  Prince of Wales: February 27, 1962-May 25, 1963   (582)

        Barker, Felix. Evening News, February 28, 1962, p.
            5h.
        Cashin, Fergus. Daily Sketch, March 1, 1962, p. 4a.
        Darlington, W. A. Daily Telegraph, February 28,
            1962, p. 14c.
        Gascoigne, Bamber. Spectator, March 9, 1962, p. 306.
        Gellert, Roger. New Statesman, March 9, 1962, p.
            346.
        Hobson, Harold. Sunday Times, March 4, 1962, p. 39d.
        Hope-Wallace, Philip. Manchester Guardian, February
            28, 1962, p. 7f.
        Keown, Eric. Punch, March 7, 1962, p. 403.
        Levin, Bernard. Daily Express, February 28, 1962,
            p. 4f.
        Nathan, David. Daily Herald, February 28, 1962, p.
            5c.
        Shulman, Milton. Evening Standard, February 28,
            1962, p. 18b.
        The Times, February 28, 1962, p. 5a.
        Trewin, J. C. Illustrated London News, March 10,
            1962, p. 386.
        Tynan, Kenneth. Observer, March 4, 1962, p. 26d.
        Worsley, T. C. Financial Times, February 28, 1962,
            p. 18c.

The Gingerbread Lady.
Phoenix: October 23, 1974-April 5, 1975 (180)

    Barker, Felix. Evening News, October 24, 1974, p.
       31a.
    Billington, Michael. Manchester Guardian, October
       24, 1974, p. 12e.
    Cushman, Robert. Observer, October 27, 1974, p. 28a.
    Hobson, Harold. Sunday Times, October 27, 1974, p.
       31d.
    Hurren, Kenneth. Spectator, November 2, 1974, p.
       576.
    Kretzmer, Herbert. Daily Express, October 24, 1974,
       p. 12g.
    Nightingale, Benedict. New Statesman, November 1,
       1974, pp. 628-629.
    Thirkell, Arthur. Daily Mirror, October 24, 1974,
       p. 18c.
    Tinker, Jack. Daily Mail, October 24, 1974, p. 30a.
    Trewin, J. C. Illustrated London News, January 1975,
       p. 69.
    Wardle, Irving. The Times, October 24, 1974, p. 15c.
    Young, B. A. Financial Times, October 24, 1974, p.
       3a.

Little Me. See: Coleman, Cy

The Odd Couple.
Queen's: October 12, 1966-September 23, 1967 (405)

    Barker, Felix. Evening News, October 13, 1966, p.
       4g.
    Bryden, Ronald. Observer, October 16, 1966, p. 25b.
    Darlington, W. A. Daily Telegraph, October 13, 1966,
       p. 19e.
    Higgins, John. Financial Times, October 14, 1966,
       p. 28b.
    Hope-Wallace, Philip. Manchester Guardian, October
       13, 1966, p. 9e.
    Jones, D. A. N. New Statesman, October 21, 1966,
       p. 599.
    Kingston, Jeremy. Punch, October 19, 1966, pp. 599-
       600.
    Kretzmer, Herbert. Daily Express, October 13, 1966,
       p. 4a.
    Lambert, J. W. Sunday Times, October 16, 1966, p.
       51d.
    Nathan, David. Sun, October 13, 1966, p. 8f.
    Norman, Barry. Daily Mail, October 14, 1966, p. 14b.
    Shulman, Milton. Evening Standard, October 13, 1966,
       p. 4e.
    Spurling, Hilary. Spectator, October 21, 1966, p.
       517.
    The Times, October 13, 1966, p. 18a.
    Trewin, J. C. Illustrated London News, October 22,
       1966, p. 50.

Plaza Suite.
Lyric: February 18, 1969-November 1, 1969   (294)

    Barber, John. Daily Telegraph, February 19, 1969,
       p. 19a.
    Barker, Felix. Evening News, February 19, 1969, p.
       8a.
    Bryden, Ronald. Observer, February 23, 1969, p. 24f.
    Hobson, Harold. Sunday Times, February 23, 1969, p.
       57c.
    Kingston, Jeremy. Punch, February 26, 1969, p. 322.
    Lewis, Peter. Daily Mail, February 29, 1969, p. 14c.
    Nathan, David. Sun, February 19, 1969, p. 9c.
    Shulman, Milton. Evening Standard, February 19,
       1969, p. 5c.
    Spurling, Hilary. Spectator, February 28, 1969, pp.
       279-280.
    Trewin, J. C. Illustrated London News, May 1, 1969,
       p. 29.
    Young, B. A. Financial Times, February 19, 1969,
       p. 3g.

Promises, Promises. See: Bacharach, Burt

The Sunshine Boys.
Piccadilly: May 7, 1975-July 12, 1975   (77)

    Barber, John. Daily Telegraph, May 8, 1975, p. 13a.
    Billington, Michael. Manchester Guardian, May 8,
       1975, p. 10d.
    Frame, Colin. Evening News, May 8, 1975, p. 4f.
    Hurren, Kenneth. Spectator, May 17, 1975, p. 617.
    Kretzmer, Herbert. Daily Express, May 6, 1975, p.
       10g.
    Lewis, Peter. Daily Mail, May 8, 1975, p. 20c.
    Morley, Sheridan. Punch, May 21, 1975, p. 904.
    Nightingale, Benedict. New Statesman, May 16, 1975,
       p. 670.
    Shulman, Milton. Evening Standard, May 8, 1975, p.
       19d.
    Spurling, Hilary. Observer, May 11, 1975, p. 29a.
    Thirkell, Arthur. Daily Mirror, May 8, 1975, p. 18d.
    Trewin, J. C. Illustrated London News, July 1975,
       p. 66.
    Wardle, Irving. The Times, May 8, 1975, p. 9g.
    Young, B. A. Financial Times, May 8, 1976, p. 3a.

Sweet Charity. See: Coleman, Cy

SMITH, Robert Paul
   The Tender Trap. See: Shulman, Max

SMITH, William Henry
   The Drunkard. See: Huycke, Lorne, The Wayward Way

SONDHEIM, Stephen
   Company. Book by George Furth; music and lyrics by
   Stephen Sondheim.
   Her Majesty's: January 18, 1972-September 30, 1972
   (303)*

      B., J. Daily Telegraph, January 19, 1972, p. 9a.
      Billington, Michael. Manchester Guardian, January
         19, 1972, p. 8e.
      Dawson, Helen. Observer, January 23, 1972, p. 27a.
      Higgins, John. The Times, January 29, 1972, p. 10d.
      Hobson, Harold. Sunday Times, January 23, 1972, p.
         27a.
      Hurren, Kenneth. Spectator, January 29, 1972, p.
         165.
      Kingston, Jeremy. Punch, January 26, 1972, pp. 125-
         126.
      Kretzmer, Herbert. Daily Express, January 19, 1972,
         p. 10a.
      Lewis, Peter. Daily Mail, January 20, 1972, p. 17e.
      Nightingale, Benedict. New Statesman, January 28,
         1972, p. 121.
      Pankhurst, H. J. Evening News, January 19, 1972,
         p. 3f.
      Shulman, Milton. Evening News, January 19, 1972,
         p. 20e.
      Trewin, J. C. Illustrated London News, March 1972,
         p. 58.
      Young, B. A. Financial Times, January 19, 1972, p.
         3a.

   A Funny Thing Happened on the Way to the Forum. Music
   and lyrics by Stephen Sondheim; book by Burt Shevelove
   and Larry Gelbart. Based on the plays of Plautus.
   Strand: October 3, 1963-July 31, 1965 (762)

      Barker, Felix. Evening News, October 4, 1963, p. 5a.
      Bryden, Ronald. New Statesman, October 11, 1963, p.
         500.
      Darlington, W. A. Daily Telegraph, October 4, 1963,
         p. 16d.
      Gascoigne, Bamber. Observer, October 6, 1963, p.
         27e.
      Hobson, Harold. Sunday Times, October 6, 1963, p.
         33b.
      Hope-Wallace, Philip. Manchester Guardian, October
         4, 1963, p. 9a.
      Kretzmer, Herbert. Daily Express, October 4, 1963,
         p. 4a.
      Nathan, David. Daily Herald, October 4, 1963, p.
         9c.
      Rutherford, Malcolm. Spectator, October 19, 1963,
         p. 460.
      Shulman, Milton. Evening Standard, October 4, 1963,
         p. 4b.
      The Times, October 4, 1963, p. 16a.

Trewin, J. C. Illustrated London News, October 19,
    1963, p. 652.
Worsley, T. C. Financial Times, October 5, 1963, p.
    7a.
Young, B. A. Punch, October 9, 1963, p. 539.

Gypsy. See: Styne, Jule

A Little Night Music. Book by Hugh Wheeler, suggested
by the film "Smiles of a Summer Night" by Ingmar Bergman.
Lyrics and music by Stephen Sondheim.
Adelphi: April 15, 1975-April 3, 1976 (406)

    Barber, John. Daily Telegraph, April 16, 1975, p.
        13a.
    Barker, Felix. Evening News, April 16, 1975, p. 14d.
    Billington, Michael. Manchester Guardian, April 16,
        1975, p. 10d.
    Cushman, Robert. Observer, April 20, 1975, p. 28a.
    Hurren, Kenneth. Spectator, April 26, 1975, p. 518.
    Kretzmer, Herbert. Daily Express, April 16, 1975,
        p. 12g.
    Morley, Sheridan. Punch, April 23, 1975, p. 731.
    Nightingale, Benedict. New Statesman, April 25,
        1975, p. 560.
    Shulman, Milton. Evening Standard, April 16, 1975,
        p. 19c.
    Thirkell, Arthur. Daily Mirror, April 16, 1975, p.
        18b.
    Tinker, Jack. Daily Mail, April 16, 1975, p. 36a.
    Wardle, Irving. The Times, April 16, 1975, p. 12c.
    Young, B. A. Financial Times, April 16, 1975, p.
        3c.

West Side Story. See: Bernstein, Leonard

SPEWACK, Bella
    See: Spewack, Sam and Bella

SPEWACK, Sam
    Under the Sycamore Tree.
    Aldwych: April 23, 1952-October 4, 1952 (189)

    Barber, John. Daily Express, April 24, 1952, p. 3f.
    Brown, Ivor. Observer, April 27, 1952, p. 6a.
    Conway, Harold. Evening Standard, April 24, 1952,
        p. 5c.
    Darlington, W. A. Daily Telegraph, April 24, 1952,
        p. 16d.
    Hayes, Walter. Daily Sketch, April 24, 1952, p. 7.
    Hobson, Harold. Sunday Times, April 27, 1952, p. 7a.
    Hope-Wallace, Philip. Manchester Guardian, April
        25, 1952, p. 5a.
    Keown, Eric. Punch, May 7, 1952, p. 572.
    Mannock, P. L. Daily Herald, April 24, 1952, p. 3f.
    The Times, April 24, 1952, p. 6f.

Trewin, J. C. Illustrated London News, May 10, 1952,
    p. 812.
Tynan, Kenneth. Spectator, May 9, 1952, p. 608.
Williams, Stephen. Evening News, April 24, 1952, p.
    2f.
Wilson, Cecil. Daily Mail, April 24, 1952, p. 4c.
Worsley, T. C. New Statesman, May 3, 1952, p. 524.

SPEWACK, Sam and Bella
    My Three Angels. By Sam and Bella Spewack. Based on
    Albert Husson's Cusine des Anges.
    Lyric: May 12, 1955-November 26, 1955 (128)

    Barber, John. Daily Express, May 13, 1955, p. 5f.
    Darlington, W. A. Daily Telegraph, May 13, 1955,
        p. 9f.
    Granger, Derek. Financial Times, May 13, 1955, p.
        7c.
    Hartley, Anthony. Spectator, May 20, 1955, p. 646.
    Hobson, Harold. Sunday Times, May 15, 1955, p. 7b.
    Hope-Wallace, Philip. Manchester Guardian, May 14,
        1955, p. 5a.
    Keown, Eric. Punch, May 25, 1955, pp. 659-660.
    Shulman, Milton. Evening Standard, May 13, 1955,
        p. 20d.
    The Times, May 13, 1955, p. 5c.
    Trewin, J. C. Illustrated London News, May 28, 1955,
        p. 982.
    Tynan, Kenneth. Observer, May 15, 1955, p. 15a.
    Williams, Stephen. Evening News, May 13, 1955, p.
        5d.
    Wilson, Cecil. Daily Mail, May 13, 1955, p. 11c.
    Worsley, T. C. New Statesman, June 4, 1955, p. 781.

    Spring Song.
    Saville: September 4, 1950-September 30, 1950 (32)

    Bishop, George W. Daily Telegraph, September 5,
        1950, p. 6e.
    Conway, Harold. Evening Standard, September 5, 1950,
        p. 5c.
    Hayes, Walter. Daily Sketch, September 5, 1950, p.
        5b.
    Lewin, David. Daily Express, September 5, 1950, p.
        3a.
    Mannock, P. L. Daily Herald, September 5, 1950, p.
        3f.
    The Times, September 5, 1950, p. 8d.
    Trewin, J. C. Illustrated London News, September
        23, 1950, p. 498.
    Trewin, J. C. Observer, September 10, 1950, p. 6b.
    W., M. Daily Mail, September 5, 1950, p. 5d.

SPIGELGLASS, Leonard
    A Majority of One.
    Phoenix: March 9, 1960-September 24, 1960 (227)

Alvarez, A. New Statesman, March 19, 1960, p. 398.
Barnes, Clive. Daily Express, March 10, 1960, p.
    12h.
Carthew, Anthony. Daily Herald, March 10, 1960, p.
    3e.
Darlington, W. A. Daily Telegraph, March 10, 1960,
    p. 14f.
Hobson, Harold. Sunday Times, March 13, 1960, p.
    25g.
Hope-Wallace, Philip. Manchester Guardian, March
    11, 1960, p. 9d.
Keown, Eric. Punch, March 16, 1960, p. 401.
Pryce-Jones, Alan. Observer, March 13, 1960, p. 23e.
Shulman, Milton. Evening Standard, March 10, 1960,
    p. 20e.
The Times, March 10, 1960, p. 6c.
Trewin, J. C. Illustrated London News, March 28,
    1960, p. 522.
Wilson, Cecil. Daily Mail, March 10, 1960, p. 3f.
Worsley, T. C. Financial Times, March 10, 1960, p.
    17e.

STEIN, Joseph
    Fiddler on the Roof. See: Bock, Jerry
    Plain and Fancy. See: Hague, Albert
    Zorba. See: Kander, John

STEVENS, Leslie
    The Marriage-Go-Round.
    Piccadilly: October 29, 1959-April 30, 1960 (210)

    Alvarez, A. New Statesman, November 7, 1959, p. 624.
    Barker, Felix. Evening News, October 30, 1959, p.
        6d.
    Brien, Alan. Spectator, November 6, 1959, p. 630.
    Darlington, W. A. Daily Telegraph, October 30,
        1959, p. 14e.
    Hobson, Harold. Sunday Times, November 1, 1959,
        p. 25b.
    Jones, Mervyn. Observer, November 1, 1959, p. 23a.
    Keown, Eric. Punch, November 4, 1959, p. 412.
    Levin, Bernard. Daily Express, October 30, 1959,
        p. 13f.
    Nathan, David. Daily Herald, October 30, 1959, p.
        3b.
    Shulman, Milton. Evening Standard, October 30,
        1959, p. 20b.
    The Times, October 30, 1959, p. 4a.
    Trewin, J. C. Illustrated London News, November 14,
        1959, p. 656.
    Wilson, Cecil. Daily Mail, October 30, 1959, p. 3g.
    Worsley, T. C. Financial Times, October 30, 1959,
        p. 17g.

STEWART, Donald Ogden
    Honour Bright.
    Lyric, Hammersmith: June 17, 1958-July 12, 1958 (31)

Barber, John. Daily Express, June 18, 1958, p. 7b.
Barker, Felix. Evening News, June 18, 1958, p. 5d.
Boothroyd, J. B. Punch, June 25, 1958, p. 850.
Gibbs, Patrick. Daily Telegraph, June 18, 1958, p.
    10d.
Goring, Edward. Daily Mail, June 18, 1958, p. 3a.
Hobson, Harold. Sunday Times, June 22, 1958, p. 11c.
Hope-Wallace, Philip. Manchester Guardian, June 19,
    1958, p. 5f.
Robinson, Robert. Spectator, June 27, 1958, p. 833.
Shulman, Milton. Evening Standard, June 18, 1958,
    p. 8a.
The Times, June 18, 1958, p. 5e.
Trewin, J. C. Illustrated London News, June 28,
    1958, p. 114.
Tynan, Kenneth. Observer, June 22, 1958, p. 15c.
Weaver, Harry. Daily Herald, June 18, 1958, p. 3d.
Worsley, T. C. Financial Times, June 18, 1958, p.
    13g.
Worsley, T. C. New Statesman, June 28, 1958, p.
    835.

The Kidders.
Arts: November 12, 1957-   . Reopened at St. Martin's:
March 18, 1958-April 26, 1958 (46)

Arts:
Barber, John. Daily Express, November 13, 1957, p.
    5e.
Darlington, W. A. Daily Telegraph, November 13,
    1957, p. 10e.
Granger, Derek. Financial Times, November 13, 1957,
    p. 2g.
Hobson, Harold. Sunday Times, November 17, 1957, p.
    25b.
Hope-Wallace, Philip. Manchester Guardian, November
    14, 1957, p. 7c.
Keown, Eric. Punch, November 20, 1957, p. 610.
Shulman, Milton. Evening Standard, November 13,
    1957, p. 8c.
The Times, November 13, 1957, p. 3d.
Trewin, J. C. Illustrated London News, November 23,
    1957, p. 898.
Tynan, Kenneth. Observer, November 17, 1957, p. 15a.
Watt, David. Spectator, November 22, 1957, p. 690.
Wilson, Cecil. Daily Mail, November 13, 1957, p. 5a.
Worsley, T. C. New Statesman, November 23, 1957, pp.
    691-692.

St. Martin's:
Barber, John. Daily Express, March 19, 1958, p. 4c.
Brien, Alan. Spectator, March 28, 1958, p. 389.
Gibbs, Patrick. Daily Telegraph, March 19, 1958,
    p. 10c.
H., J. Evening News, March 19, 1958, p. 7d.
Hope-Wallace, Philip. Manchester Guardian, March
    20, 1958, p. 9a.

Keown, Eric. Punch, March 26, 1958, p. 425.
Lambert, J. W. Sunday Times, March 23, 1958, p. 11b.
The Times, March 19, 1958, p. 3d.
Trewin, J. C. Illustrated London News, April 5,
    1958, p. 564.
Tynan, Kenneth. Observer, March 23, 1958, p. 15c.

STEWART, Michael
  Bye-Bye Birdie. See: Strouse, Charles
  Carnival. See: Merrill, Bob
  Hello, Dolly! See: Herman, Jerry

STONE, Peter
  1776. By Peter Stone and Sherman Edwards.
  New: June 16, 1970-October 31, 1970 (168)

    Barber, John. Daily Telegraph, June 18, 1970, p.
        16f.
    Bryden, Ronald. Observer, June 21, 1970, p. 28f.
    Frame, Colin. Evening News, June 17, 1970, p. 3e.
    Hobson, Harold. Sunday Times, June 21, 1970, p. 32c.
    Hope-Wallace, Philip. Manchester Guardian, June 17,
        1970, p. 12c.
    Kretzmer, Herbert. Daily Express, June 17, 1970,
        p. 16h.
    Lewis, Peter. Daily Mail, June 18, 1970, p. 12b.
    Nightingale, Benedict. New Statesman, July 10, 1970,
        p. 29.
    Shulman, Milton. Evening Standard, June 17, 1970,
        p. 21e.
    Trewin, J. C. Illustrated London News, June 27,
        1970, p. 36.
    Wardle, Irving. The Times, June 17, 1970, p. 8g.
    Young, B. A. Financial Times, June 17, 1970, p. 3b.

STOTHART, Herbert
  Rose Marie. See: Friml, Rudolf

STROUSE, Charles
  Applause. Book by Betty Comden and Adolph Green based
  on the film "All About Eve" and an original story by
  Mary Orr. Lyrics by Lee Adams with music by Charles
  Strouse.
  Her Majesty's: November 16, 1972-October 6, 1973 (382)

    Barber, John. Daily Telegraph, November 11, 1972,
        p. 14b.
    Billington, Michael. Manchester Guardian, November
        17, 1972, p. 12f.
    Cashin, Fergus. Sun, November 17, 1972, p. 5e.
    Dawson, Helen. Observer, November 19, 1972, p. 37c.
    Green, James. Evening News, November 17, 1972, p.
        2e.
    Hobson, Harold. Sunday Times, November 19, 1972,
        p. 37b.
    Hurren, Kenneth. Spectator, November 25, 1972, p.
        851.

Kingston, Jeremy. Punch, November 29, 1972, p. 810.
Kretzmer, Herbert. Daily Express, November 17, 1972,
    p. 13a.
Nightingale, Benedict. New Statesman, November 24,
    1972, p. 785.
Shulman, Milton. Evening Standard, November 17,
    1972, p. 20c.
Trewin, J. C. Illustrated London News, January
    1973, p. 62.
Wardle, Irving. The Times, November 17, 1972, p.
    11c.
Young, B. A. Financial Times, November 17, 1972,
    p. 3a.

Bye-Bye Birdie. Libretto by Michael Stewart; lyrics by
Lee Adams.
Her Majesty's: June 15, 1961-February 3, 1962 (268)

Barker, Felix. Evening News, June 16, 1961, p. 4d.
Darlington, W. A. Daily Telegraph, June 16, 1961,
    p. 16d.
Gellert, Roger. New Statesman, June 30, 1961, p.
    1060.
Hobson, Harold. Sunday Times, June 18, 1961, p. 35b.
Keown, Eric. Punch, June 21, 1961, pp. 950-951.
Levin, Bernard. Daily Express, June 16, 1961, p.
    19f.
Muller, Robert. Daily Mail, June 16, 1961, p. 3c.
Nathan, David. Daily Herald, June 16, 1961, p. 4h.
Thompson, J. W. M. Evening Standard, June 16, 1961,
    p. 19a.
The Times, June 16, 1961, p. 18g.
Trewin, J. C. Illustrated London News, July 1,
    1961, p. 30.
Tynan, Kenneth. Observer, June 18, 1961, p. 27b.
Wall, Michael. Manchester Guardian, June 17, 1961,
    p. 5d.
Worsley, T. C. Financial Times, June 16, 1961, p.
    22d.

Golden Boy. Music by Charles Strouse; lyrics by Lee
Adams; book by Clifford Odets and William Gibson. Based
on Odets' play, Golden Boy.
Palladium: June 4, 1968-September 14, 1968 (136)

Barker, Felix. Evening News, June 5, 1968, p. 3b.
Bryden, Ronald. Observer, June 9, 1968, p. 31b.
Darlington, W. A. Daily Telegraph, June 5, 1968,
    p. 17a.
French, Philip. New Statesman, June 14, 1968, p.
    811.
Hope-Wallace, Philip. Manchester Guardian, June 5,
    1968, p. 6a.
Kingston, Jeremy. Punch, June 12, 1968, p. 860.
Kretzmer, Herbert. Daily Express, June 5, 1968,
    p. 5c.

Lambert, J. W. Sunday Times, June 9, 1968, p. 53a.
Lewis, Peter. Daily Mail, June 6, 1968, p. 12b.
Nathan, David. Sun, June 5, 1968, p. 3a.
Shulman, Milton. Evening Standard, June 5, 1968,
      p. 4e.
Trewin, J. C. Illustrated London News, June 15,
      1968, p. 30.
Wardle, Irving. The Times, June 5, 1968, p. 11a.

I and Albert. Book by Jay Allen; lyrics by Lee Adams;
music by Charles Strouse.
Piccadilly: November 6, 1972-February 10, 1973 (112)

Barber, John. Daily Telegraph, November 7, 1972,
      p. 12b.
Barker, Felix. Evening News, November 7, 1972, p.
      7d.
Billington, Michael. Manchester Guardian, November
      7, 1972, p. 10a.
Dawson, Helen. Observer, November 12, 1972, p. 24g.
Hobson, Harold. Sunday Times, November 12, 1972, p.
      37f.
Hurren, Kenneth. Spectator, November 11, 1972, p.
      769.
Kingston, Jeremy. Punch, November 15, 1972, p. 729.
Kretzmer, Herbert. Daily Express, November 7, 1972,
      p. 4e.
Nightingale, Benedict. New Statesman, November 24,
      1972, p. 785.
Shulman, Milton. Evening Standard, November 7,
      1972, p. 23d.
Trewin, J. C. Illustrated London News, January
      1973, p. 62.
Wardle, Irving. The Times, November 7, 1972, p.
      12c.
Young, B. A. Financial Times, November 7, 1972,
      p. 3a.

STYNE, Jule
    Bells Are Ringing. Music by Jule Styne; book and lyrics
    by Betty Comden and Adolph Green.
    Coliseum: November 14, 1957-July 26, 1958 (292)

Barber, John. Daily Express, November 15, 1957, p.
      5a.
Barker, Felix. Evening News, November 15, 1957, p.
      4a.
Darlington, W. A. Daily Telegraph, November 15,
      1957, p. 10f.
Granger, Derek. Financial Times, November 15, 1957,
      p. 2g.
Hobson, Harold. Sunday Times, November 17, 1957, p.
      25a.
Keown, Eric. Punch, November 20, 1957, p. 610.
Shulman, Milton. Evening Standard, November 15,
      1957, p. 6a.

The Times, November 15, 1957, p. 3a.
Trewin, J. C. Illustrated London News, November 30,
     1957, p. 946.
Tynan, Kenneth. Observer, November 17, 1957, p. 15b.
Watt, David. Spectator, November 22, 1957, p. 690.
Wilson, Cecil. Daily Mail, November 15, 1957, p. 3h.
Worsley, T. C. New Statesman, November 23, 1957, p.
     692.

Do Re Mi. Music by Jule Styne; lyrics by Betty Comden
and Adolph Green; book by Garson Kanin.
Prince of Wales: October 12, 1961-February 24, 1962
(170)

     Barker, Felix. Evening News, October 13, 1961, p.
          9g.
     Darlington, W. A. Daily Telegraph, October 13, 1961,
          p. 16d.
     Gascoigne, Bamber. Spectator, October 20, 1961, p.
          541.
     Gellert, Roger. New Statesman, October 20, 1961, p.
          573.
     Hobson, Harold. Sunday Times, October 15, 1961, p.
          41d.
     Hope-Wallace, Philip. Manchester Guardian, October
          13, 1961, p. 9g.
     Keown, Eric. Punch, October 18, 1961, pp. 584-585.
     Levin, Bernard. Daily Express, October 13, 1961,
          p. 16f.
     Muller, Robert. Daily Mail, October 13, 1961, p. 3f.
     Piler, Jack. Daily Herald, October 13, 1961, p. 5b.
     Shulman, Milton. Evening Standard, October 13, 1961,
          p. 21a.
     The Times, October 13, 1961, p. 18a.
     Trewin, J. C. Illustrated London News, October 28,
          1961, p. 740.
     Tynan, Kenneth. Observer, October 15, 1961, p. 26h.
     Worsley, T. C. Financial Times, October 13, 1961,
          p. 20a.

Funny Girl. Music by Jule Styne; lyrics by Bob Merrill;
book by Isabel Lennart.
Prince of Wales: April 13, 1966-July 16, 1966   (109)

     Barker, Felix. Evening News, April 14, 1966, p. 9a.
     Darlington, W. A. Daily Telegraph, April 14, 1966,
          p. 19a.
     Fay, Gerard. Manchester Guardian, April 14, 1966,
          p. 8f.
     Gilliatt, Penelope. Observer, April 17, 1966, p.
          25c.
     Hobson, Harold. Sunday Times, April 17, 1966, p.
          31a.
     Kretzmer, Herbert. Daily Express, April 14, 1966,
          p. 6f.
     Lewis, Peter. Daily Mail, April 15, 1966, p. 18b.

Nathan, David. Sun, April 14, 1966, p. 8f.
Shulman, Milton. Evening Standard, April 14, 1966,
     p. 8e.
The Times, April 14, 1966, p. 17a.
Young, B. A. Financial Times, April 15, 1966, p.
     30c.

Gentlemen Prefer Blondes. Lyrics by Leo Robin; book by
Anita Loos.
Princess: August 20, 1962-November 3, 1962, transferred
to Strand: November 7, 1962-March 2, 1963 (220)

Barker, Felix. Evening News, August 21, 1962, p. 3a.
Fay, Gerard. Manchester Guardian, August 21, 1962,
     p. 5b.
Gellert, Roger. New Statesman, August 31, 1962, p.
     265.
Higgins, John. Financial Times, August 22, 1962,
     p. 16a.
Lambert, J. W. Sunday Times, August 26, 1962, p.
     25a.
Levin, Bernard. Daily Mail, August 21, 1962, p. 3c.
Nathan, David. Daily Herald, August 21, 1962, p.
     7b.
Shulman, Milton. Evening Standard, August 21, 1962,
     p. 4a.
The Times, August 21, 1962, p. 11c.
Trewin, J. C. Illustrated London News, September
     15, 1962, p. 414.
Tynan, Kenneth. Observer, August 26, 1962, p. 19a.
Young, B. A. Punch, August 29, 1962, p. 316.

Gypsy. Book by Arthur Laurents, based on the autobiogra-
phy by Gypsy Rose Lee. Lyrics by Stephen Sondheim; music
by Jule Styne.
Piccadilly: May 29, 1973-March 2, 1974 (300)

Barker, Felix. Evening News, May 30, 1973, p. 5a.
Billington, Michael. Manchester Guardian, May 30,
     1973, p. 12a.
Cushman, Robert. Observer, June 3, 1973, p. 34a.
Hurren, Kenneth. Spectator, June 9, 1973, p. 719.
Kingston, Jeremy. Punch, June 13, 1973, p. 888.
Kretzmer, Herbert. Daily Express, May 30, 1973,
     p. 8d.
Lambert. J. W. Sunday Times, June 3, 1973, p. 37b.
Nightingale, Benedict. New Statesman, June 15, 1973,
     p. 902.
O'Connor, Garry. Financial Times, May 30, 1973, p.
     3a.
Shulman, Milton. Evening Standard, May 30, 1973,
     p. 27d.
Tinker, Jack. Daily Mail, May 31, 1973, p. 25a.
Trewin, J. C. Illustrated London News, August 1973,
     p. 67.
Wardle, Irving. The Times, May 30, 1973, p. 11d.

SWERLING, Jo
    <u>Guys and Dolls</u>. See: Loesser, Frank

SWIFT, David
    <u>Gomes</u>. By David Swift and Sidney Shelton.
    Queen's: November 20, 1973-November 24, 1973 (5)

        Barber, John. <u>Daily Telegraph</u>, November 21, 1973,
            p. 15c.
        Barker, Felix. <u>Evening News</u>, November 21, 1973, p.
            4e.
        Hobson, Harold. <u>Sunday Times</u>, November 25, 1973,
            p. 37d.
        Kingston, Jeremy. <u>Punch</u>, November 28, 1973, p. 839.
        Kretzmer, Herbert. <u>Daily Express</u>, November 21, 1973,
            p. 12e.
        Lewsen, Charles. <u>The Times</u>, November 21, 1973, p.
            11h.
        Shulman, Milton. <u>Evening Standard</u>, November 21,
            1973, p. 24e.
        Tinker, Jack. <u>Daily Mail</u>, November 21, 1973, p. 3f.
        Trewin, J. C. <u>Illustrated London News</u>, February
            1974, p. 59.
        Young, B. A. <u>Financial Times</u>, November 21, 1973, p.
            3a.

TARLOFF, Frank
    <u>The First Fish</u>.
    Savoy: July 8, 1964-August 8, 1964 (34)

        Barker, Felix. <u>Evening News</u>, July 9, 1964, p. 4e.
        Darlington, W. A. <u>Daily Telegraph</u>, July 9, 1964,
            p. 16e.
        Gascoigne, Bamber. <u>Observer</u>, July 12, 1964, p. 24g.
        Kingston, Jeremy. <u>Punch</u>, July 15, 1964, p. 100.
        Kretzmer, Herbert. <u>Daily Express</u>, July 9, 1964, p.
            4b.
        Lambert, J. W. <u>Sunday Times</u>, July 12, 1964, p. 25a.
        Nightingale, Benedict. <u>Manchester Guardian</u>, July 9,
            1964, p. 7d.
        Norman, Barry. <u>Daily Mail</u>, July 9, 1964, p. 10e.
        Shulman, Milton. <u>Evening Standard</u>, July 9, 1964,
            p. 4a.
        <u>The Times</u>, July 9, 1964, p. 7d.

TAYLOR, Christopher
    <u>Wings of the Dove</u>. Based on the novel by Henry James.
    Lyric: December 3, 1963-April 4, 1964, transferred to
    Haymarket: April 6, 1964-September 12, 1964 (324)

        Cashin, Fergus. <u>Daily Sketch</u>, December 5, 1963, p.
            4f.
        Darlington, W. A. <u>Daily Telegraph</u>, December 4,
            1963, p. 18e.
         Gascoigne, Bamber. <u>Observer</u>, December 8, 1963, p.
            28e.

Gellert, Roger. New Statesman, December 13, 1963,
    p. 889.
Hobson, Harold. Sunday Times, December 8, 1963, p.
    35a.
Hope-Wallace, Philip. Manchester Guardian, December
    4, 1963, p. 9c.
Kretzmer, Herbert. Daily Express, December 4, 1963,
    p. 4d.
Levin, Bernard. Daily Mail, December 5, 1963, p.
    22a.
Nathan, David. Daily Herald, December 4, 1963, p.
    3c.
Pryce-Jones, David. Spectator, December 13, 1963,
    p. 792.
Shulman, Milton. Evening Standard, December 4, 1963,
    p. 4a.
The Times, December 4, 1963, p. 15a.
Trewin, J. C. Illustrated London News, December 21,
    1963, p. 1044.
Worsley, T. C. Financial Times, December 5, 1963,
    p. 22a.
Young, B. A. Punch, December 11, 1963, pp. 863-864.

TAYLOR, Samuel
    The Happy Time.
    St. James: January 30, 1952-March 1, 1952 (34)

    Barber, John. Daily Express, January 31, 1952, p.
        3d.
    Conway, Harold. Evening Standard, January 31, 1952,
        p. 5c.
    Darlington, W. A. Daily Telegraph, January 31,
        1952, p. 6f.
    Hayes, Walter. Daily Sketch, January 31, 1952, p.
        5c.
    Hobson, Harold. Sunday Times, February 3, 1952, p.
        2e.
    Hope-Wallace, Philip. Manchester Guardian, February
        1, 1952, p. 5c.
    Keown, Eric. Punch, February 20, 1952, p. 268.
    Mannock, P. L. Daily Herald, January 31, 1952, p.
        3e.
    Raymond, John. New Statesman, February 9, 1952, p.
        153.
    The Times, January 31, 1952, p. 6e.
    Trewin, J. C. Observer, February 3, 1952, p. 6b.
    Tynan, Kenneth. Spectator, February 8, 1952, p.
        173.
    Williams, Stephen. Evening News, January 31, 1952,
        p. 2f.
    Wilson, Cecil. Daily Mail, January 31, 1952, p. 4c.

No Strings. See: Rodgers, Richard

Pleasure of His Company.
Haymarket: April 23, 1959-April 9, 1960 (403)

Barker, Felix. Evening News, April 24, 1959, p. 13g.
Brien, Alan. Spectator, May 1, 1959, p. 615.
Carthew, Anthony. Daily Herald, April 24, 1959, p.
    3f.
Clurman, Harold. Observer, April 26, 1959, p. 21d.
Gibbs, Patrick. Daily Telegraph, April 24, 1959,
    p. 14d.
Hobson, Harold. Sunday Times, January 26, 1959, p.
    25c.
Hope-Wallace, Philip. Manchester Guardian, April
    25, 1959, p. 5f.
Keown, Eric. Punch, May 6, 1959, pp. 625-626.
Shulman, Milton. Evening Standard, April 24, 1959,
    p. 13e.
Thompson, John. Daily Express, April 24, 1959, p.
    7h.
The Times, April 24, 1959, p. 6a.
Trewin, J. C. Illustrated London News, May 9, 1959,
    p. 810.
Wilson, Cecil. Daily Mail, April 24, 1959, p. 3c.
Worsley, T. C. Financial Times, April 24, 1959, p.
    17g.

Sabrina Fair.
Palace: August 4, 1958-December 11, 1958   (149)

Boothroyd, J. B. Punch, August 18, 1958, p. 241.
Brown, Ivor. Observer, August 8, 1958, p. 6a.
Darlington, W. A. Daily Telegraph, August 5, 1958,
    p. 8f.
Granger, Derek. Financial Times, August 5, 1958,
    p. 5d.
Hartley, Anthony. Spectator, August 13, 1958, p.
    193.
Hobson, Harold. Sunday Times, August 8, 1958, p.
    9a.
Hope-Wallace, Philip. Manchester Guardian, August
    6, 1958, p. 3c.
Lewin, David. Daily Express, August 5, 1958, p. 3c.
R., J. N. B. New Statesman, August 21, 1958, p.
    209.
Shulman, Milton. Evening Standard, August 5, 1958,
    p. 3b.
The Times, August 5, 1958, p. 8e.
Trewin, J. C. Illustrated London News, August 21,
    1958, p. 308.
Williams, Stephen. Evening News, August 5, 1958,
    p. 5g.
Wilson, Cecil. Daily Mail, August 5, 1958, p. 6a.

A Touch of Spring.
Comedy: May 13, 1975-January 3, 1976   (300)

Barber, John. Daily Telegraph, May 15, 1975, p. 6d.
Frame, Colin. Evening News, May 14, 1975, p. 4c.
Hurren, Kenneth. Spectator, May 24, 1975, p. 642.

Kretzmer, Herbert. <u>Daily Express</u>, May 14, 1975, p.
     10d.
Morley, Sheridan. <u>Punch</u>, May 21, 1975, p. 904.
Nightingale, Benedict. <u>New Statesman</u>, May 23, 1975,
     p. 702.
Shulman, Milton. <u>Evening Standard</u>, May 14, 1975,
     p. 11a.
Spurling, Hilary. <u>Observer</u>, May 18, 1975, p. 29b.
Thirkell, Arthur. <u>Daily Mirror</u>, May 14, 1975, p.
     16b.
Tinker, Jack. <u>Daily Mail</u>, May 14, 1975, p. 30e.
Trewin, J. C. <u>Illustrated London News</u>, July 1975,
     p. 66.
Wardle, Irving. <u>The Times</u>, May 14, 1975, p. 9d.
Young, B. A. <u>Financial Times</u>, May 14, 1975, p. 3a.

TEBELAK, John-Michael
  <u>Godspell</u>. See: Schwartz, Stephen

TEICHMANN, Howard
  <u>The Solid Gold Cadillac</u>. By Howard Teichmann and George
  S. Kaufman.
  Saville: May 4, 1965-September 4, 1965 (142)

     Barker, Felix. <u>Evening News</u>, May 5, 1965, p. 7f.
     Burgess, Anthony. <u>Spectator</u>, May 14, 1965, p. 633.
     Cashin, Fergus. <u>Daily Sketch</u>, May 5, 1964, p. 3a.
     Gilliatt, Penelope. <u>Observer</u>, May 9, 1965, p. 25g.
     Hope-Wallace, Philip. <u>Manchester Guardian</u>, May 5,
          1965, p. 9a.
     Kingston, Jeremy. <u>Punch</u>, May 12, 1965, pp. 711-712.
     Kretzmer, Herbert. <u>Daily Express</u>, May 5, 1965, p.
          4a.
     Levin, Bernard. <u>Daily Mail</u>, May 6, 1965, p. 16b.
     Shulman, Milton. <u>Evening Standard</u>, May 5, 1965, p.
          4a.
     <u>The Times</u>, May 5, 1965, p. 15a.
     Trewin, J. C. <u>Illustrated London News</u>, May 15, 1965,
          p. 30c.
     Young, B. A. <u>Financial Times</u>, May 5, 1965, p. 30c.

THOMAS, Brandon
  <u>Charley's Aunt</u>. See: Loesser, Frank

THOMPSON, Fred
  <u>Lady Be Good</u>. See: Gershwin, George

THOMPSON, Jay
  <u>Once Upon a Mattress</u>. See: Rodgers, Mary

THRONSON, Ron
  <u>Mother Earth</u>. See: Shearer, Toni

THURBER, James
  <u>The Thirteen Clocks</u>. See: Loewe, Frank

A Thurber Carnival. Music by Don Elliott.
Savoy: April 11, 1962-April 28, 1962   (18)

    Barker, Felix. Evening News, April 12, 1962, p. 11h.
    Daily Sketch, April 13, 1962, p. 6a.
    Darlington, W. A. Daily Telegraph, April 12, 1962,
       p. 16d.
    Gellert, Roger. New Statesman, April 20, 1962, p.
       573.
    Hobson, Harold. Sunday Times, April 15, 1962, p.
       41c.
    Keown, Eric. Punch, April 18, 1962, p. 622.
    Levin, Bernard. Daily Express, April 12, 1962, p.
       4e.
    Muller, Robert. Daily Mail, April 13, 1962, p. 3f.
    Nathan, David. Daily Herald, April 12, 1962, p. 5c.
    Shulman, Milton. Evening Standard, April 12, 1962,
       p. 21a.
    The Times, April 12, 1962, p. 17f.
    Trewin, J. C. Illustrated London News, April 28,
       1962, p. 678.
    Tynan, Kenneth. Observer, April 15, 1962, p. 27g.
    Weatherby, W. J. Manchester Guardian, April 12,
       1962, p. 9c.
    Worsley, T. C. Financial Times, April 13, 1962,
       p. 22a.

TRAVER, Ben
    Man With a Load of Mischief. See: Clifton, John

TRUMBO, Dalton
    The Biggest Thief in Town.
New Boltons: July 17, 1951 (opened)
Duchess: August 14, 1951, transferred to Fortune:
December 17, 1951-January 19, 1952   (173)

    Conway, Harold. Evening Standard, August 15, 1951,
       p. 5b.
    Hayes, Walter. Daily Sketch, August 15, 1951, p.
       3c.
    Hobson, Harold. Sunday Times, July 22, 1951, p. 2f.
    Keown, Eric. Punch, August 8, 1951, p. 160.
    Mannock, P. L. Daily Herald, August 15, 1951, p.
       3e.
    R., J. N. B. New Statesman, July 28, 1951, p. 98.
    The Times, July 18, 1951, p. 8e.
    Trewin, J. C. Illustrated London News, August 4,
       1951, p. 186.
    Trewin, J. C. Observer, July 22, 1951, p. 6a.
    Tynan, Kenneth. Spectator, August 24, 1951, p. 239.
    Williams, Stephen. Evening News, August 15, 1951,
       p. 2h.
    Wilson, Cecil. Daily Mail, August 15, 1951, p. 4f.

TRZCINSKI, Edmund
    Stalag 17. See: Bevan, Donald J.

VAN DRUTEN, John
    Cabaret. See: Kander, John

VAN ITALLIE, Jean-Claude
    America Hurrah.
    Royal Court: August 2, 1967-October 14, 1967 (74)

        Barker, Felix. Evening News, August 3, 1967, p. 9a.
        Bryden, Ronald. Observer, August 6, 1967, p. 18c.
        Darlington, W. A. Daily Telegraph, August 3, 1967,
            p. 17a.
        Hobson, Harold. Sunday Times, August 6, 1967, p.
            21a.
        Hope-Wallace, Philip. Manchester Guardian, August
            3, 1967, p. 5e.
        Kingston, Jeremy. Punch, August 9, 1967, p. 215.
        Kretzmer, Herbert. Daily Express, August 3, 1967,
            p. 4g.
        Lewis, Peter. Daily Mail, August 4, 1967, p. 10b.
        Mortimer, John. New Statesman, August 11, 1967, p.
            181.
        Nathan, David. Sun, August 3, 1967, p. 6d.
        Shulman, Milton. Evening Standard, August 3, 1967,
            p. 5a.
        Spurling, Hilary. Spectator, August 11, 1967, p.
            168.
        Trewin, J. C. Illustrated London News, August 12,
            1967, p. 28.
        Wardle, Irving. The Times, August 3, 1967, p. 6d.
        Young, B. A. Financial Times, August 4, 1967, p.
            20c.

VEILLER, Bayard
    Trial of Mary Dugan (Revival).
    Savoy: July 2, 1958-September 6, 1958 (76)

        Barber, John. Daily Express, July 3, 1958, p. 7a.
        Boorne, Bill. Evening News, July 3, 1958, p. 7g.
        Brien, Alan. Spectator, July 18, 1958, p. 85.
        Darlington, W. A. Daily Telegraph, July 3, 1958,
            p. 10f.
        Hobson, Harold. Sunday Times, July 6, 1958, p. 9b.
        Keown, Eric. Punch, July 9, 1958, p. 57.
        Shulman, Milton. Evening Standard, July 3, 1958,
            p. 10f.
        The Times, July 3, 1958, p. 5a.
        Trewin, J. C. Illustrated London News, July 19,
            1958, p. 122.
        Tynan, Kenneth. Observer, July 6, 1958, p. 15d.
        Wilson, Cecil. Daily Mail, July 3, 1958, p. 3h.
        Worsley, T. C. Financial Times, July 3, 1958, p.
            15f.
        Worsley, T. C. New Statesman, July 12, 1958, p.
            46.

VIDAL, Gore
   <u>Visit to a Small Planet</u>.
   Westminster: February 25, 1960-March 5, 1960   (12)

       Alvarez, A. <u>New Statesman</u>, March 5, 1960, p. 329.
       Barnes, Clive. <u>Daily Express</u>, February 26, 1960,
          p. 4f.
       Darlington, W. A. <u>Daily Telegraph</u>, February 26,
          1960, p. 15c.
       Findlater, Richard. <u>Financial Times</u>, February 26,
          1960, p. 19f.
       Hobson, Harold. <u>Sunday Times</u>, February 28, 1960,
          p. 26b.
       Keown, Eric. <u>Punch</u>, March 9, 1960, p. 368.
       Nathan, David. <u>Daily Herald</u>, February 26, 1960, p.
          3d.
       Pryce-Jones, Alan. <u>Observer</u>, February 28, 1960, p.
          23a.
       Shulman, Milton. <u>Evening Standard</u>, February 26,
          1960, p. 14e.
       <u>The Times</u>, February 26, 1960, p. 15b.
       Trewin, J. C. <u>Illustrated London News</u>, March 12,
          1960, p. 446.
       Wainwright, David. <u>Evening News</u>, February 26, 1960,
          p. 7c.
       Wilson, Cecil. <u>Daily Mail</u>, February 26, 1960, p.
          7a.

WALLACH, Ira
   <u>Out of the Question</u>. (American title: <u>Absence of a</u>
   <u>Cello</u>.)
   St. Martin's: October 15, 1968-July 19, 1969   (316)

       Barker, Felix. <u>Evening News</u>, October 16, 1968, p.
          11e.
       Bryden, Ronald. <u>Observer</u>, October 20, 1968, p. 26f.
       Christie, Ian. <u>Daily Express</u>, October 16, 1968, p.
          20e.
       Hobson, Harold. <u>Sunday Times</u>, October 20, 1968, p.
          57b.
       Kingston, Jeremy. <u>Punch</u>, October 23, 1968, p. 593.
       Nathan, David. <u>Sun</u>, October 16, 1968, p. 7d.
       Nightingale, Benedict. <u>New Statesman</u>, October 25,
          1968, p. 556.
       Norman, Barry. <u>Daily Mail</u>, October 17, 1968, p.
          14b.
       Pritchett, Oliver. <u>Manchester Guardian</u>, October 16,
          1968, p. 8f.
       Shulman, Milton. <u>Evening Standard</u>, October 17,
          1968, p. 19a.
       Spurling, Hilary. <u>Spectator</u>, October 25, 1968, p.
          598.
       Trewin, J. C. <u>Illustrated London News</u>, October 26,
          1968, p. 32.
       Wardle, Irving. <u>The Times</u>, October 16, 1968, p.
          16c.

WALLOP, Douglas
    Damn Yankees. See: Adler, Richard

WARD, Larry and GORDON, Russell
    Masterpiece.
    Royalty: January 26, 1961-February 25, 1961 (35)

        Barker, Felix. Evening News, January 27, 1961, p.
            3b.
        Craig, H. A. L. New Statesman, February 3, 1961,
            pp. 190-191.
        Darlington, W. A. Daily Telegraph, January 27, 1961,
            p. 16d.
        Gascoigne, Bamber. Spectator, February 3, 1961, p.
            148.
        Hobson, Harold. Sunday Times, January 29, 1961, p.
            31b.
        Hope-Wallace, Philip. Manchester Guardian, January
            28, 1961, p. 5e.
        Keown, Eric. Punch, February 1, 1961, p. 222.
        Levin, Bernard. Daily Express, January 27, 1961,
            p. 8g.
        Muller, Robert. Daily Mail, January 27, 1961, p. 5c.
        Nathan, David. Daily Herald, January 27, 1961, p.
            3a.
        Shulman, Milton. Evening Standard, January 27, 1961,
            p. 14e.
        The Times, January 27, 1961, p. 16a.
        Trewin, J. C. Illustrated London News, February 11,
            1961, p. 242.
        Wardle, Irving. Observer, January 29, 1961, p. 30b.
        Worsley, T. C. Financial Times, January 27, 1961,
            p. 19d.

WEIDMAN, Jerome
    Fiorello! See: Bock, Jerry

WEINSTOCK, Jack
    How to Succeed in Business Without Really Trying. See:
    Loesser, Frank

WELLER, Michael
    Cancer.
    Royal Court: September 14, 1970-October 17, 1970 (36)

        Barber, John. Daily Telegraph, September 16, 1970,
            p. 12e.
        Chamberlain, Michael. New Statesman, September 18,
            1970, p. 345.
        Christie, Ian. Daily Express, September 15, 1970,
            p. 12e.
        Dawson, Helen. Observer, September 20, 1970, p. 25a.
        Hope-Wallace, Philip. Manchester Guardian, September
            15, 1970, p. 8a.
        Hurren, Kenneth. Spectator, September 26, 1970, p.
            342.

Kingston, Jeremy. Punch, September 23, 1970, pp.
    444-445.
Lambert, J. W. Sunday Times, September 20, 1970, p.
    29d.
Shulman, Milton. Evening Standard, September 15,
    1970, p. 17e.
Wardle, Irving. The Times, September 15, 1970, p.
    13a.
Young, B. A. Financial Times, September 15, 1970,
    p. 3a.

WELLES, Orson
    Moby Dick. Based on Herman Melville's novel, Moby Dick.
    Duke of York's: June 16, 1955-July 9, 1955 (25)
    Limited engagement of 3 weeks.

    Barber, John. Daily Express, June 17, 1955, p. 3c.
    Darlington, W. A. Daily Telegraph, June 17, 1955,
        p. 11f.
    Fay, Gerard. Manchester Guardian, June 18, 1955,
        p. 5f.
    Forster, Peter. Financial Times, June 17, 1955, p.
        7d.
    Hobson, Harold. Sunday Times, June 19, 1955, p. 9a.
    Holt, Paul. Daily Herald, June 17, 1955, p. 3a.
    Inglis, Brian. Spectator, June 24, 1955, p. 800.
    Keown, Eric. Punch, June 25, 1955, p. 775.
    Shulman, Milton. Evening Standard, June 17, 1955,
        p. 6a.
    The Times, June 17, 1955, p. 12a.
    Trewin, J. C. Illustrated London News, July 2,
        1955, p. 34.
    Tynan, Kenneth. Observer, June 19, 1955, p. 11a.
    Williams, Stephen. Evening News, June 17, 1955, p.
        5c.
    Wilson, Cecil. Daily Mail, June 17, 1955, p. 5e.
    Worsley, T. C. New Statesman, June 25, 1955, pp.
        886, 888.

WHEELER, Hugh
    Big Fish, Little Fish.
    Duke of York's: September 18, 1962-September 29, 1962
    (14)

    Barker, Felix. Evening News, September 19, 1962,
        p. 5b.
    Gascoigne, Bamber. Spectator, September 28, 1962,
        p. 438.
    Hobson, Harold. Sunday Times, September 23, 1962,
        p. 39c.
    Hope-Wallace, Philip. Manchester Guardian, September
        19, 1962, p. 11f.
    Kretzmer, Herbert. Daily Express, September 19,
        1962, p. 4e.
    Levin, Bernard. Daily Mail, September 19, 1962, p.
        3e.

Nathan, David. Daily Herald, September 19, 1962, p.
    7g.
Shulman, Milton. Evening Standard, September 19,
    1962, p. 4d.
The Times, September 19, 1962, p. 16a.
Trewin, J. C. Illustrated London News, September
    29, 1962, p. 494.
Tynan, Kenneth. Observer, September 23, 1962, p.
    27a.
Worsley, T. C. Financial Times, September 20, 1962,
    p. 24d.
Young, B. A. Punch, September 26, 1962, p. 464.

A Little Night Music. See: Sondheim, Stephen

WILBUR, Richard
    Candide. See: Bernstein, Leonard

WILDER, Thornton
    The Ides of March. See: Kilty, Jerome

    The Matchmaker.
    Haymarket: November 4, 1954-July 2, 1955 (275)

        Darlington, W. A. Daily Telegraph, November 5,
            1954, p. 8e.
        Granger, Derek. Financial Times, November 5, 1954,
            p. 5e.
        Hartley, Anthony. Spectator, November 12, 1954, p.
            573.
        Hewins, Ralph. Daily Express, November 5, 1954, p.
            3h.
        Hobson, Harold. Sunday Times, November 7, 1954, p.
            11b.
        Keown, Eric. Punch, November 12, 1954, p. 610.
        Manchester Guardian, November 6, 1954, p. 4e.
        Shulman, Milton. Evening Standard, November 5,
            1954, p. 10f.
        The Times, November 5, 1954, p. 7f.
        Trewin, J. C. Illustrated London News, November 20,
            1954, p. 901.
        Tynan, Kenneth. Observer, November 7, 1954, p. 11b.
        Wilson, Cecil. Daily Mail, November 5, 1954, p. 4e.
        Worsley, T. C. New Statesman, November 13, 1954,
            p. 612.

WILLIAMS, Lawrence
    Bride of Denmark Hill. By Lawrence Williams and Nell
    O'Day.
    Royal Court: July 2, 1952, transferred to Comedy:
    August 11, 1952-August 23, 1952 (16)

        Barber, John. Daily Express, July 3, 1952, p. 3e.
        Brown, Ivor. Observer, July 6, 1952, p. 6a.
        Conway, Harold. Evening Standard, July 3, 1952, p.
            5c.

D., H. B. Daily Sketch, August 12, 1952, p. 3a.
Darlington, W. A. Daily Telegraph, July 3, 1952,
    p. 6c.
Fay, Gerard. Manchester Guardian, July 4, 1952, p.
    5e.
Fay, Gerard. Spectator, July 11, 1952, p. 65.
Keown, Eric. Punch, July 16, 1952, p. 127.
Mannock, P. L. Daily Herald, July 3, 1952, p. 3c.
R., J. N. B. New Statesman, July 12, 1952, p. 41.
The Times, July 3, 1952, p. 9c.
Trewin, J. C. Illustrated London News, July 19,
    1952, p. 108.
Williams, Stephen. Evening News, July 3, 1952, p.
    2e.
Wiltshire, Maurice. Daily Mail, July 3, 1952, p.
    4f.

WILLIAMS, Tennessee
    Camino Real.
    Phoenix: April 8, 1957-June 1, 1957   (64)

    Barber, John. Daily Express, April 9, 1957, p. 7f.
    Darlington, W. A. Daily Telegraph, April 9, 1957,
        p. 10d.
    Fay, Gerard. Manchester Guardian, April 10, 1957,
        p. 7a.
    Granger, Derek. Financial Times, April 9, 1957, p.
        11a.
    Hobson, Harold. Sunday Times, April 14, 1957, p.
        19e.
    Keown, Eric. Punch, April 17, 1957, p. 518.
    Shulman, Milton. Evening Standard, April 9, 1957,
        p. 6d.
    The Times, April 9, 1957, p. 3d.
    Trewin, J. C. Illustrated London News, April 27,
        1957, p. 702.
    Tynan, Kenneth. Observer, April 14, 1957, p. 13e.
    Watt, David. Spectator, April 12, 1957, p. 488.
    Williams, Stephen. Evening News, April 9, 1957, p.
        5e.
    Wilson, Cecil. Daily Mail, April 9, 1957, p. 3c.
    Worsley, T. C. New Statesman, April 13, 1957, pp.
        473-474.

    Cat on a Hot Tin Roof.
    Comedy: January 30, 1958-May 25, 1958   (132)

    Barber, John. Daily Express, January 31, 1958, p.
        7h.
    Barker, Felix. Evening News, January 31, 1958, p.
        3c.
    Darlington, W. A. Daily Telegraph, January 31,
        1958, p. 10c.
    Granger, Derek. Financial Times, January 31, 1958,
        p. 11f.
    Hobson, Harold. Sunday Times, February 2, 1958, p.
        21a.

Hope-Wallace, Philip. <u>Manchester Guardian</u>, February
     1, 1958, p. 2f.
Inglis, Brian. <u>Spectator</u>, February 7, 1958, p. 174.
Keown, Eric. <u>Punch</u>, February 5, 1958, p. 218.
Shulman, Milton. <u>Evening Standard</u>, January 31, 1958,
     p. 6a.
<u>The Times</u>, January 31, 1958, p. 3c.
Trewin, J. C. <u>Illustrated London News</u>, February 15,
     1958, p. 276.
Tynan, Kenneth. <u>Observer</u>, February 2, 1958, p. 13d.
Weaver, Harry. <u>Daily Herald</u>, January 31, 1958, p.
     2e.
Wilson, Cecil. <u>Daily Mail</u>, January 31, 1958, p. 3f.
Worsley, T. C. <u>New Statesman</u>, February 8, 1958, p.
     166.

<u>Garden District</u>.
Arts: September 16, 1958-October 28, 1958 (49)

Barber, John. <u>Daily Express</u>, September 17, 1958,
     p. 8h.
Barker, Felix. <u>Evening News</u>, September 18, 1958,
     p. 5c.
Brien, Alan. <u>Spectator</u>, September 26, 1958, pp.
     401-402.
Crisp, Clement. <u>Financial Times</u>, September 17,
     1958, p. 13e.
Darlington, W. A. <u>Daily Telegraph</u>, September 17,
     1958, p. 10f.
Hobson, Harold. <u>Sunday Times</u>, September 21, 1958,
     p. 11a.
Hope-Wallace, Philip. <u>Manchester Guardian</u>, September
     18, 1958, p. 5e.
Keown, Eric. <u>Punch</u>, September 24, 1958, p. 416.
Nevard, Mike. <u>Daily Herald</u>, September 17, 1958,
     p. 3e.
Robinson, Robert. <u>New Statesman</u>, September 27,
     1958, p. 407.
Shulman, Milton. <u>Evening Standard</u>, September 17,
     1958, p. 14d.
<u>The Times</u>, September 17, 1958, p. 6a.
Trewin, J. C. <u>Illustrated London News</u>, September
     27, 1958, p. 534.
Tynan, Kenneth. <u>Observer</u>, September 21, 1958, p.
     17a.
Wilson, Cecil. <u>Daily Mail</u>, September 17, 1958, p.
     5f.

<u>The Glass Menagerie</u> (Revival).
Haymarket: December 1, 1965-January 8, 1966 (43)

Barker, Felix. <u>Evening News</u>, December 2, 1965, p.
     7b.
Benedictus, David. <u>Observer</u>, December 5, 1965, p.
     24d.
Bryden, Ronald. <u>New Statesman</u>, December 10, 1965,
     p. 445.

Darlington, W. A. Daily Telegraph, December 2, 1965,
     p. 18d.
Hobson, Harold. Sunday Times, December 5, 1965, p.
     45e.
Hope-Wallace, Philip. Manchester Guardian, December
     3, 1965, p. 11e.
Kingston, Jeremy. Punch, December 8, 1965, p. 855.
Kretzmer, Herbert. Daily Express, December 2, 1965,
     p. 6b.
Nathan, David. Sun, December 2, 1965, p. 5d.
Shulman, Milton. Evening Standard, December 2, 1965,
     p. 4f.
Spurling, Hilary. Spectator, December 10, 1965, p.
     778.
The Times, December 2, 1965, p. 15c.
Trewin, J. C. Illustrated London News, December 11,
     1965, p. 41.
Young, B. A. Financial Times, December 3, 1965, p.
     28c.

The Night of the Iguana.
Ashcroft, Croydon: February 17, 1965
Savoy: March 24, 1965-May 29, 1965 (76)

Barker, Felix. Evening News, February 18, 1965, p.
     8e.
Darlington, W. A. Daily Telegraph, February 18,
     1965, p. 18e.
Driver, Christopher. Manchester Guardian, February
     18, 1965, p. 9a.
Hobson, Harold. Sunday Times, February 21, 1965,
     p. 45b.
Kingston, Jeremy. Punch, February 24, 1965, p. 289.
The Times, February 18, 1965, p. 16d.
Walsh, Michael. Daily Express, February 18, 1965,
     p. 4c.

Savoy:
Barker, Felix. Evening News, March 25, 1965, p. 11c.
Bryden, Ronald. New Statesman, April 2, 1965, p.
     546.
Darlington, W. A. Daily Telegraph, March 25, 1965,
     p. 18d.
Gilliatt, Penelope. Observer, March 28, 1965, p.
     25d.
Hope-Wallace, Philip. Manchester Guardian, March
     25, 1965, p. 9c.
Lambert, J. W. Sunday Times, March 28, 1965, p.
     27c.
Nathan, David. Sun, March 25, 1965, p. 8c.
Shulman, Milton. Evening Standard, March 25, 1965,
     p. 4d.
The Times, March 25, 1965, p. 16b.
Young, B. A. Financial Times, March 26, 1965, p.
     30a.

Orpheus Descending.
Royal Court: May 14, 1959-June 27, 1959 (52)

   Alvarez, A. New Statesman, May 23, 1959, pp. 771-
      772.
   Atkinson, Alex. Punch, May 27, 1959, p. 727.
   Barker, Felix. Evening News, May 14, 1959, p. 9a.
   Brien, Alan. Spectator, May 22, 1959, pp. 725-726.
   Clurman, Harold. Observer, May 17, 1959, p. 19a.
   Gibbs, Patrick. Daily Telegraph, May 15, 1959, p.
      14f.
   Goring, Edward. Daily Mail, May 15, 1959, p. 16g.
   Hope-Wallace, Philip. Manchester Guardian, May 16,
      1959, p. 5e.
   Lambert, J. W. Sunday Times, May 17, 1959, p. 21a.
   Nathan, David. Daily Herald, May 15, 1959, p. 3d.
   Shulman, Milton. Evening Standard, May 15, 1959,
      p. 8a.
   Thompson, John. Daily Express, May 15, 1959, p. 7h.
   The Times, May 15, 1959, p. 6a.
   Trewin, J. C. Illustrated London News, May 30, 1959,
      p. 942.
   Worsley, T. C. Financial Times, May 15, 1959, p.
      19g.

Period of Adjustment.
Royal Court: June 13, 1962-July 7, 1962, transferred
to Wyndham's: July 10, 1962-November 3, 1962 (164)

   Barker, Felix. Evening News, June 14, 1962, p. 4a.
   Darlington, W. A. Daily Telegraph, June 14, 1962,
      p. 16e.
   Foreman, Carl. New Statesman, June 22, 1962, p.
      917.
   Gascoigne, Bamber. Spectator, June 22, 1962, pp.
      823, 826.
   Hope-Wallace, Philip. Manchester Guardian, June
      14, 1962, p. 7c.
   Keown, Eric. Punch, June 30, 1962, p. 951.
   Kretzmer, Herbert. Daily Express, June 14, 1962,
      p. 4e.
   Lambert, J. W. Sunday Times, June 17, 1962, p. 37a.
   Muller, Robert. Daily Mail, June 14, 1962, p. 3f.
   Nathan, David. Daily Herald, June 14, 1962, p. 7a.
   Shulman, Milton. Evening Standard, June 14, 1962,
      p. 17a.
   The Times, June 14, 1962, p. 6b.
   Trewin, J. C. Illustrated London News, June 30,
      1962, p. 1058.
   Tynan, Kenneth. Observer, June 17, 1962, p. 28g.

The Rose Tattoo.
New: January 15, 1959-April 4, 1959 (92)

   Alvarez, A. Observer, January 18, 1959, p. 19d.
   Barker, Felix. Evening News, January 16, 1959, p.
      9c.

Brien, Alan. Spectator, January 23, 1959, pp. 103-
    104.
Carthew, Anthony. Daily Herald, January 16, 1959,
    p. 3a.
Darlington, W. A. Daily Telegraph, January 16, 1959,
    p. 12c.
Hobson, Harold. Sunday Times, January 18, 1959, p.
    17c.
Hope-Wallace, Philip. Manchester Guardian, January
    16, 1959, p. 7e.
Keown, Eric. Punch, January 21, 1959, p. 138.
Shulman, Milton. Evening Standard, January 16, 1959,
    p. 8d.
Thompson, John. Daily Express, January 16, 1959, p.
    7d.
The Times, January 16, 1959, p. 3c.
Trewin, J. C. Illustrated London News, January 31,
    1959, p. 150.
Wilson, Cecil. Daily Mail, January 16, 1959, p. 3h.
Worsley, T. C. Financial Times, January 16, 1959,
    p. 15g.
Worsley, T. C. New Statesman, January 24, 1959, p.
    104.

Small Craft Warnings.
Hampstead Theatre Club: January 29, 1973-February 26,
1973 (26); revived at Comedy: March 13, 1973-May 5,
1973 (60)

Barker, Felix. Evening News, January 30, 1973, p.
    2d.
Billington, Michael. Manchester Guardian, March 14,
    1973, p. 10f.
Brustein, Robert. Observer, February 4, 1973, p.
    35a.
Hobson, Harold. Sunday Times, February 4, 1973, p.
    36b.
Hurren, Kenneth. Spectator, February 3, 1973, p.
    142.
Jongh, Nicholas De. Manchester Guardian, January
    30, 1973, p. 10e.
Kingston, Jeremy. Punch, February 7, 1973, p. 184.
Kretzmer, Herbert. Daily Express, January 30, 1973,
    p. 8d.
Nightingale, Benedict. New Statesman, February 9,
    1973, p. 208.
Tinker, Jack. Daily Mail, March 14, 1973, p. 33e.
Trewin, J. C. Illustrated London News, April 1973,
    p. 99.
Wardle, Irving. The Times, January 30, 1973, p. 9c.
Young, B. A. Financial Times, January 30, 1973, p.
    3a.

A Streetcar Named Desire (Revival).
Piccadilly: March 14, 1974-October 12, 1974 (243)

Barber, John. Daily Telegraph, March 15, 1974, p.
     13a.
Billington, Michael. Manchester Guardian, March 15,
     1974, p. 12e.
Christie, Ian. Daily Express, March 15, 1974, p.
     12d.
Cushman, Robert. Observer, March 17, 1974, p. 35c.
Frame, Colin. Evening News, March 15, 1974, p. 11a.
Hobson, Harold. Sunday Times, March 17, 1974, p.
     37a.
Hurren, Kenneth. Spectator, March 23, 1974, pp.
     368-369.
Kingston, Jeremy. Punch, March 27, 1974, p. 519.
Nightingale, Benedict. New Statesman, March 22,
     1974, p. 421.
Shulman, Milton. Evening Standard, March 15, 1974,
     p. 23c.
Thirkell, Arthur. Daily Mirror, March 15, 1974, p.
     18b.
Tinker, Jack. Daily Mail, March 15, 1974, p. 20a.
Trewin, J. C. Illustrated London News, May 1974,
     p. 75.
Wardle, Irving. The Times, March 15, 1974, p. 15d.
Young, B. A. Financial Times, March 15, 1974, p.
     3c.

Summer and Smoke.
Lyric, Hammersmith: November 22, 1951-December 22,
1951, transferred to Duchess: January 24, 1952-March
1, 1952 (43)

Barber, John. Daily Express, November 23, 1951, p.
     3e.
Brown, Ivor. Observer, November 25, 1951, p. 6b.
Conway, Harold. Evening Standard, November 23,
     1951, p. 5d.
Darlington, W. A. Daily Telegraph, November 23,
     1951, p. 7f.
Hayes, Walter. Daily Sketch, November 23, 1951, p.
     3c.
Hobson, Harold. Sunday Times, November 25, 1951,
     p. 2e.
Keown, Eric. Punch, December 5, 1951, p. 650.
Mannock, P. L. Daily Herald, November 23, 1951, p.
     3g.
The Times, November 23, 1951, p. 2f.
Trewin, J. C. Illustrated London News, December 8,
     1951, p. 952.
Tynan, Kenneth. Spectator, December 7, 1951, p. 772.
Williams, Stephen. Evening News, November 23, 1951,
     p. 2g.
Wilson, Cecil. Daily Mail, November 23, 1951, p.
     6a.
Worsley, T. C. New Statesman, December 8, 1951, p.
     664.

Duchess:
    Darlington, W. A. Daily Telegraph, January 25, 1952,
       p. 7b.
    Evening Standard, January 25, 1952, p. 9f.
    Keown, Eric. Punch, February 6, 1952, p. 211.
    Mannock, P. L. Daily Herald, January 25, 1952, p.
       3e.
    The Times, January 25, 1952, p. 7a.
    Williams, Stephen. Evening News, January 25, 1952,
       p. 4e.

This Property is Condemned. See: Albee, Edward, Zoo
Story (Arts: August 25, 1960)

Two-Character Play.
Hampstead Theatre Club: November 27, 1967-December 12,
1967 (24)

    French, Philip. New Statesman, December 26, 1967,
       pp. 886-887.
    Hobson, Harold. Sunday Times, December 17, 1967,
       p. 23d.
    Trewin, J. C. Illustrated London News, December 23,
       1967, p. 30.
    Wade, David. The Times, December 12, 1967, p. 9d.

WILLSON, Meredith
    The Music Man. Book, music, and lyrics by Meredith
    Willson.
    Adelphi: March 16, 1961-February 24, 1962 (395)

    Barker, Felix. Evening News, March 17, 1961, p. 7a.
    Darlington, W. A. Daily Telegraph, March 17, 1961,
       p. 16e.
    Gascoigne, Bamber. Spectator, March 24, 1961, p.
       401.
    Hobson, Harold. Sunday Times, March 19, 1961, p.
       41c.
    Hope-Wallace, Philip. Manchester Guardian, March
       18, 1961, p. 5d.
    Keown, Eric. Punch, March 22, 1961, pp. 474-475.
    Levin, Bernard. Daily Express, March 17, 1961, p.
       16g.
    Muller, Robert. Daily Mail, March 17, 1961, p. 3d.
    Nathan, David. Daily Herald, March 17, 1961, p. 3g.
    Shulman, Milton. Evening Standard, March 17, 1961,
       p. 4a.
    The Times, March 17, 1961, p. 18a.
    Trewin, J. C. Illustrated London News, April 1,
       1961, p. 556.
    Tynan, Kenneth. Observer, March 19, 1961, p. 29b.
    Worsley, T. C. Financial Times, March 17, 1961, p.
       20f.

WILSON, Earl, Jr.
    Let My People Come. Music and lyrics by Earl Wilson, Jr.
    Regent; August 29, 1974-July 30, 1977 (1,171)

        Barber, John. Daily Telegraph, August 30, 1974, p.
            11d.
        Billington, Michael. Manchester Guardian, August
            30, 1974, p. 8a.
        Coveney, Michael. Financial Times, August 30, 1974,
            p. 3g.
        Frame, Colin. Evening News, August 30, 1974, p. 4f.
        Hagerty, Bill. Daily Mirror, August 30, 1974, p.
            16a.
        Hurren, Kenneth. Spectator, September 7, 1974, p.
            313.
        Kingston, Jeremy. Punch, September 11, 1974, p.
            419.
        Lambert, J. W. Sunday Times, September 1, 1974,
            p. 30c.
        Lewsen, Charles. The Times, August 30, 1974, p. 9d.
        Radin, Victoria. Observer, September 1, 1974, p.
            24c.
        Tinker, Jack. Daily Mail, August 30, 1974, p. 17f.

WISE, Jim
    Dames at Sea. Music by Jim Wise; book and lyrics by
    George Haimsohn and Robin Miller.
    Duchess: August 27, 1969-December 6, 1969 (127)

        Barber, John. Daily Telegraph, August 28, 1969, p.
            19a.
        Barnes, Caryl. Manchester Guardian, August 28,
            1969, p. 8e.
        Billington, Michael. The Times, August 28, 1969,
            p. 5d.
        Dawson, Helen. Observer, August 31, 1969, p. 19c.
        Frame, Colin. Evening News, August 28, 1969, p. 2h.
        Kingston, Jeremy. Financial Times, August 28, 1969,
            p. 3c.
        Kingston, Jeremy. Punch, September 17, 1969, p.
            470.
        Lambert, J. W. Sunday Times, August 31, 1969, p.
            25f.
        Lewis, Peter. Daily Mail, August 29, 1969, p. 12d.
        Nathan, David. Sun, August 28, 1969, p. 5a.
        Shulman, Milton. Evening Standard, August 28, 1969,
            p. 6c.
        Spurling, Hilary. Spectator, September 6, 1969, p.
            312.
        Trewin, J. C. Illustrated London News, September 6,
            1969, p. 30.

WISHENGRAD, Morton
    Rope Dancers.
    Arts: July 9, 1959-August 4, 1959 (30)*

Brien, Alan. <u>Spectator</u>, July 24, 1959, p. 101.
Darlington, W. A. <u>Daily Telegraph</u>, July 15, 1959,
    p. 8d.
Hobson, Harold. <u>Sunday Times</u>, July 19, 1959, p.
    13c.
Hope-Wallace, Philip. <u>Manchester Guardian</u>, July 15,
    1959, p. 5a.
Pryce-Jones, Alan. <u>Observer</u>, July 19, 1959, p. 10c.
<u>The Times</u>, July 15, 1959, p. 8d.

WODEHOUSE, P. G.
    <u>Oh, Kay</u>! See: Gershwin, George

WOUK, Herman
    <u>The Caine Mutiny Court-Martial</u>.
    Hippodrome: June 13, 1956-October 6, 1956 (133)

Barber, John. <u>Daily Express</u>, June 14, 1956, p. 3h.
C., A. V. <u>Spectator</u>, June 22, 1956, p. 855.
Darlington, W. A. <u>Daily Telegraph</u>, June 14, 1956,
    p. 8d.
Fay, Gerard. <u>Manchester Guardian</u>, June 15, 1956,
    p. 7d.
Granger, Derek. <u>Financial Times</u>, June 14, 1956, p.
    7g.
Hobson, Harold. <u>Sunday Times</u>, June 17, 1956, p. 13a.
Keown, Eric. <u>Punch</u>, June 20, 1956, pp. 747-748.
Pearce, Emery. <u>Daily Herald</u>, June 14, 1956, p. 7c.
Shulman, Milton. <u>Evening Standard</u>, June 14, 1956,
    p. 16c.
<u>The Times</u>, June 14, 1956, p. 5e.
Trewin, J. C. <u>Illustrated London News</u>, June 30,
    1956, p. 836.
Tynan, Kenneth. <u>Observer</u>, June 17, 1956, p. 9a.
Williams, Stephen. <u>Evening News</u>, June 14, 1956, p.
    5c.
Wilson, Cecil. <u>Daily Mail</u>, June 14, 1956, p. 3g.
Worsley, T. C. <u>New Statesman</u>, June 23, 1956, p.
    728.

WRIGHT, Robert
    <u>The Great Waltz</u>. See: Korngold, Eric

    <u>Kismet</u>. By Robert Wright and George Forrest. Book by
    Charles Lederer and Luther Davis. Musical based on an
    earlier play by Edward Knoblock.
    Stoll: April 20, 1955-December 1, 1956 (648)

Barber, John. <u>Daily Express</u>, April 21, 1955, p. 3d.
Darlington, W. A. <u>Daily Telegraph</u>, April 21, 1955,
    p. 10e.
Granger, Derek. <u>Financial Times</u>, April 21, 1955, p.
    7c.
Hartley, Anthony. <u>Spectator</u>, April 29, 1955, p.
    538.
Holt, Paul. <u>Daily Herald</u>, April 21, 1955, p. 3d.

Hope-Wallace, Philip. <u>Manchester Guardian</u>, April
     22, 1955, p. 5f.
Keown, Eric. <u>Punch</u>, April 27, 1955, p. 538.
Lambert, J. W. <u>Sunday Times</u>, April 24, 1955, p. 7c.
Shulman, Milton. <u>Evening Standard</u>, April 21, 1955,
     p. 6a.
<u>The Times</u>, April 21, 1955, p. 4g.
Trewin, J. C. <u>Illustrated London News</u>, May 7, 1955,
     p. 842.
Williams, Stephen. <u>Evening News</u>, April 21, 1955, p.
     9c.
Wilson, Cecil. <u>Daily Mail</u>, April 21, 1955, p. 8b.

YAFFE, James
   The Deadly Game.
   Ashcroft, Croydon: April 8, 1963-April 20, 1963   (13)

     Barker, Felix. <u>Evening News</u>, April 9, 1963, p. 9c.
     Gellert, Roger. <u>New Statesman</u>, April 19, 1963, p.
          608.
     Jacobs, Eric. <u>Manchester Guardian</u>, April 9, 1963,
          p. 7d.
     Pacey, Ann. <u>Daily Herald</u>, April 9, 1963, p. 9g.
     Pryce-Jones, David. <u>Financial Times</u>, April 10,
          1963, p. 26b.
     Shorter, Eric. <u>Daily Telegraph</u>, April 9, 1963, p.
          16d.
     Thompson, John. <u>Evening Standard</u>, April 9, 1963,
          p. 4d.
     <u>The Times</u>, April 9, 1963, p. 15a.

   The Deadly Game.
   Savoy: April 26, 1967-June 3, 1967   (45)

     Barker, Felix. <u>Evening News</u>, April 27, 1967, p. 3a.
     Bryden, Ronald. <u>Observer</u>, April 30, 1967, p. 25g.
     Darlington, W. A. <u>Daily Telegraph</u>, April 27, 1967,
          p. 19a.
     Hobson, Harold. <u>Sunday Times</u>, April 30, 1967, p.
          49c.
     Hope-Wallace, Philip. <u>Manchester Guardian</u>, April
          27, 1967, p. 9d.
     Kingston, Jeremy. <u>Punch</u>, May 3, 1967, pp. 653-654.
     Kretzmer, Herbert. <u>Daily Express</u>, April 27, 1967,
          p. 6d.
     Lewis, Peter. <u>Daily Mail</u>, April 27, 1967, p. 14b.
     Pacey, Ann. <u>Sun</u>, April 27, 1967, p. 7b.
     Shulman, Milton. <u>Evening Standard</u>, April 27, 1967,
          p. 4e.
     Spurling, Hilary. <u>Spectator</u>, May 5, 1967, p. 534.
     Trewin, J. C. <u>Illustrated London News</u>, May 6, 1967,
          p. 31.
     Wardle, Irving. <u>The Times</u>, April 27, 1967, p. 8g.
     Young, B. A. <u>Financial Times</u>, April 28, 1967, p.
          30a.

YORDAN, Philip
    Anna Lucasta.
    Prince of Wales: August 24, 1953-September 12, 1953
    (36)

        Forster, Peter. Observer, August 30, 1953, p. 6f.
        R., G. Daily Telegraph, August 25, 1953, p. 7e.
        The Times, August 25, 1953, p. 2f.

    Anna Lucasta (Revival).
    Hippodrome: January 26, 1954-March 27, 1954 (106)

        Barber, John. Daily Express, January 27, 1954, p.
           3a.
        Holt, Paul. Daily Herald, January 27, 1954, p. 3f.
        Keown, Eric. Punch, February 3, 1954, p. 190.
        Trewin, J. C. Illustrated London News, February 13,
           1954, p. 244.

YOUMANS, Vincent
    No, No Nanette. Book by Otto Harbach and Frank Mandel;
    lyrics by Irving Caesar and Otto Harbach; music by
    Vincent Youmans.
    Drury Lane: May 15, 1973-January 12, 1974 (277)

        Barker, Felix. Evening News, May 16, 1973, p. 2d.
        Billington, Michael. Manchester Guardian, May 16,
           1973, p. 10c.
        Hobson, Harold. Sunday Times, May 20, 1973, p. 37a.
        Hurren, Kenneth. Spectator, May 26, 1973, p. 656.
        Kingston, Jeremy. Punch, May 23, 1973, p. 737.
        Kretzmer, Herbert. Daily Express, May 16, 1973, p.
           8d.
        Nightingale, Benedict. New Statesman, June 15, 1973,
           p. 902.
        Shulman, Milton. Evening Standard, May 16, 1973, p.
           26c.
        Tinker, Jack. Daily Mail, May 17, 1973, p. 23d.
        Trewin, J. C. Illustrated London News, July 1973,
           p. 87.
        Wardle, Irving. The Times, May 16, 1973, p. 11c.
        Young, B. A. Financial Times, May 16, 1973, p. 3c.

ZINDEL, Paul
    The Effect of Gamma Rays on Man-in-the-Moon Marigolds.
    Hampstead Theatre Club: November 13, 1972-December 4,
    1972 (23)

        Brustein, Robert. Observer, November 19, 1972, p.
           37b.
        Hobson, Harold. Sunday Times, November 19, 1972,
           p. 7d.
        Kingston, Jeremy. Punch, November 22, 1972, p. 767.
        Kretzmer, Herbert. Daily Express, November 14, 1972,
           p. 16g.
        Trewin, J. C. Illustrated London News, January 1973,
           p. 62.

Wardle, Irving. <u>The Times</u>, November 14, 1972, p.
    12d.
Young, B. A. <u>Financial Times</u>, November 14, 1972,
    p. 3a.

ZOGHBY, Emil Dean
    <u>Catch My Soul</u>. See: Good, Jack

PART II

★ CHRONOLOGY ★

This section gives a list of works produced during each year included in the study; namely, 1950-1975. Only the author's name and the title of the work are given. For full information one should look at the entry in section one.

1950

Gorney, Jay. Touch and Go.
Heggen, Thomas. Mister Roberts.
Kingsley, Sidney. Detective Story.
Odets, Clifford. Awake and Sing.
Rodgers, Richard. Carousel.
Spewack, Sam. Spring Song.

1951

Hertzog, Arthur. Mary Had a Little.
Porter, Cole. Kiss Me Kate.
Rodgers, Richard. South Pacific.
Trumbo, Dalton. The Biggest Thief in Town.
Williams, Tennessee. Summer and Smoke.

1952

Archibald, William. The Innocents.
Baker, Dorothy. Two Loves I Have.
Barry, Philip. Second Threshold.
Bellak, George. The Trouble-Makers.
Berlin, Irving. Call Me Madam.
Dinelli, Mel. The Man.
Dowling, Jennette. The Young Elizabeth.
Gershwin, George. Porgy and Bess.
Hellman, Lillian. Montserrat.
Lindsay, Howard. Remains To Be Seen.
Odets, Clifford. Winter Journey.
Rosenthal, Andrew. Red Letter Day.
Rosenthal, Andrew. Third Person.
Spewak, Sam. Under the Sycamore Tree.
Taylor, Samuel. The Happy Time.

Williams, Lawrence. The Bride of Denmark Hill.
Williams, Tennessee. Summer and Smoke.

1953

Axelrod, George. The Seven Year Itch.
Bevan, Donald. Stalag 17.
Herbert, F. Hugh. The Moon Is Blue.
Kramm, Joseph. The Shrike.
Loesser, Frank. Guys and Dolls.
Loewe, Frederick. Paint Your Wagon.
Rodgers, Richard. The King and I.
Rome, Harold. Wish You Were Here.
Yordan, Philip. Anna Lucasta.

1954

Goetz, Ruth. The Immoralist.
Hayes, Alfred. The Girl on the Via Flaminia.
Morris, Edmund. The Wooden Dish.
Odets, Clifford. The Big Knife.
Patrick, John. The Teahouse of the August Moon.
Porter, Cole. Can-Can.
Regan, Sylvia. The Fifth Season.
Rodgers, Richard. Pal Joey.
Taylor, Samuel. Sabrina Fair.
Wilder, Thornton. The Matchmaker.
Yordan, Philip. Anna Lucasta.

1955

Anderson, Maxwell. The Bad Seed.
Bernstein, Leonard. Wonderful Town.
Chodorov, Jerome. Anniversary Waltz.
Hayes, Joseph. The Desperate Hours.
O'Brien, Liam. The Remarkable Mr. Pennypacker.
O'Neill, Eugene. Mourning Becomes Electra.
Osborn, Paul. Morning's at Seven.
Ross, Jerry. The Pajama Game.
Schulman, Max. The Tender Trap.
Spewack, Sam. My Three Angels.
Welles, Orson. Moby Dick.
Wright, Robert. Kismet.

1956

Bemberg, George. Someone to Talk to.
Benson, Sally. The Young and the Beautiful.
Foote, Horton. The Trip to Bountiful.
Goodrich, Frances. The Diary of Anne Frank.
Hague, Albert. Plain and Fancy.
Hellman, Lillian. The Children's Hour.
Levin, Ira. No Time for Sergeants.
Loos, Anita. Gigi.
Miller, Arthur. The Crucible.
Miller, Arthur. A View From the Bridge.

1956 (cont.)

Nash, N. Richard. The Rainmaker.
Rome, Harold. Fanny.
Wouk, Herman. The Caine Mutiny.

1957

Anderson, Robert. Tea and Sympathy.
Crichton, Kyle. The Happiest Millionaire.
Faulkner, William. Requiem for a Nun.
Fields, Joseph. The Tunnel of Love.
Gazzo, Michael V. A Hatful of Rain.
Green, Carolyn. Janus.
McCullers, Carson. The Member of the Wedding.
Ross, Jerry. Damn Yankees.
Styne, Jules. Bells Are Ringing.
Williams, Tennessee. Camino Real.

1958

Ardrey, Robert. Shadow of Heroes.
Bernstein, Leonard. West Side Story.
Connelly, Marcus. Hunter's Moon.
Gibson, William. Two for the Seesaw.
Hughes, Langston. Simply Heaven.
Lawrence, Jerome. Auntie Mame.
Loesser, Frank. Where's Charley?
Loewe, Frederick. My Fair Lady.
O'Neill, Eugene. The Iceman Cometh.
O'Neill, Eugene. Long Day's Journey into Night.
Rodgers, Richard. Cinderella.
Stewart, Donald Ogden. Honour Bound.
Stewart, Donald Ogden. The Kidders.
Veiller, Bayard. Trial of Mary Duggan.
Williams, Tennessee. Cat on a Hot Tin Roof.
Williams, Tennessee. Garden District.

1959

Barkentin, Marjorie. Ulysses in Nighttime.
Bernstein, Leonard. Candide.
Donleavy, J. P. The Ginger Man.
Hansberry, Lorraine. A Raisin in the Sun.
Kurnitz, Harry. Once More With Feeling.
Osborn, Paul. The World of Suzie Wong.
Stevens, Leslie. The Marriage-Go-Round.
Taylor, Samuel. The Pleasure of His Company.
Williams, Tennessee. Orpheus Descending.
Williams, Tennessee. The Rose Tattoo.
Wishengrad, Morton. The Rope Dancers.

1960

Albee, Edward. The Zoo Story. Presented with This
    Property is Condemned, by Tennessee Williams.

1960 (cont.)

Barnes, Billy. The Billy Barnes Revue.
Broderick, Patricia. Admiration of Life.
Donleavy, J. P. The Fairy Tales of New York.
Friml, Rudolf. Rose Marie.
Frings, Ketti. Look Homeward Angel.
Hellman, Lillian. Toys in the Attic.
Lawrence, Jerome. Inherit the Wind.
Loesser, Frank. The Most Happy Fella.
O'Neill, Eugene. A Moon for the Misbegotten.
Rodgers, Mary. Once Upon a Mattress.
Rodgers, Richard. Cinderella.
Rodgers, Richard. Flower Drum Song.
Rosenthal, Andrew. Horses in Midstream.
Rosenthal, Andrew. Innocent as Hell.
Saroyan, William. Sam the Highest Jumper of Them All.
Saroyan, William. Settled Out of Court.
Spieglass, Leonard. A Majority of One.
Vidal, Gore. Visit to a Small Planet.

1961

Albee. Edward. The American Dream and The Death of
    Bessie Smith.
Chayefsky, Paddy. The Tenth Man.
Donleavy, J. P. Fairy Tales of New York.
Gelber, Jack. The Connection.
Gibson, William. The Miracle Worker.
Goldman, James. They Might Be Giants.
Inge, William. The Dark at the Top of the Stairs.
Kopit, Arthur. Oh, Dad, Poor Dad, Mamma's Hung You in
    the Closet and I'm Feeling So Sad.
Levin, Ira. Critic's Choice.
Levitt, Saul. The Andersonville Trial.
MacLeish, Archibald. J. B.
O'Neill, Eugene. Mourning Becomes Electra.
Rice, Elmer. The Winner.
Rodgers, Richard. The Sound of Music.
Schisgal, Murray. Ducks and Lovers.
Schmidt, Harvey. The Fantasticks.
Strouse, Charles. Bye Bye, Birdie.
Styne, Jule. Do Re Mi.
Ward, Larry. Masterpiece.
Willson, Meredith. The Music Man.

1962

Besoyan, Rick. Little Mary Sunshine.
Bock, Jerry. Fiorello!
Flicker, Theodore. The Premise.
Frings, Ketti. Look Homeward Angel.
Gershe, Leonard. Miss Pell Is Missing.
Hughes, Langston. Black Nativity.
Inge, William. A Loss of Roses.

1962 (cont.)

Saroyan, William. Two Plays: Talking to You, and
    Across the Board on Tomorrow Morning.
Simon, Neil. Come Blow Your Horn.
Styne, Jule   Gentlemen Prefer Blondes.
Thurber, James. A Thurber Carnival.
Wheeler, Hugh. Big Fish, Little Fish.
Williams, Tennessee. Period of Adjustment.

1963

Bernstein, Leonard. On the Town.
Donleavy, J. P. The Ginger Man.
Gilbroy, Frank. Who'll Save the Plowboy?
Goell, Kermit. Pocahontas.
Kerr, Jean. Mary, Mary.
Kilty, Jerome. The Ides of March.
Loesser, Frank. How to Succeed in Business Without
    Really Trying.
Long, Arthur Sumner. Never Too Late.
Looking for the Action.
Merrill, Bob. Carnival.
O'Neill, Eugene. Hughie (a Triple Bill which included:
    In the Zone, Before Breakfast, and Hughie).
O'Neill, Eugene. A Touch of the Poet.
Rodgers, Richard. The Boys From Syracuse.
Rodgers, Richard. No Strings.
Schisgal, Murray. Luv.
Sondheim, Stephen. A Funny Thing Happened on the Way
    to the Forum.
Taylor, Christopher. Wings of the Dove.
Yaffe, James. The Deadly Game.

1964

Aidman, Charles. Spoon River.
Albee, Edward. Who's Afraid of Virginia Woolf.
Bock, Jerry. She Loves Me.
Brown, Kenneth. The Brig.
Coleman, Cy. Little Me.
Donleavy, J. P. A Singular Man.
Duberman, Martin. In White America.
Gardner, Herb. A Thousand Clowns.
Hughes, Langston. Black Nativity.
Hunter, Evan. The Easter Man.
Huycke, Lorne. The Wayward Way.
Loewe, Frederick. Camelot.
Patrick, John. Everybody Loves Opal.
Rose, Reginald. Twelve Angry Men.
Schisgal, Murray. The Tiger and the Typists.
Tarloff, Frank. The First Fish.

1965

Albee, Edward. The Zoo Story. Presented with George
    Dandin by Molière.
Baldwin, James. The Amen Corner.
Baldwin, James. Blues for Mr. Charlie.
Feiffer, Jules. Crawling Arnold. Presented with Miss
    Julie by Strindberg.
Herman, Jerry. Hello, Dolly!
Huycke, Lorne. The Wayward Way.
Kopit, Arthur. Oh, Dad, Poor Dad, Mamma's Hung You in
    the Closet and I'm Feeling So Sad.
Miller, Arthur. The Crucible.
Patinkin, Sheldon. The Star Spangled Jack Show.
Resnik, Muriel. Any Wednesday.
Simon, Neil. Barefoot in the Park.
Teichmann, Howard. The Solid Gold Cadillac.
Williams, Tennessee. The Glass Menagerie.
Williams, Tennessee. The Night of the Iguana.

1966

Bellow, Saul. The Bellow Plays: Out From Under, Orange
    . Souffle, The Wen.
Fisher, Bob. The Impossible Years.
Kesselring, Joseph. Arsenic and Old Lace.
Loewe, Frank. The Thirteen Clocks.
Manhoff, Bill. The Owl and the Pussycat.
Miller, Arthur. Incident at Vichy.
Sackler, Howard. The Pastime of Monsieur Robert.
Simon, Neil. The Odd Couple.
Styne, Jule. Funny Girl.

1967

Bock, Jerry. Fiddler on the Roof.
Burrows, Abe. Cactus Flower.
Coleman, Cy. Sweet Charity.
Feiffer, Jules. Little Murders.
Foster, Paul. Tom Paine.
Garson, Barbara. Macbird!
Hirson, Roger. World War 2-1/2.
Jones, LeRoi. The Dutchman. Presented with Neighbors,
    by James Saunders.
Lowell, Robert. Benito Cereno.
O'Neill, Eugene. Mourning Becomes Electra.
Romberg, Sigmund. The Desert Song.
Schmidt, Harvey. 110 in the Shade.
Van Itallie, Jean-Claude. America Hurrah.
Williams, Tennessee. Two-Character Play.
Yaffe, James. The Deadly Game.

1968

Anderson, Robert. <u>You Know I Can't Hear You When the Water's Running</u>.
Chayefsky, Paddy. <u>The Latent Heterosexual</u>.
Clifton, John. <u>Man With a Load of Mischief</u>.
Cryer, Gretchen. <u>Grass Roots</u>.
Feiffer, Jules. <u>God Bless</u>.
Gershwin, George. <u>Lady Be Good</u>.
Gesner, Clark. <u>You're a Good Man, Charlie Brown</u>.
Hillier, Robert P. <u>Jamie Jackson</u>.
Kander, John. <u>Cabaret</u>.
Kopit, Arthur. <u>Indians</u>.
Leigh, Mitch. <u>Man of LaMancha</u>.
McClure, Michael. <u>The Beard</u>.
McDermot, Galt. <u>Hair</u>.
Schmidt, Harvey. <u>I Do! I Do!</u>
Strouse, Charles. <u>Golden Boy</u> (A musical version of Odets' play).
Wallach, Ira. <u>Out of the Question</u>.

1969

Albee, Edward. <u>A Delicate Balance</u>.
Allen, Steve. <u>Belle Starr</u>.
Allen, Woody. <u>Play It Again, Sam</u>.
Bacharach, Burt. <u>Promises, Promises</u>.
Crowley, Mart. <u>The Boys in the Band</u>.
Green, Mawby. <u>Pyjama Tops</u>.
Herman, Jerry. <u>Mame</u>.
Hester, Hal. <u>Your Own Thing</u>.
Miller, Arthur. <u>The Price</u>.
Myers, Robert Manson. <u>The Spoils of Poynton</u>.
Porter, Cole. <u>Anything Goes</u>.
Simon, Neil. <u>Plaza Suite</u>.
Wise, Jim. <u>Dames at Sea</u>.

1970

Albee, Edward. <u>Tiny Alice</u>.
Anderson, Robert. <u>I Never Sang for My Father</u>.
Gershe, Leonard. <u>Butterflies Are Free</u>.
Good, Jack. <u>Catch My Soul</u>.
Korngold, Eric. <u>The Great Waltz</u>.
MacDermot, Galt. <u>Isabel's a Jezebel</u>.
McCullers, Carson. <u>The Square Root of Wonderful</u>.
Porter, Cole. <u>Kiss Me Kate</u>.
Stone, Peter. <u>1776</u>.
Weller, Michael. <u>Cancer</u>.

1971

<u>El Coca-Cola Grande</u>.
Eyren, Tom. <u>The Dirtiest Show in Town</u>.
Gelbart, Larry. <u>Jump</u>.
Gohman, Don. <u>Ambassador</u>.
Guare, John. <u>A Day for Surprises</u>.

1971 (cont.)

Kern, Jerome. Show Boat.
Lowell, Robert. Prometheus Bound.
Marasco, Robert. Child's Play.
McNally, Terrence. Next and Sweet Eros.
Melfi, Leonard. Birdbath.
Odets, Clifford. Awake and Sing.
O'Neill, Eugene. Long Day's Journey Into Night.
Porter, Cole. Kiss Me Kate.
Schwartz, Stephen. Godspell.

1972

Albee, Edward. All Over.
Greer, Herb. Po' Miss Julie.
Hecht, Ben. The Front Page.
Krasna, Norman. Bunny.
Miller, Arthur. All My Sons.
Pontac, Perry. The Old Man's Comforts.
Rome, Harold. Gone with the Wind.
Rossett, Alan. High Time.
Shearer, Toni. Mother Earth.
Sherwood, Robert. Reunion in Vienna.
Sondheim, Stephen. Company.
Strouse, Charles. Applause.
Strouse, Charles. I and Albert.
Zindel, Paul. The Effect of Gamma Rays on Man-in-the-
    moon Marigolds.

1973

Eyren, Tom. Sarah B. Divine.
Jacobs, Jim. Grease.
Kander, John. Zorba.
Kanin, Garson. Born Yesterday.
Kerr, Jean. Finishing Touches.
Kilty, Jerome. Dear Love.
MacDermot, Galt. Two Gentlemen of Verona.
Magdalany, Peter. Section Nine.
Rodgers, Richard. The King and I.
Schwartz, Stephen. Pippin.
Shepard, Sam. The Unseen Hand.
Styne, Jule. Gypsy.
Swift, David. Gomes.
Williams, Tennessee. Small Craft Warnings.
Youmans, Vincent. No, No, Nanette.

1974

Bernstein, Leonard. West Side Story.
Gershwin, George. Oh, Kay!
Gillette, William. Sherlock Holmes.
Gurney, A. R., Jr. Children.
Kelly, George. The Show-off.
Loesser, Frank. Hans Anderson.

1974 (cont.)

MacDermot, Galt. Hair.
Miller, Jason. That Championship Season.
Patrick, Robert. Kennedy's Children.
Shepard, Sam. Tooth of Crime.
Simon, Neil. The Gingerbread Lady.
Williams, Tennessee. A Streetcar Named Desire.
Wilson, Earl, Jr. Let My People Come.

1975

Barry, Julian. Lenny.
Chase, Mary. Harvey.
Clark, Ronald. Norman, Is That You?
MacDermot, Galt. Hair.
Nash, N. Richard. The Rainmaker.
Patrick, Robert. Play by Play.
Rintels, David. Clarence Darrow.
Schwartz, Stephen. Godspell.
Simon, Neil. The Sunshine Boys.
Sondheim, Stephen. A Little Night Music.
Taylor, Samuel. A Touch of Spring.

PART III

★ TITLE INDEX ★

Absence of a Cello (See:
    Out of the Question)
        Ira Wallach

All My Sons
        Arthur Miller

All Over
        Edward Albee

Ambassador
        Don Gohman

The Amen Corner
        James Baldwin

America Hurrah
        Jean Claude Van Itallie

The American Dream
        Edward Albee

The Andersonville Trial
        Saul Levitt

Anna Lucasta
        Philip Yordan

Anniversary Waltz
        Jerome Chodorov
        and Joseph Fields

Any Wednesday
        Muriel Resnick

Anything Goes
        Cole Porter

Applause
        Charles Strouse

Arsenic and Old Lace
        Joseph Kesselring

Auntie Mame
        Jerome Lawrence

Awake and Sing
        Clifford Odets

The Bad Seed
        Maxwell Anderson

Ballad of a Sad Cafe
        Edward Albee

Barefoot in the Park
        Neil Simon

The Beard
        Michael McClure

Before Breakfast
        Eugene O'Neill
        (See: Hughie)

Belle Starr
        Steve Allen

Bells Are Ringing
        Jule Styne

Benito Cereno
        Robert Lowell

Big Fish, Little Fish
        Hugh Wheeler

The Big Knife
        Clifford Odets

The Biggest Thief in Town
        Dalton Trumbo

Billy Barnes Revue
        Billy Barnes

Birdbath
    Leonard Melfi

Black Nativity
    Langston Hughes

Blues for Mr. Charlie
    James Baldwin

Born Yesterday
    Garson Kanin

The Boys From Syracuse
    Richard Rodgers

The Boys in the Band
    Mart Crowley

Bride of Denmark Hill
    Lawrence Williams
    and Nell O'Day

The Brig
    Kenneth H. Brown

Bunny
    Norman Krasna

Butterflies Are Free
    Leonard Gershe

Bye-Bye Birdie
    Charles Strouse

Cabaret
    John Kander

Cactus Flower
    Abe Burrows

The Caine Mutiny Court-
Martial
    Herman Wouk

Call Me Madam
    Irving Berlin

Camelot
    Frederick Loewe and
    Alan Jay Lerner

Camino Real
    Tennessee Williams

Can-Can
    Cole Porter

Cancer
    Michael Weller

Candide
    Leonard Bernstein

Carnival
    Bob Merrill

Carousel
    Richard Rodgers

Cat on a Hot Tin Roof
    Tennessee Williams

Catch My Soul
    Jack Good

Children
    A. R. Gurney

The Children's Hour
    Lillian Hellman

Child's Play
    Robert Marasco

Cinderella
    Richard Rodgers

Clarence Darrow
    David Rintels

Come Blow Your Horn
    Neil Simon

Company
    Stephen Sondheim

The Connection
    Jack Gelber

The Country Girl (See:
Winter Journey)
    Clifford Odets

Crawling Arnold
    Jules Feiffer

Critic's Choice
    Ira Levin

The Crucible
    Arthur Miller

Dames at Sea
        Jim Wise

Damn Yankees
        Jerry Ross

Dark at the Top of the Stairs
        William Inge

A Day for Surprises
        John Guare

The Deadly Games
        James Yaffe

Dear Love
        Jerome Kilty

The Death of Bessie Smith
        Edward Albee

A Delicate Balance
        Edward Albee

The Desert Song
        Sigmund Romberg

The Desperate Hours
        Joseph Hayes

Detective Story
        Sidney Kingsley

The Diary of Anne Frank
        Frances Goodrich and
        Albert Hackett

The Dirtiest Show in Town
        Tom Eyren

Do Re Mi
        Jule Styne

Ducks and Lovers
        Murray Schisgal

The Dutchman
        LeRoi Jones

The Easter Man
        Evan Hunter

The Effect of Gamma Rays on
Man-in-the-Moon Marigolds
        Paul Zindel

Everybody Loves Opal
        John Patrick

Fairy Tales of New York
        J. P. Donleavy

Fanny
        Harold Rome

The Fantasticks
        Harvey Schmidt

Fiddler on the Roof
        Jerry Bock

The Fifth Season
        Sylvia Regan

Finishing Touches
        Jean Kerr

Fiorello!
        Jerry Bock

The First Fish
        Frank Tarloff

Flower Drum Song
        Richard Rodgers

The Front Page
        Ben Hecht

Funny Girl
        Jule Styne

A Funny Thing Happened on
the Way to the Forum
        Stephen Sondheim

Garden District
        Tennessee Williams

Gentlemen Prefer Blondes
        Jule Styne

Gigi
        Anita Loos

The Ginger Man
        J. P. Donleavy

The Girl on the Via Flaminia
        Alfred Hayes

Glass Menagerie
          Tennessee Williams

God Bless
          Jules Feiffer

Godspell
          Stephen Schwartz

Golden Boy
          Charles Strouse

Gomes
          David Swift

Gone With the Wind
          Harold Rome

Grass Roots
          Gretchen Cryer

Grease
          Jim Jacobs

The Great Waltz
          Eric Korngold

Guys and Dolls
          Frank Loesser

Gypsy
          Jule Styne

Hair
          Galt MacDermot

Hans Anderson
          Frank Loesser

The Happiest Millionaire
          Kyle Critchton

The Happy Time
          Samuel Taylor

Harvey
          Mary Chase

A Hatful of Rain
          Michael Gazzo

Hello, Dolly!
          Jerry Herman

High Time
          Alan Rossett

Honour Bright
          Donald Ogden Stewart

Horses in Midstream
          Andrew Rosenthal

How to Succeed in Business
Without Really Trying
          Frank Loesser

Hughie
          Eugene O'Neill

Hunter's Moon
          Marcus Cook Connelly

I and Albert
          Charles Strouse

I Do! I Do!
          Harvey Schmidt

I Never Sang for My Father
          Robert Anderson

The Iceman Cometh
          Eugene O'Neill

The Ides of March
          Jerome Kilty

The Immoralist
          Ruth Goetz

The Impossible Years
          Bob Fisher

In the Zone (See: Hughie)
          Eugene O'Neill

In White America
          Martin B. Duberman

Incident at Vichy
          Arthur Miller

Indians
          Arthur Kopit

Inherit the Wind
          Jerome Lawrence

Innocent as Hell
          Andrew Rosenthal

The Innocents
          William Archibald

Mister Roberts
    Thomas Heggen

Moby Dick
    Orson Welles

Montserrat
    Lillian Hellman

Moon for the Misbegotten
    Eugene O'Neill

The Moon Is Blue
    Frederick Hugh Herbert

Morning's at Seven
    Paul Osborne

The Most Happy Fella
    Frank Loesser

Mourning Becomes Electra
    Eugene O'Neill

The Music Man
    Meredith Willson

My Fair Lady
    Frederick Loewe and
    Alan Jay Lerner

My Three Angels
    Sam Spewack

Never Too Late
    Arthur Sumner Long

Next
    Terence McNally

The Night of the Iguana
    Tennessee Williams

No, No, Nanette
    Vincent Youmans

Norman, Is That You?
    Ronald Clark

No Strings
    Richard Rodgers

No Time for Sergeants
    Ira Levin

The Odd Couple
    Neil Simon

Oh Dad, Poor Dad, Mamma's
Hung You in the Closet and
I'm Feeling So Sad
    Arthur Kopit

Oh, Kay!
    George Gershwin

On the Town
    Leonard Bernstein

Once More With Feeling
    Harry Kurnitz

Once Upon a Mattress
    Mary Rodgers

110 in the Shade
    Harvey Schmidt

Orpheus Descending
    Tennessee Williams

Out from Under, Orange
Souffle, The Wen
    Saul Bellow

Out of the Question
    Ira Wallach

The Owl and the Pussycat
    Bill Manhoff

Paint Your Wagon
    Frederick Loewe and
    Alan Jay Lerner

The Pajama Game
    Jerry Ross

Pal Joey
    Richard Rodgers

The Pastime of Monsieur
Robert
    Howard Sackler

Period of Adjustment
    Tennessee Williams

Pippin
    Stephen Schwartz

Plain and Fancy
    Albert Hauge

The Solid Gold Cadillac
        Howard Teichmann and
        George S. Kaufman

Someone to Talk To
        George Bemberg

The Sound of Music
        Richard Rodgers

South Pacific
        Richard Rodgers

The Spoils of Poynton
        Robert Manson Myers

Spoon River
        Charles Aidman

Spring Song
        Sam and Bella Spewack

The Square Root of Wonderful
        Carson McCullers

Stalag 17
        Donald Bevan

The Star Spangled Jack Show
        Sheldon Patinkin

Summer and Smoke
        Tennessee Williams

The Sunshine Boys
        Neil Simon

Sweet Charity
        Cy Coleman

Sweet Eros
        Terence McNally

Tea and Sympathy
        Robert Anderson

The Teahouse of the August
Moon
        John Patrick

The Tender Trap
        Max Schulman

The Tenth Man
        Paddy Chayefsky

That Championship Season
        Jason Miller

They Might Be Giants
        James Goldman

Third Person
        Andrew Rosenthal

The Thirteen Clocks
        Frank Loewe

A Thousand Clowns
        Herb Gardner

A Thurber Carnival
        James Thurber

The Tiger and the Typist
        Murray Sxhisgal

Tiny Alice
        Edward Albee

Tom Paine
        Paul Foster

Tooth of Crime
        Sam Shepard

Touch and Go
        Jay Gorney

A Touch of Spring
        Samuel Taylor

A Touch of the Poet
        Eugene O'Neill

Toys in the Attic
        Lillian Hellman

Trial of Mary Dugan
        Bayard Veiller

The Trip to the Bountiful
        Horton Foote

The Trouble-Makers
        George Bellak

The Tunnel of Love
        Joseph Fields

Twelve Angry Men
        Reginald Rose

APPENDIX I

Twenty-five Longest Running American ★ Productions in London, 1950-1975 ★

(Note: This list includes both musical shows and plays.)

	Title	Author	Year Produced	Run
1.	Pyjama Tops	Mawby Green & Ed Feilbert	1969	2,498
2.	The Sound of Music	Richard Rodgers & Oscar Hammerstein II	1961	2,385
3.	My Fair Lady	Frederick Loewe & Alan Lerner	1958	2,281
4.	Fiddler on the Roof	Jerry Bock & Sheldon Harnick	1967	2,030
5.	Hair	Galt MacDermot & Gerome Ragni	1968	1,998
6.	Let My People Come	Earl Wilson, Jr.	1974	1,171
7.	Godspell	Stephen Schwartz & John-Michael Tebelak	1971	1,128
8.	West Side Story	Leonard Bernstein & Stephen Sondheim	1958	1,039
9.	Teahouse of the August Moon	John Patrick	1954	964
10.	The King and I	Richard Rodgers & Oscar Hammerstein II	1953	926
11.	Show Boat	Jerome Kern & Oscar Hammerstein II	1971	910
12.	The World of Suzie Wong	Paul Osborn	1959	823
13.	South Pacific	Richard Rodgers & Oscar Hammerstein II	1951	802
14.	Hello, Dolly!	Jerry Herman	1965	794

LONGEST RUNNING AMERICAN PRODUCTIONS (con't)

Title	Author	Year Produced	Run
15. A Funny Thing Happened on the Way to the Forum	Stephen Sondheim	1963	761
16. The Great Waltz	Eric Korngold, George Forrest, & Robert Wright	1970	706
17. Kismet	Robert Wright	1955	648
18. Pajama Game	Jerry Ross & Richard Adler	1955	588
19. Come Blow Your Horn	Neil Simon	1962	582
20. Carousel	Richard Rodgers & Oscar Hammerstein II	1950	567
21. Tunnel of Love	Joseph Fields & Peter DeVries	1957	563
22. Guys and Dolls	Frank Loesser	1953	545
23. How to Succeed in Business Without Really Trying	Frank Loesser	1963	520
24. Camelot	Frederick Loewe & Alan Lerner	1964	518
25. Kiss Me Kate	Cole Porter	1951	501

APPENDIX II

Twenty-five Longest Running American
★ **Musicals in London, 1950-1975** ★

	Title	Composer	Year Produced	Run
1.	The Sound of Music	Richard Rodgers	1961	2,385
2.	My Fair Lady	Frederick Loewe	1958	2,281
3.	Fiddler on the Roof	Jerry Bock	1967	2,030
4.	Hair	Galt MacDermot	1968	1,998
5.	Let My People Come	Earl Wilson, Jr.	1974	1,171
6.	Godspell	Stephen Schwartz	1971	1,128 ·
7.	West Side Story	Leonard Bernstein	1958	1,039
8.	The King and I	Richard Rodgers	1953	926
9.	Show Boat	Jerome Kern	1971	910
10.	South Pacific	Richard Rodgers	1951	802
11.	Hello, Dolly!	Jerry Herman	1965	794
12.	A Funny Thing Happened on the Way to the Forum	Stephen Sondheim	1963	761
13.	The Great Waltz	Eric Korngold	1970	706
14.	Kismet	Robert Wright	1955	648
15.	The Pajama Game	Jerry Ross	1955	588
16.	Promises, Promises	Burt Bacharach	1969	569
17.	Carousel	Richard Rodgers	1950	567
18.	Guys and Dolls	Frank Loesser	1953	545

LONGEST RUNNING AMERICAN MUSICALS (cont.)

	Title	Composer	Year Produced	Run
19.	How to Succeed in Business Without Really Trying	Frank Loesser	1963	520
20.	Camelot	Frederick Loewe	1964	518
21.	Kiss Me Kate	Cole Porter	1951	501
22.	Call Me Madam	Irving Berlin	1952	485
23.	Sweet Charity	Cy Coleman	1967	484
24.	Paint Your Wagon	Frederick Loewe	1953	478
25.	Flower Drum Song	Richard Rodgers	1960	464

APPENDIX III

Twenty-five Longest Running American
★   **Plays in London, 1950-1975**   ★

	Title	Author	Year Produced	Run
1.	Pyjama Tops	Mawby Green & Ed Feilbert	1969	2,498
2.	The Teahouse of the August Moon	John Patrick	1954	964
3.	The World of Suzie Wong	Paul Osborn	1959	823
4.	The Dirtiest Show in Town	Tom Eyren	1971	795
5.	Come Blow Your Horn	Neil Simon	1962	582
6.	The Tunnel of Love	Joseph Fields & Peter DeVries	1957	563
7.	The Young Elizabeth	Jennette Dowling & Francis Letton	1952	498
8.	Who's Afraid of Virginia Woolf?	Edward Albee	1964	489
9.	The Remarkable Mr. Pennypacker	Liam O'Brien	1955	421
10.	No Time for Sergeants	Ira Levin	1956	411
11.	The Odd Couple	Neil Simon	1966	405
12.	The Price	Arthur Miller	1969	404
13.	The Pleasure of His Company	Samuel Taylor	1959	403
14.	Mary, Mary	Jean Kerr	1963	396
14.	The Boys in the Band	Mart Crowley	1969	396

LONGEST RUNNING AMERICAN PLAYS (cont.)

	Title	Author	Year Produced	Run
15.	Play It Again, Sam	Woody Allen	1969	355
16.	The Seven Year Itch	George Axelrod	1953	331
17.	The Wings of the Dove	Christopher Taylor	1963	324
18.	Out of the Question	Ira Wallach	1968	316
19.	Auntie Mame	Jerome Lawrence & Robert E. Lee	1958	301
20.	Arsenic and Old Lace	Joseph Kesselring	1966	300
20.	A Touch of Spring	Samuel Taylor	1975	300
21.	Plaza Suite	Neil Simon	1969	294
22.	The Matchmaker	Thornton Wilder	1954	275
23.	The Miracle Worker	William Gibson	1961	267
24.	Winter Journey	Clifford Odets	1952	243
24.	Barefoot in the Park	Neil Simon	1965	243
24.	A Streetcar Named Desire	Tennessee Williams	1974	243
25.	The Rainmaker	N. Richard Nash	1956	228

APPENDIX IV

★ New York Productions ★

This list includes the theatre, the opening and closing dates, and the number of performances of the first New York productions of works cited in this bibliography.

Play	Place	Date	Run
Absence of a Cello	Ambassador	9/21/64-1/2/65	120
Across the Board on Tomorrow Morning and Talking to You	Belasco	8/17/42-8/22/42	8
All My Sons	Coronet	6/29/47-11/8/47	328
All Over	Martin Beck	3/28/71-5/1/71	42
Ambassador	Lunt-Fontanne	11/19/72-11/25/72	19
The Amen Corner	Ethel Barrymore	4/15/65-6/26/65	84
America Hurrah	Pocket Theatre	11/6/66-5/5/68	634
American Dream with the Death of Bessie Smith	York Playhouse	1/24/61-1/7/62	370
Anna Lucasta	Mansfield	8/30/44-11/30/46	957
The Andersonville Trial	Henry Miller	12/29/59-6/1/60	179
Anniversary Waltz	Broadhurst	4/7/54-9/14/55	615
Any Wednesday	Music Box	2/18/64-6/26/66	982
Anything Goes	Alvin	11/21/34-11/16/35	420
Applause	Palace	3/30/70-5/27/72	896
Arsenic and Old Lace	Fulton	1/10/41-6/17/44	1,444

NEW YORK PRODUCTIONS (cont.)

Play	Place	Date	Run
Auntie Mame	Broadhurst	10/31/56-6/28/58	639
Awake and Sing	Belasco	2/19/35-9/28/35	209
The Bad Seed	46th Street	12/8/54-9/24/55	332
Ballad of a Sad Cafe	Martin Beck	10/30/63-2/15/64	123
Barefoot in the Park	Biltmore	10/23/63-6/25/67	1,530
The Beard	Evergreen	10/24/67-1/14/68	100
Before Breakfast (on a bill with Hughie)			
Belle Starr	No NY prod.		
Bells Are Ringing	Shubert	11/29/56-3/7/59	924
Benito Cereno	American Place	11/1/64-12/12/64	36
Big Fish, Little Fish	ANTA Theatre	3/15/61-6/10/61	101
The Big Knife	National	2/24/49-5/28/49	108
The Biggest Thief in Town	Mansfield	3/30/49-4/9/49	13
Billy Barnes Revue	John Golden	8/4/59-10/17/59	87
Birdbath	Martinique	4/11/66-4/23/66	16
Black Nativity	41st Street	12/11/61-1/28/62	57
Blues for Mr. Charlie	ANTA Theatre	4/23/64-8/29/64	148
Born Yesterday	Lyceum	2/4/46-12/31/49	1,642
The Boys From Syracuse	Alvin	11/23/38-6/10/39	235
The Boys in the Band	Theater Four	4/15/68-9/6/70	1,001
Bride of Denmark Hill	No NY prod.		
The Brig	Living Theatre	5/15/63-10/16/63	177
Bunny	No NY prod.		

NEW YORK PRODUCTIONS (cont.)

Play	Place	Date	Run
Butterflies Are Free	Booth Theater	10/21/69-7/2/72	1,128
Bye Bye, Birdie	Martin Beck	4/14/60-10/7/61	607
Cabaret	Broadhurst	11/20/66-9/6/69	1,165
Cactus Flower	Royale	12/8/65-11/23/68	1,234
The Caine Mutiny Court Martial	Plymouth	1/20/54-1/15/55	412
Call Me Madam	Imperial	10/12/50-4/3/52	644
Camelot	Majestic	12/3/60-1/5/63	873
Can-Can	Shubert	5/7/53-6/25/55	892
Cancer	No NY prod.		
Candide	Martin Beck	12/1/56-2/2/57	73
Carnival	Imperial	4/13/61-1/5/63	719
Carousel	Majestic	4/19/45-5/24/47	890
Cat on a Hot Tin Roof	Morosco	3/24/55-11/17/56	694
Children	No NY prod.		
The Children's Hour	Maxine Elliott	11/20/34-7/4/36	691
Child's Play	Royale	2/17/70-12/12/70	342
Cinderella	No NY prod.		
Clarence Darrow	Helen Hayes	3/26/74-4/23/74	22
Come Blow Your Horn	Brooks Atkinson	2/22/61-10/6/62	677
The Connection	Living Theatre	7/15/59-6/4/61	722
The Country Girl (Winter Journey in London)	Lyceum	11/10/50-6/2/51	236
Crawling Arnold	No NY prod.		
Critic's Choice	Ethel Barrymore	12/14/60-5/27/61	189
The Crucible	Martin Beck	1/22/53-7/11/53	197
Dames at Sea	Bouwerie	12/20/68-5/10/70	575

NEW YORK PRODUCTIONS (cont.)

Play	Place	Date	Run
Damn Yankees	46th Street	5/5/55-10/12/57	1,020
Dark at the Top of the Stairs	Music Box	12/5/57-1/17/59	468
A Day for Surprises	No NY prod.		
The Deadly Games	Longacre	2/2/60-3/5/60	39
Dear Love	No NY prod.		
The Death of Bessie Smith	York Playhouse	3/1/61-1/7/62	328
A Delicate Balance	Martin Beck	9/22/66-1/14/67	132
The Desert Song	Imperial	11/30/26-1/7/28	471
The Desperate Hours	Ethel Barrymore	2/10/55-8/13/55	212
Detective Story	Hudson	3/23/49-8/12/50	581
The Diary of Anne Frank	Cort	10/5/55-6/22/57	717
The Dirtiest Show in Town	Astor Place	6/27/70-9/19/71	509
Do-Re-Mi	St. James	12/26/60-1/13/62	400
Ducks and Lovers	No NY prod.		
The Dutchman	Cherry Lane	3/24/64-2/6/65	366
The Easter Man	No NY prod.		
The Effect of Gamma Rays on Man-in-the-Moon Marigolds	Mercer-O'Casey	4/7/70-5/14/72	819
Everybody Loves Opal	Longacre	10/11/61-10/28/61	21
Fairy Tales of New York	No NY prod.		
Fanny	Majestic	11/4/54-12/16/56	888
The Fantasticks	Sullivan St. Playhouse	5/3/60-still running	
Fiddler on the Roof	Imperial	9/22/64-7/2/72	3,242
The Fifth Season	Cort	1/23/53-10/23/54	654

NEW YORK PRODUCTIONS (cont.)

Play	Place	Date	Run
Finishing Touches	Plymouth	2/8/73-7/1/73	164
Fiorello	Broadhurst	11/23/59-10/28/61	795
The First Fish	No NY prod.		
Flower Drum Song	St. James	12/1/58-5/7/60	600
The Front Page	Times Square	8/14/28-1/12/29	276
Funny Girl	Winter Garden	3/26/64-7/1/67	1,348
A Funny Thing Happened on the Way to the Forum	Alvin	5/8/62-8/29/64	964
Garden District	York	1/7/58-7/13/58	c. 208
Gentlemen Prefer Blondes (musical)	Ziegfeld	12/8/49-9/15/51	740
Gigi	Fulton	11/24/51-5/31/52	219
The Ginger Man	Orpheum	11/21/63-1/5/64	52
The Gingerbread Lady	Plymouth	12/13/70-5/29/71	193
The Girl on the Via Flaminia	Circle in the Square (trans. 48th St. 4/1/54)	2/9/54-5/29/54	111
The Glass Menagerie	Playhouse	3/31/45-8/3/46	561
God Bless	No NY prod.		
Godspell	Cherry Lane (trans. Broadhurst 6/22/76)	5/17/71-still running	
Golden Boy (musical)	Majestic	10/20/64-3/5/66	568
Gomes	No NY prod.		
Gone With the Wind	No NY prod.		
Grass Roots	No NY prod.		
Grease	Eden	2/14/72-still running	
Guys and Dolls	46th Street	11/24/50-11/28/53	1200

NEW YORK PRODUCTIONS (cont.)

Play	Place	Date	Run
Gypsy	Broadway	5/21/59-3/25/61	702
Hair	Biltmore	4/29/68-7/1/72	1,750
Hans Anderson	No NY prod.		
The Happiest Mil- lionaire	Lyceum	11/20/56-7/13/57	271
The Happy Time	Plymouth	1/24/50-7/14/51	614
Harvey	48th St.	11/1/44-1/15/49	1,775
A Hatful of Rain	Lyceum	11/9/55-10/13/56	398
Hello, Dolly!	St. James	1/16/64-12/27/70	2,844
High Time	No NY prod.		
Honour Bright	No NY prod.		
Horses in Midstream	Royale	4/2/53-4/4/53	4
How to Succeed in Business Without Really Trying	46th St.	10/14/61-3/6/65	1,417
Hughie	Royale	12/22/64-1/30/65	51
Hunter's Moon	No NY prod.		
I and Albert	No NY prod.		
I Do! I Do!	46th St.	12/5/66-6/15/68	560
I Never Sang For My Father	Longacre	1/25/68-5/11/68	124
The Iceman Cometh	Martin Beck	10/9/46-3/15/47	136
The Ides of March	No NY prod.		
The Immoralist	Royale	2/8/54-5/1/54	96
The Impossible Years	Playhouse	10/13/64-5/27/67	670
In the Zone (see Hughie)			
In White America	Sheridan Square Playhouse	10/31/63-	499
Incident at Vichy	Lincoln Center	12/3/64-5/7/65	99

NEW YORK PRODUCTIONS (cont.)

Play	Place	Date	Run
Indians	Brooks Atkinson	10/13/69-1/3/70	96
Inherit the Wind	National	4/22/55-6/22/57	806
Innocent as Hell	No NY prod.		
The Innocents	Playhouse	2/1/50-6/3/50	141
Isabel's a Jezebel	No NY prod.		
J. B.	ANTA Theatre	12/11/58-10/24/59	364
Jade	No NY prod.		
Jamie Jackson	No NY prod.		
Janus	Plymouth	11/24/55-6/30/56	251
Jump	No NY prod.		
Kennedy's Children	John Golden	11/3/74-1/4/76	72
The Kidders	No NY prod.		
The King and I	St. James	3/29/51-3/20/54	1,246
Kismet (musical)	Ziegfeld	12/3/53-4/23/55	583
Kiss Me Kate	New Century	12/30/48-7/28/51	1,077
Lady, Be Good	Liberty	12/1/24-9/12/25	329
The Latent Hetero- sexual	No NY prod.		
Lenny	Brooks Atkinson	5/26/71-6/24/72	455
Let My People Come	Village Gate (off Broadway)	1/8/74-7/4/76	1,008
	Morosco	7/7/76-10/2/76	101
	As of June 1, 1976, 1,122 performances		
Little Mary Sunshine	Orpheum	11/8/59-9/2/62	1,143
Little Me	Lunt-Fontanne	11/17/62-6/29/63	257
Little Murders	Broadhurst	4/25/67-4/29/67	7
A Little Night Music	Shubert	2/25/73-8/3/74	600
Long Day's Journey Into Night	Helen Hayes	11/7/56-3/29/58	390

NEW YORK PRODUCTIONS (cont.)

Play	Place	Date	Run
Look Homeward, Angel	Ethel Barrymore	11/28/57-4/4/59	564
Looking for the Action	No NY prod.		
A Loss of Roses	Eugene O'Neill	11/28/59-12/19/59	25
Lunchtime	No NY prod.		
Luv	Booth	11/11/64-1/7/67	901
Macbird!	Village Gate	2/22/67-1/21/68	386
A Majority of One	Shubert	2/16/59-6/25/60	556
Mame	Winter Garden	5/24/66-1/3/70	1,508
The Man	Fulton	1/19/50-4/8/50	92
Man of La Mancha	ANTA Theatre	11/22/65-6/26/71	2,328
Man with a Load of Mischief	Jan Hus Plyhse.	11/6/66-6/4/67	241
The Marriage-Go-Round	Plymouth	10/29/58-2/13/60	431
Mary Had a Little	No NY prod.		
Mary, Mary	Helen Hayes	3/8/61-12/12/64	1,572
Masterpiece	No NY prod.		
The Matchmaker	Royale	12/5/55-2/2/57	486
The Member of the Wedding	Empire	1/5/50-3/17/51	501
The Miracle Worker	Playhouse	10/19/59-7/1/61	700
Miss Pell Is Missing	No NY prod.		
Mister Roberts	Alvin	2/18/48-1/6/51	1,157
Moby Dick	Ethel Barrymore	11/28/62-12/8/62	13
Montserrat	Fulton	10/29/49-12/24/49	65
Moon for the Misbegotten	Bijou	5/2/57-6/29/57	68
The Moon is Blue	Henry Miller	3/8/51-5/30/53	924
Morning's at Seven	Longacre	11/30/39-1/6/40	44

NEW YORK PRODUCTIONS (cont.)

Play	Place	Date	Run
The Most Happy Fella	Imperial	5/3/56-12/14/57	676
Mother Earth	Belasco	10/19/72-10/28/72	12
Mourning Becomes Electra	Guild	10/26/31-4/16/32	150
Music Man	Majestic	12/19/57-4/15/61	1,375
My Fair Lady	Mark Hellinger	3/15/56-9/29/62	2,715
My Three Angels	Morosco	3/11/53-1/2/54	344
Never Too Late	Playhouse	11/27/62-4/24/65	1,007
Next	Greenwich Mews	2/10/69-10/18/70	707
Night of the Iguana	Royale	12/28/61-9/29/62	316
No, No Nanette	Globe	9/16/25-6/19/26	321
No Strings	54th Street	3/15/62-8/3/63	580
No Time for Sergeants	Alvin	10/20/55-9/14/57	796
Norman, Is That You?	Lyceum	2/19/70-2/28/70	12
The Odd Couple	Plymouth	3/10/65-7/2/67	964
Oh Dad, Poor Dad, Mamma's Hung You in the Closet and I'm Feeling So Sad	Phoenix	2/26/62-3/31/63	454
Oh, Kay	Imperial	11/8/26-6/18/27	256
The Old Man's Comforts	No NY prod.		
On the Town	Adelphi	12/28/44-2/2/46	463
Once More With Feeling	National	10/21/58-6/6/59	263
Once Upon a Mattress	Phoenix	5/11/59-7/2/60	460
110 in the Shade	Broadhurst	11/24/63-8/8/64	330
Orpheus Descending	Martin Beck	3/21/57-5/18/57	68

NEW YORK PRODUCTIONS (cont.)

Play	Place	Date	Run
Out from Under; Orange Souffle; The Wen (Unit title in NY Under the Weather)	Cort	10/27/66-11/5/66	12
The Owl and the Pussycat	ANTA Theatre	11/18/64-11/27/65	427
Paint Your Wagon	Shubert	11/12/51-7/19/52	289
The Pajama Game	St. James	5/13/54-11/24/56	1,063
Pajama Tops	Winter Garden	5/31/63-7/13/63	52
Pal Joey	Barrymore	12/25/40-8/16/41	270
	Shubert	9/1/41-11/29/41	104
		Total	374
Period of Adjustment	Helen Hayes	11/10/60-3/4/61	132
The Pastime of Monsieur Robert	No NY prod.		
Pippin	Imperial	10/23/72-still running	
Plain and Fancy	Mark Hellinger	1/27/55-3/3/56	461
Play by Play	No NY prod.		
Play It Again, Sam	Broadhurst	2/12/69-3/14/70	453
Plaza Suite	Plymouth	2/14/68-10/3/70	1,097
Po' Miss Julie	No NY prod.		
Pocahontas	No NY prod.		
Porgy and Bess	Alvin	10/10/35-1/18/36	124
The Price	Morosco	2/7/68-2/15/69	429
Prometheus Bound	No NY prod.		
Promises, Promises	Shubert	12/1/68-1/1/72	1,281
Pyjama Tops (see Pajama Tops)			
The Rainmaker	Cort	10/28/54-2/12/55	125
A Raisin in the Sun	Ethel Barrymore	3/11/59-6/25/60	530
Red Letter Day	No NY prod.		

NEW YORK PRODUCTIONS (cont.)

Play	Place	Date	Run
Remains to be Seen	Morosco	10/3/51-3/22/52	199
The Remarkable Mr. Pennypacker	Coronet	12/30/53-7/10/54	221
Requiem for a Nun	John Golden	1/30/59-3/7/59	43
Reunion in Vienna	Martin Beck	11/16/31-7/2/36	264
Rope Dancers	Cort	11/20/57-5/3/58	189
The Rose Tattoo	Martin Beck	2/3/51-10/27/51	306
Sabrina Fair	National	11/11/53-8/21/54	318
Sam, The Highest Jumper of Them All	No NY prod.		
Sarah B. Divine	No NY prod.		
Second Threshold	Morosco	1/2/51-4/21/51	126
Section Nine	McCarter Theater, Princeton, N.J. (Amer. premiere)	11/20/75-	14
Settled Out of Court	No NY prod.		
The Seven Year Itch	Fulton	11/20/52-8/13/55	1,141
1776	46th Street	3/16/69-2/3/72	1,217
Shadow of the Heroes	York Playhouse	12/5/61-12/22/61	20
She Loves Me	Eugene O'Neill	4/23/63-1/11/64	301
Sherlock Holmes	Garrick	11/6/99-6/16/00	256
Show Boat	Ziegfeld	12/27/27-5/4/29	572
The Show-Off	Playhouse	2/5/24-6/20/25	571
The Shrike	Cort	1/15/52-12/6/53	161
Simply Heavenly	Playhouse	8/20/57-10/12/57	62
A Singular Man	No NY prod.		
Small Craft Warnings	New	4/2/72-9/17/72	200
The Solid Gold Cadillac	Belasco	11/5/53-2/12/55	526

NEW YORK PRODUCTIONS (cont.)

Play	Place	Date	Run
Someone To Talk To	No NY prod.		
The Sound of Music	Lunt-Fontanne	11/16/59-6/15/63	1,443
South Pacific	Majestic	4/7/49-1/16/54	1,925
The Spoils of Poynton	No NY prod.		
Spoon River Anthology	Booth	9/29/63-1/4/64	111
Spring Song	No NY prod.		
The Square Root of Wonderful	National	10/30/57-12/7/57	45
Stalag 17	48th Street	5/8/51-6/21/52	472
The Star Spangled Jack Show	No NY prod.		
A Streetcar Named Desire	Ethel Barrymore	12/3/47-12/17/49	855
Summer and Smoke	Music Box	10/6/48-1/1/49	100
The Sunshine Boys	Broadhurst	12/20/72-4/21/74	538
Sweet Charity	Palace	1/29/66-7/15/67	608
Sweet Eros	Grammercy Arts	11/21/68-1/26/69	78
Tea and Sympathy	Ethel Barrymore	10/30/53-6/18/55	712
The Teahouse of the August Moon	Martin Beck	10/15/53-3/24/56	1,027
The Tender Trap	Longacre	10/13/54-1/8/55	102
The Tenth Man	Booth	11/5/59-5/13/61	623
That Championship Season	Public Theater	5/2/72-9/3/72	144
	Booth	9/14/72-4/21/74	700
		Total	844
They Might Be Giants	No NY prod.		
Third Person	No NY prod.		

NEW YORK PRODUCTIONS (cont.)

Play	Place	Date	Run
The Thirteen Clocks	No NY prod.		
A Thousand Clowns	Eugene O'Neill	4/5/62-4/13/63	428
A Thurber Carnival	ANTA Theatre	2/26/60-6/25/60	127
	reopened	9/5/60-11/26/60	96
		Total	223
The Tiger and the Typists	Orpheum	2/4/63-7/28/63	200
Tiny Alice	Billy Rose	12/29/64-5/22/65	167
Tom Paine	Stage 73	3/25/68-12/8/68	295
Tooth of Crime	Performing Garage	3/7/73-7/29/73	123
Touch and Go	Broadhurst	10/13/49-3/18/50	176
A Touch of Spring	No NY prod.		
A Touch of the Poet	Helen Hayes	10/2/58-6/13/59	284
Toys in the Attic	Hudson	2/25/60-4/8/61	556
The Trial of Mary Dugan	National	9/19/27-8/18/28	437
The Trip to Bountiful	Henry Miller	11/3/53-12/5/53	39
The Trouble-Makers	No NY prod.		
The Tunnel of Love	Royale	2/13/57-2/22/58	417
Twelve Angry Men	No NY prod.		
Two-Character Play (prod. in NY as Out Cry)	Lyceum	3/1/73-3/10/73	12
Two for the Seesaw	Booth	1/16/58-10/31/58	750
Two Gentlemen of Verona	Delacorte Thea. (Central Park)	7/22/71-8/29/71	14
	St. James	12/1/71-5/20/73	627
		Total	641
Two Loves I Have (NY title: Trio)	Belasco	12/29/44-2/24/45	67

NEW YORK PRODUCTIONS (cont.)

Play	Place	Date	Run
Ulysses in Nighttime	Rooftop	6/5/58-11/30/58 c.	206
Under the Sycamore Tree	Cricket	3/7/60-4/10/60	41
The Unseen Hand	Astor Place	4/1/70-4/18/70	21
A View from the Bridge	Coronet	9/29/55-2/4/56	149
Visit to a Small Planet	Booth	2/7/57-1/11/58	388
The Wayward Way	No NY prod.		
West Side Story	Winter Garden	9/26/57-6/27/59	732
Where's Charley?	St. James	10/11/48-9/9/50	792
Who'll Save the Plowboy?	Phoenix	1/9/62-2/25/62	56
Who's Afraid of Virginia Woolf?	Billy Rose	10/13/62-5/16/64	664
Wings of the Dove	No NY prod.		
Wish You Were Here	Imperial	6/25/52-11/28/53	598
Wonderful Town	Winter Garden	2/25/53-7/3/54	559
Wooden Dish	Booth	10/6/55-10/15/55	12
The World of Suzie Wong	Broadhurst	10/14/58-1/2/60	508
World War 2-1/2	Martinique	3/24/69	1
You Know I Can't Hear You When the Water's Running	Ambassador	3/13/67-1/4/69	756
The Young and the Beautiful	Longacre	10/1/55-11/26/55	65
The Young Elizabeth	No NY prod.		
Your Own Thing	Orpheum	1/13/68-4/5/70	933
You're a Good Man, Charlie Brown	Theatre 80	3/7/67-2/4/71	1,597

NEW YORK PRODUCTIONS (cont.)

Play	Place	Date	Run
The Zoo Story	Provincetown Playhouse	1/14/60-5/21/61	582
Zorba	Imperial	11/17/68-8/9/69	305

APPENDIX V

★ London Theatres ★

The intent of this list is to provide information about the theatres cited in the bibliography. Major commercial theatres, and a few club and experimental theatres are included, but the list is not an exhaustive directory of London theatres. Several theatres in the bibliography have been demolished or converted to movie theatres. These houses comprise a supplement at the end of the main list. The number of seats for each theatre appears in parentheses.

Adelphi
Strand, W. C. 2
(1,481)

Albery
St. Martin's Lane, WC2N 4AH
(877)

Aldwych
Aldwych, WC2B 4DF
(1,024)

Ambassadors
West Street, W. C. 2
(453)

Apollo
Shaftesbury Avenue, W. 1
(796)

Arts Theatre Club
6/7 Great Newport Street,
                    W. C. 2
(347)

Ashcroft
Park Lane, Croydon
(748)

Cambridge
Earlham Street, WC2 9HU
(1,281)

Coliseum
St. Martin's Lane, W. C. 2
(2,358)

Comedy
Panton Street, S. W. 1
(820)

Criterion
Piccadilly Circus, W1V 9LB
(592)

Drury Lane Theatre Royal
Catherine Street, W. C. 2
(2,283)

Duchess
Catherine Street, W. C. 2
(474)

Duke of York's
St. Martin's Lane, W. C. 2
(700)

Fortune
Russell Street, W. C. 2
(440)

Garrick
Charing Cross Road, W. C. 2
(800)

Globe
Shaftesbury Avenue, W. 1
(907)

Greenwich
Crooms Hill, S. E. 10
(426)

Greenwood
55 Weston Street, S. E. 1
(466)

Hampstead Theatre Club
Swiss Cottage Centre, N. W. 3
(157)

Haymarket, Theatre Royal
Haymarket, S. W. 1
(906)

Her Majesty's
Haymarket
(1,261)

Jeanetta Cochrane
Southampton Row, W. C. 1
(344)

King's Head Theatre Club
115 Upper Street
Islington, N. 1
(85)

Palladium
Argyll Street, W. 1
(2,325)

Lyric
Shaftesbury Avenue, W. 1
(948)

Mayfair
Stratton Street, W. 1
(310)

Mermaid
Puddledock
Blackfriars, E. C. 4
(498)

New
Drury Lane and Parker Street,
                          WC2B 5PW
(907)

Old Vic
Waterloo Road, S. E. 1
(948)

Open Space
32 Tottenham Court Road, W. 1
(200) (Note: Present quarters
to be demolished to make way
for a new shopping center.)

Palace
Shaftesbury Avenue, W. 1
(1,450)

Phoenix
Charing Cross Road, W. C. 2
(1,012)

Piccadilly
Denman Street, W1V 8DY
(1,130)

The Place
17 Dukes Road, W. C. 1
(255)

Players
Villiers Street, W. C. 2
(300)

Prince of Wales
Coventry Street, W. 1
(1,139)

Queen's
Shaftesbury Avenue, W. 1
(989)

The Regent
Regent Street, W. 1   ·
(528)

The Round House
Chalk Farm Road, NW1 8BG
(700)

Royal Court
Sloane Square, S. W. 1
(401)

Royalty
Portugal Street, Kingsway,
                      W. C. 2
(922)

Sadler's Wells
Rosebery Avenue, EC1R 4TN
(1,499)

St. Martin's
West Street, W. C. 2
(550)

Savoy
Savoy Court, Strand, W. C. 2
(1,122)

Shaftesbury
Shaftesbury Avenue, W. C. 2
(1,250)

Shaw
100 Euston Road, NW1 2AJ
(510)

Strand
Aldwych, W. C. 2
(1,082)

Theatre Royal, Stratford
Stratford, E. 15
(500)

Vaudeville
Strand, W. C. 2
(659)

Victoria Palace
Victoria Street, SW1E 5EA
(1,565)

Westminster
Palace Street, SW1E 5JB
(600)

Whitehall
14 Whitehall, S. W. 1
(628)

Wyndhams
Charing Cross Road, WC2H 0DA
(760)

Young Vic
66 The Cut, SE1 8LP
(456)

Supplement list: Theatres cited in the bibliography which
have been demolished, converted to movie theatres, or have
ceased to function.

Casino
Old Compton Street, W. 1
(1,800)
Now a movie house.

Hippodrome
Cranbourne Street, W. C. 2
(1,340)
In 1958 became The Talk of
the Town, a nightclub.

Leatherhead Theatre Club
Leatherhead
Ended in 1969.

Lyric, Hammersmith
Bradmore Grove, Hammersmith,
                      W. 6
(750)
Demolished in the 1960s.

New Lindsey
Palace Gardens Terrace
London, W. 8
(164)

Pembroke, Croydon
Wellesley Road, Croydon
Closed, 1962.

Prince Charles
Leicester Place, W. C. 2
(420)
Now a movie theatre.

Princess
Shaftesbury Avenue, W. C. 2
(1,500)
Became Shaftesbury Theatre in
1963.

St. James   Stoll
King Street, S. W. 1   Kingsway, W. C. 2
(950)   (2,420)
Demolished in 1957.   Demolished in 1957.

Saville   Winter Garden
Shaftesbury Avenue, W. C. 2   Drury Lane, W. C. 2
(1,067)   (1,581)
Last live performance Dec.   Closed, 1960.
17, 1969; now a movie theatre.

Note: Additional information on London theatres, past and
present, appears in a variety of sources, but the following
titles are essential for those seeking reliable and thorough
directory listings in a conveniently accessible form.

British Theatre Directory. Eastbourne, Eng.: Vance-Offord,
    1972-1975.

    Although the last issue of this directory appeared in
    1975 it is still useful. The first section provides an
    alphabetical listing of London theatres with telephones,
    names of managers, policy, and a variety of technical
    details. Other sections provide the same information
    for provincial theatres arranged by city and then by the
    name of the theatre, giving the same fullness.

Howard, Diana. London Theatres and Music Halls, 1850-1950.
    London: The Library Association, 1970.

    A detailed, easy to follow retrospective directory.

Mander, Raymond and Mitchenson. The Theatres of London.
    Illustrated by Timothy Birdsall. 2d ed. London: Hart-
    Davis, 1963.

    Readable and reliable accounts of each theatre enhanced
    by drawings of facades and other details.

Who's Who in the Theatre. 16th ed. London: Pittman, 1977.

    A directory of principal London theatres, giving addresses
    and technical specifications, including opening dates and
    shows. Principal New York theatres are also given with
    opening information. Older editions of this series have
    charts of seating plans at the major London theatres.

ABOUT THE COMPILER

William T. Stanley, Assistant Professor at the School of Library Sciences, University of Southern California, has specialized in the study of American theatre in Great Britain. He has published in the *Bulletin of Bibliography*.